THE LABAN
WORKBOOK
FOR ACTORS

THE LABAN WORKBOOK FOR ACTORS

A Practical Training Guide with Video

**KATYA BLOOM,
BARBARA ADRIAN,
TOM CASCIERO,
JENNIFER MIZENKO,
AND CLAIRE PORTER**

Series Editors: David Carey
and Rebecca Clark Carey

methuen | drama

LONDON • NEW YORK • OXFORD • NEW DELHI • SYDNEY

METHUEN DRAMA
Bloomsbury Publishing Plc
50 Bedford Square, London, WC1B 3DP, UK
1385 Broadway, New York, NY 10018, USA
29 Earlsfort Terrace, Dublin 2, Ireland

BLOOMSBURY, METHUEN DRAMA and the Methuen Drama logo
are trademarks of Bloomsbury Publishing Plc

First published 2018
Reprinted by Methuen Drama

Cover design: Louise Dugdale

Cover image: LeAnn Schmidt Yannelli, William McKinley, Claire Porter and
Mackie Boblette by Jay Anderson

For legal purposes the Acknowledgements on p. vii constitute
an extension of this copyright page.

British Library Cataloguing-in-Publication Data
A catalogue record for this book is available from the British Library.

ISBN: HB: 978-1-4742-2066-8
PB: 978-1-4742-2067-5
ePDF: 978-1-4742-2069-9
eBook: 978-1-4742-2068-2

Library of Congress Cataloging-in-Publication Data
A catalog record for this book is available from the Library of Congress.

Series: Theatre Arts Workbooks

Typeset by Fakenham Prepress Solutions, Fakenham, Norfolk NR21 8NN

To find out more about our authors and books visit
www.bloomsbury.com and sign up for our newsletters.

CONTENTS

Appendix A 257

General Overview of Laban Movement Analysis Vocabulary

Appendix B 261

Body, Effort, Shape, and Space Charts

ACKNOWLEDGMENTS

This book began with an invitation from David and Rebecca Carey, editors for the *Theatre Arts Workbooks Series*, to write a *Laban Workbook*, as I had been the long-time "Laban Lady" at the Royal Academy of Dramatic Art, working alongside the Careys. I decided to invite colleagues to join me in writing this book, to give the reader a variety of perspectives on how Laban's work has been applied to acting. I'd like to thank the Careys for the invitation, and for their enthusiasm for the multiple-author idea, and Bloomsbury for their agreement and suggestion that, as I was now back in my native USA, the co-contributors be American colleagues.

Thanks above all go to the wonderful, creative team of co-contributors—Barbara Adrian, Tom Casciero, Jennifer Mizenko, and Claire Porter—for sharing their expertise in writing chapters, and for all their hard work, generosity, and good humor during the process of co-creating a book and co-editing each other's work. It has been a pleasure getting to know and work with you, in person, on Skype, and via email.

We all wish to thank John O'Donovan, our editor at Bloomsbury, who has been extremely supportive throughout the making of this book.

Katya Bloom

FOREWORD

Eve Best

"Stamp!"

What?

"Stamp the floor." She hitches up her trousers and with her tiny bare feet starts to stamp, prodding at the studio floor as if it is made of clay and it is her job to mold it. As we follow her lead and start stamping too, something miraculous happens. A role reversal in my whole being takes place—my head, so used to being in charge, for the first time in its chatty life had to take a back seat, its numerous anxious voices dissolve, and my feet, free and stampy and wild, take over.

I learnt many wonderful things at RADA. But without doubt my favorite class was Laban.

When I arrived at drama school I was, as many teachers told me, "too in my head."

"What do you mean too in my head?" I spluttered. I'd go away and think about it. Three years at Oxford studying English, analyzing texts, and writing about literature, I'd had lots of practice in working out intellectually where a character was coming from. I could write an essay about Juliet or Masha, I had many clever thoughts about Lady Macbeth, but I had never approached a character from the way that they breathed, or how fast they walked, or how they held a knife.

In Laban classes I found, at last, I was taking off my head and leaving it outside the room. It was the greatest relief imaginable. I felt as if I was stepping back inside my body again for the first time since childhood. I was learning—or re-learning—how the body "talks" to us, leads our thoughts and emotions. I was letting the physical world come first again, as a child does.

In our first year at RADA, there was a great deal of focus on the teaching of Stanislavski and on working meticulously from the inside-out, something I've come across in the professional theater world too. In Laban classes, however, we worked from both inside and outside—usually moving first, then noticing the feeling; and I discovered an outside-in approach for the first time. It was like switching on a light. It was intensely freeing—a relinquishing of control. The mind, so used in my case to feeling that it had to lead, to organize, simply became a witness to the body.

When I played Masha In *Three Sisters* at the National Theatre, we did a great deal of rigorous text work and behind-the-scenes improvisation with the director, but I didn't feel I was getting anywhere. One morning I remembered a class we'd done in Laban on Time, Weight, and Flow, and I felt my body saying "Slow down, get heavy." I walked across the room with a completely new energy and the director immediately said "Yes, that's it, keep that." I love how our physical state so strongly affects and transforms our mental and emotional one. Learning about Laban has helped me beyond words, not just as an actor, but in my whole life.

It's something so fundamental, and yet something that in our mainly mind- and intellect-driven society gets so often drummed out of us. It is our body that connects us with the natural world, with the unseen and the unfathomable, and in the end, it's always our body that knows best.

One day in my third year at RADA, I was feeling muddled and confused about something, stomping along a London street, hunched over my bags, staring angrily at the pavement, and the muddle and the confusion just seemed to be getting worse—and suddenly, I heard Katya's voice: "Look up!" I did. And in that moment, my entire world changed. I didn't change my ideas, I simply made a small shift in my physicality—and immediately, almost miraculously, I found my whole being had completely shifted. By simply paying attention to my body, I had literally changed my mind.

Eve Best
Olivier Award (2005), Drama Desk Award (2007), Tony Award
nominations (2007 and 2015)

INTRODUCTION

The Laban Workbook for Actors is a compendium of practical exercises inspired by the movement concepts of theorist and visionary, Rudolf Laban. The workbook highlights the many ways in which Laban's frameworks can enrich the art of acting and theater making.

The book functions as a hands-on workbook, offering instant access to multiple ways Laban Movement Analysis (LMA) can support actors, directors, movement, voice and acting teachers and coaches in their creative processes, whether working with an established text or on the creation of a new work. The Laban frameworks provide a wonderful array of possibilities for actor training, combining discipline and detail with spontaneity and freedom.

The beauty of Laban's analysis of movement is that his work is not prescriptive. Although his frameworks and terminology are very clear and precise, Laban did not dictate a codified method or technique for the application of his principles and categories. His work can therefore provide unlimited starting points to stimulate actors' creativity, supporting them in making bolder, more nuanced choices, and in developing range and specificity.

Who was Rudolf Laban?

Rudolf Laban (1879–1958) spent his lifetime investigating human movement and describing its components. Laban was a key figure in the German expressionist dance/theater of the 1920s. Years of touring, teaching, and choreographing internationally for dance, theater, and opera led him to be appointed Director of Movement at the State Theater in Berlin in 1930.

During the Second World War, Laban immigrated to England, where his influence spread to the fields of physical education and industry.

While in England, Laban worked with some prominent theater practitioners. He strongly influenced Joan Littlewood and her innovative Theatre Workshop, as well as Yat Malmgren, Geraldine Stephenson and Jean Newlove, who all applied his ideas in UK theater and in actor training. Laban's work remains a primary pedagogy at most British drama schools today. In the USA, training in Laban Movement Analysis is an increasingly central element in university theater departments.

Principles of movement in Laban's work

Laban uncovered basic principles of human movement and provided a detailed vocabulary for describing these, on stage and off. His focus was on the *process* of movement, as a means of developing awareness of the body, its range of dynamic expression, and the body's relationship to space.

In more recent years, the acronym BESS has been coined to describe four basic categories of Laban Studies: Body, Effort, Shape, and Space. Although these four categories are all interrelated and not really separable, they provide different lenses through which to explore movement.

The **Body** component concentrates on increasing our body awareness and physical articulation, including breath support, grounding, body connectedness, and organization. **Effort** refers to the energy and dynamics of our movement; it is the window through which the psyche is revealed. **Shape** describes our ongoing changes in bodily shaping as we relate to ourselves, to others, and to our surroundings. The **Space** component promotes our deep awareness of and connection to the three-dimensional space around us.

You can think of the Body component as relating to precisely *what* the body does; Effort as pertaining to *how* the movement is done, with what psychological and emotional qualities; Space as relating to *where* the movement goes in relation to the outside world; and Shape giving clues as to *why* you play an action toward someone using a particular bodily shape. This is, of course, an extremely simplified shorthand. The BESS elements are expanded on and interpreted in uniquely individual ways within the chapters.

We also include two Appendices that readers will find to be very handy references. The first presents a general overview of BESS terms, and the second presents a visual diagram for each element of BESS.

In his book *The Mastery of Movement on Stage*, Laban cites the power of movement to express the inner life of man: his thoughts, feelings and strivings. His first and primary application of his movement theories was to "the artistic enhancement of human action" in the theater.[1]

When applied to actor training, the psychophysical work of LMA increases actors' embodied sense of self and expands their personal expressive potential. Through the use of movement, the interrelationships between one's inner world and the external and interpersonal world—from the perspectives of both the actor and the character—are enriched.

Chapter summaries

The Laban Workbook for Actors includes five contributors, all Certified Movement Analysts (CMA) from the Laban/Bartenieff Institute of Movement Studies (LIMS) in New York. All have used Laban Movement Analysis (LMA) extensively, as a creative resource for teaching, coaching and directing actors, and for making their own work. The authors write from their own unique perspectives, each developing a particular focus and theme. Thus, the book illustrates some of the many ways Laban's frameworks have inspired both teachers and performers to enhance their creative processes. You will be stimulated by the ways Laban's vocabulary of movement has provided jumping-off points for many different kinds of explorations.

Each chapter in *The Laban Workbook for Actors* includes a short contextual essay followed by a series of insight-bearing exercises. Some chapters also include video links in which student actors explore selected exercises. Although we have presented the chapters in a particular sequence, readers should feel free to dip in and skip around, to choose which portions of the book are most relevant to their immediate needs.

The book begins with **Tom Casciero**'s "A Physical Foundation for the Actor." The focus here is to introduce and explore a set of foundational concepts and principles of movement via the Bartenieff Fundamentals[SM]. Irmgard Bartenieff brought Laban's work to the United States, and her Fundamentals develop the physical underpinnings for the body level component of Laban's work. These re-educational principles bolster your physical awareness, power and expressivity in significant ways, leading to a state in which you are relaxed, listening and responding from deeper places in the body.

This is followed by **Katya Bloom**'s chapter, "*Moving Into Character*." Here we find a wealth of improvisational exercises for exploring not only the physical life, but also the psychological and emotional complexity of characters: their motivations, actions and relationships. The chapter is divided into two parts. First, exercises are aimed at *tuning* your body through mindful movement improvisation. This is followed by exercises that support *transforming* into character. Laban's Effort framework for movement dynamics is emphasized as the source for most explorations.

Next, **Barbara Adrian**'s chapter, "Moving Your Voice: Expanding Your Vocal Creative Potential Through LMA," offers a series of practical explorations based in LMA, through which you are instructed how to increase your expressive range both vocally and physically, and apply that range to text. Devised LMA exercises guide you toward developing the breath, tone, range, articulation and expression needed to tell a story. Methods for examining text for vocal and physical movement clues are explored to lead you toward making active choices, choices that can be seen, heard, and felt.

LMA is put in the context of existing acting pedagogies in "Links Between LMA and Key Acting Techniques" by **Jennifer Mizenko**. Mizenko focuses on examining the major concepts and method-ologies of Stanislavski, Chekhov and Meisner in relation to the Laban themes of Inner/Outer, Exertion/Recuperation, Function/Expression, and Stability/Mobility. Exercises are presented to help you, as an actor or actor trainer, to apply LMA themes to these key acting techniques commonly used in the profession. The exercises help you embody acting techniques through the prism of LMA.

Finally, **Claire Porter** writes about using LMA to create your own work. In "Building a Movement and Text Performance," you will be generating your own movement material and text, experimenting with ways to perform these studies, and finding ways to create your own methods for developing a full evening piece.

The importance of Laban Movement Analysis (LMA) for actor training

The art of movement on stage embraces the whole range of bodily expression including speaking, acting, miming and dancing. (Laban 1950: 4)

Using the exercises in *The Laban Workbook for Actors*, you will come to know yourself more fully, through the medium of movement. As your understanding and embodiment deepen, so will your ability to express inner realities on stage in clearer, more authentic ways. A character's thoughts, feelings, motivations and intentions will manifest more clearly in your vocal and physical expressions.

By exploring these playful exercises, you will learn to recognize your own movement habits and strengths. You can then develop your range of movement and expressivity, while at the same time acquiring specific terminology to describe and reproduce movement. You will be able to make conscious choices to either use your own strengths and preferences effectively, or to call on your training to discover new movement patterns that are truer to your character's history and circumstances.

LMA promotes easeful alignment, the release of tension and deep support for breath, thus bringing power and grace to movement and strength and flexibility to the voice. You will find support for becoming more grounded and connected to a physical center, as you also become more sensitive to physical sensations. These are valuable assets to your imaginative work on stage. In all, you will have more physical tools to express the work of your imagination and the intention of the playwright.

In actor training a distinction is sometimes made between acting from the *inside-out* or from the *outside-in*. From a Laban perspective, the two are really inseparable. What we see or hear or do on the outside affects us internally, both physically and emotionally. Similarly, what we sense and feel internally informs both the way we move and the way we perceive and interact with the outer world. The gift of approaching movement and acting through LMA exercises is that you will be training yourself to work from *inside-out* and *outside-in* simultaneously.

The material presented in *The Laban Workbook for Actors* promotes many skills for acting and for life. In addition to becoming more physically and vocally articulate, LMA will support the development of your observation skills, your psychological and imaginative freedom, and your emotional depth. This will enrich all your relationships. And, last but not least, your ability to learn from mistakes will be enhanced, as you widen your scope for playing with possibilities.

Our hope is that this book will not only offer an exciting collection of new ideas, but will inspire readers to discover their own applications of the Laban material to their working or teaching processes.

Note

1 Ullman, L., Preface to the 2nd Edition of *The Mastery of Movement,* vii (Boston: Plays, Inc., 1960).

1
A PHYSICAL FOUNDATION FOR THE ACTOR

Tom Casciero

Human movement, with all its physical, emotional, and mental implications, is the common denominator of the dynamic art of theatre.

(LABAN 1980: 7)

Introduction

The focus of this chapter is to introduce and explore a set of Foundational Principles of Movement that support the actor's work in the training studio and on stage. These principles are at the heart of Rudolf Laban's inquiry into the nature of human movement. He strove to analyze and identify it as a way to bring clarity and credibility to the study of movement, especially in theater and dance. It was Irmgard Bartenieff who established the physical underpinnings for the Body Level aspects of Laban's work. After studying with him and bringing his theories and practices to the United States in the 1930s, she developed the Bartenieff Fundamentals, a set of body re-education exercises that engage and strengthen foundational movement principles.

The Bartenieff Fundamentals (BF) are a set of "movement sequences for training or retraining a person's functional and expressive capacities" (Woodruff 1989: 8). They emerged as Bartenieff applied Rudolf Laban's work to rehabilitating polio patients in New York City and were later distilled by Bartenieff and Dori Lewis from the many variations of the Fundamentals that she taught. They have their roots in developmental movement and physical therapy and can balance and improve an actor's physical structure and movement skill. "The goal is to reawaken a student's awareness of muscles and joints that are not used, used inadequately or misused so that she or he can extend movement possibilities in both energy and expressivity" (Bartenieff 1980: 230).

The Bartenieff Fundamentals provide a clear and concrete set of exercises and movement principles (described later) that establish the physical foundations for the body level aspects of Laban's work. "Fundamentals are directed not to skill-building, but to the functional ingredients of skills" (Woodruff 1989: 9). The BF are the building blocks of more complex movement and patterns of movement. They are not the tennis serve itself, for example, but the ability of the player to be *grounded*, use *breath* to *initiate* and *support* the movement, and to have an *intention* in space that *organizes* the body to complete the task.

The movement foundations in the BF may not at first appear to be directly related to the skills of developing a character, creating a devised piece of physical theater, or to performing a monologue or scene. However, the BF provide the functional ingredients of those skills, just as they did with the tennis serve. Because they work to strengthen the foundational aspects of an actor's movement, they ultimately provide a platform from which, and on which, other skills may be built. As such, they have great value in creating physical character and in enriching movement and voice.

The Bartenieff Fundamentals lead to and bolster an actor's physical awareness, power, expressivity, and range of movement in significant ways. They help the actor to become aware of and eliminate or re-pattern inefficient movement habits. And they lead to a state in which the actor is relaxed, and listening and responding from deeper places in the body.

As actors become embodied in their own physical forms through the Bartenieff Fundamentals exercises, they become present within themselves and present in the moment. This is perhaps one of simplest, yet most vital skills of the actor. Each actor also becomes aware of and sensitive to their inner life and its relationship to the outer world. By understanding themselves through movement, they come to understand the characters whose thoughts, feelings, and values they must bring to life. And that's a good thing.

Here's how I've laid out the chapter:

First, we'll clear the body of tension so everything that follows is more accessible and efficient.

Then we'll go straight to a physical exploration of the spiral, because a three-dimensional spiral in space engages many of the Foundational Principles of Movement. This will also provide a large muscle warm-up and increase flexibility. We'll follow that by defining the foundational movement principles and identifying how they are at work as the building blocks that make the spiral possible.

Next we'll explore the Bartenieff Fundamentals, both those that Bartenieff described as the "Basic Six," and other exercises inspired by her work. The Foundational Principles of Movement will be identified as they occur in the BF and used to inform and strengthen your awareness and range of movement. We'll then go back to the spiral, this time with the added support of the Fundamentals and their underlying movement principles and see what happens.

The chapter wouldn't be complete without with some playful applications to acting. So we'll take the movement principles and all you've learned on your feet and use them to create physical characters. We'll put them in open scenes and see what happens. Then, as one of these new characters, you'll deliver one of your own favorite scripted monologues. Let's get started.

Tension and tension release

Two kinds of obstructions are possible; the physical and the mental inhibition ... (Laban 1980: 120)

Physical tension can mute expression, restricting the flow of feeling and thought to the audience and other actors. It can inhibit the ability to be in touch with oneself physically and emotionally, limiting access to the depth and breadth of the human experience. And tension stands in the way of incoming information, compromising the actor's ability to listen and respond fully to others. The actor must become aware of and neutralize unnecessary tensions to be efficient on stage and in life.

In order to lessen tension, it's important to understand the source of that tension. Acute, but temporary, tensions caused by falling asleep in an unusual position are easily remedied. Chronic tensions that are developed over time and through habitual use, or compensation for an injury, dampen or mute expression the most. The sources of tension are myriad—postures or movement modeled on family traits, past emotional events, conflicting values, body image, and cultural factors. Worrying about the past and future, the stress of expectations, hectic schedules, and lack of sleep also create tension. It is by recognizing the source of tension and taking charge of your inner life that you begin diffusing tension and moving toward a freedom of movement that is your birthright.

The following release exercises are helpful in regaining that freedom of movement. Some are Bartenieff's preparations for the Fundamentals. Others are my own discoveries, and some are from other sources.

Exercise 1: Using the Heel Rock to locate tension

The Heel Rock is actually a preparatory exercise for the Fundamentals. Bartenieff refers to it as "Rock and Roll." The rock is used here as a tool for locating tension and gently releasing it. In rocking the skeleton, we expose holding patterns in the musculature. If the movement is not sequencing through the body, a misalignment or holding pattern in the musculature is responsible. Work in partners and in bare feet.

1 **Partner A** lies on the floor face up. **Partner B** kneels or sits at her feet and grasps each ankle by wrapping the hand around the ankle just below the prominent anklebones. The fingers will be on one side and the thumb on the other. Partner B must also be grounded and aligned while working.

2 **Partner B** gently presses down—this grounds the heel to the earth. While pressing, pull your hands toward you and the foot will point slightly. While still grounding the heel, push your

hands away from you and the foot will flex slightly. Make this a continuous movement and the whole skeleton will "rock" back and forth. Allow your wrists to be flexible and their foot to hinge.

3   Rock for 1 minute. Pause, and both A and B inhale and release a few breaths.

4   Rock the partner again for 1 minute.

5   Allow **Partner A** to describe the areas of tension she felt. **Partner B** then describes the holding places she saw or felt.

6   Repeat with **Partner B** on the floor.

Tips for spotting tension:

1   Does the chest look open and relaxed and is the breath freely flowing? No? Check to see if the jaw is held shut, or there is tension in the chest or shoulder/shoulder blades.

2   Is the head free and rocking? If not the spine may be misaligned or the neck tense.

3   If the pelvis doesn't rock toward you and away from you, check for low back tension.

4   Are the thighs tense? Often the knees are hyperextended. Roll a towel and place it under the knees.

5   Use the following tension release exercises to address your findings.

After some practice with a partner, this exercise can also be done on one's own. Be sure to initiate from the ankle, flexing and extending.

Exercise 2: The Shake Out

1   Lie on your back on the floor with the knees up and feet flat on the floor.

2   Lift and shake the feet. Let them rise up toward the ceiling, shaking until the whole leg (into pelvis) is involved. Shake for 10 seconds and then allow the legs to float downward.

3   Repeat three times. Shake gently at first and more vigorously
     on the repetitions.

4   Add the hands and arms. Shake the hands with the feet, and
     arms with the legs as they rise toward the ceiling. Allow the
     movement to affect the shoulders and pelvis. Shake for 10
     seconds and then allow the legs to float downward.

5   Repeat three times. Shake gently at first and then more
     vigorously.

Exercise 3: Somatic rolling — exterior awareness

1   Lie on the floor on your back. Begin rolling across the floor.
     Bring your focus to the surfaces of your body as they contact
     the floor. As you roll the surfaces will change — first your side,
     then abdomen, other side, etc. Note any areas of tension and
     breathe into that area. Exhale and allow the tension to release.

2   When you arrive at the other side of the room, stop, sit up and
     watch others roll.

3   When everyone has completed rolling, lie down again in the
     same position and begin rolling in the opposite direction.

4   When stopped, notice the sensations and attunement to
     yourself and the environment.

Exercise 4: Somatic rolling — interior awareness

1   Lie on the floor on your back.

2   Begin rolling across the floor. This time bring your focus to your
     internal organs as you roll. Feel the effects of gravity on your
     heart, and lungs, brain, intestines, etc. as they fall toward the
     floor. They will be falling toward the floor continuously, but in
     different directions in the body — sometimes front, or side, or
     back, etc.

3   With each turn of the roll, note your sense of fullness as their
     weight shifts within you.

4 When everyone has completed rolling, lie down again in the same position and begin rolling in the opposite direction.

5 When everyone has completed rolling in this direction, stand and walk about the room.

6 Is the perspective from which you now view the world different from before the roll? Are you more aware? Present? Grounded? If so, how? Can this state be useful to the actor? If so, how? Share your observations with one another.

Exercise 5: Releasing the shoulder blades

The shoulder blades (scapulae) and collarbones support the functional and expressive movement of the arms. If restricted, the arm's mobility will be reduced or the arm will fatigue more readily.

1 Lie on your back with the knees up, feet flat on the floor, and the arms out to the sides, perpendicular to the trunk. Let the palms be flat on the floor with the thumbs pointing downward (relative to your body, i.e., toward your feet).

2 Rotate the arms and hands by initiating from the shoulder blade. Let the hand turn over, the palm will be facing up and thumb will now be pointing in the direction of the top of the head.

3 Continuing rotating in the *same direction* once more so that the thumb is again pointing toward the feet and the arms are very twisted.

4 Hold this position for 20 seconds. During that time, breathe into your back between the shoulder blades and release as you exhale. On the next breath, feel the ribs widen and release. And on the third breath, allow the arms to rotate back to their original position. Note the relationship of the shoulder blades to the floor.

5 Repeat three times or as needed to induce release.

Exercise 6: The Sock Rock—pelvis/low back

This release is for the lower back and sacrum, an area laced with nervous system fibers and muscular attachments. This exercise massages the area, encouraging muscular release and stimulating the nervous system. It releases the spine, helping to reintegrate the upper and lower body and to restore grounding between the lower body and the earth.

1 Use a soft rubber, foam, or tennis ball, or a pair of rolled-up socks.

2 Lie on your back, knees up, feet flat on the floor.

3 Press into the floor with your feet and lift the pelvis off the floor. Place the sock under the triangle formed by the tailbone and the two bumps at the back of the hipbones.

4 Adjust the ball/sock until the pelvis is "floating" on it, teeter-tottering from side to side and up to down. Let your breath be soft and spine long. After 2 minutes lift the pelvis, remove the sock, and lower the pelvis. Notice the relationship of the pelvis to the floor.

5 Slowly roll over, kneel, and come to a standing position. Begin walking. Avoid returning to habitual ways of walking or standing. Notice any difference and discuss what you find.

Spiraling through space

The spiral is one of the most beautiful forms in nature. There is a visual beauty to its three-dimensional curve through space that reflects a mathematical beauty within. Its path radiates outward in a mathematical constancy associated with the Fibonacci sequence of numbers and with the Golden Mean (1.618033).

All of the foundational principles I'll be discussing and you'll be experiencing in this chapter are engaged when moving in the spiral. Following the path of the spiral through space requires a complex combination of physical body support, three-dimensional shape changes in the body, and an attention to, and relationship with, space. So let's get to it and I'll explain the relationships afterward.

See: 1 Demonstration of the spiral
https://vimeo.com/channels/thelabanworkbook/199987581

Exercise 1: Spiraling downward, right hand to left foot

Initiate and lead with the hand. The goal is to spiral around and down and touch the toe. For those less flexible, make any needed adjustments. Please see the video example for more clarity.

1 Begin standing, arms and legs in the shape of an X. To begin the spiral, initiate with the right hand and sweep forward in a curve across your body, to the left, and down as you go.

2 Exhale throughout the movement; with less air in your body, you'll be able to condense more and thus go deeper and farther into the twist.

3 Spatial intent—track your hand with your eyes as it traces along the spiral through space. This will engage the head and spine, etc. and help to organize the movement.

4 Allow your feet to pivot as you turn and knees to bend deeper as you lower.

5 If possible, tuck the right knee slightly under the left. This will allow the torso to sink and twist more.

6 When you arrive, the head is down and you're looking at your right hand and right toes.

Exercise 2: Spiraling upward—right hand, return to standing

Initiate the movement in the lower body. The movement is supported by the breath and is initiated by the tailbone. It sequences through the pelvis, belly, chest, shoulder blade, and out through the arm and hand.

1 In this rather twisted position there is limited space in the torso

for breath in the lungs. So as you inhale, the lungs will expand and change the shape of the torso, helping it to rise and untwist.

2   Initiate with the tailbone, tucking it down and under as your legs press into the earth to drive the pelvis upward.

3   The upper lungs will fill as you continue breathing in. This will widen and lengthen the torso to support your rise.

4   The shoulder, arm, and hand are drawn upward by the torso as it rises and unwinds.

5   The arm swings outward and the hand travels along the same spiral it rode downward. Track your hand with your eyes as it moves along the spiral.

6   Allow a pivot on the balls of the feet as you turn.

7   As your torso unwinds and faces forward, its expansion is complete and the shoulder blade now takes over as the source of the initiation of the movement.

8   As the arm continues rising on the spiral pathway, the sequencing of the movement flows through the elbow and wrist as they unbend. This returns you to the X position.

Exercise 3: Repeat right hand spiral downward and upward

1   Repeat the steps in Exercises 1 and 2, spiraling down and back up five times.

2   Make any adjustments needed in order to maintain your balance and alignment.

Exercise 4: Spiraling downward—left hand to right foot

Begin standing, arms and legs in the shape of an X. This time initiate with the left hand, reaching out to spiral forward, to the right, and down as you go.

1   Repeat the rest of the sequence as described in Exercise 1. Simply substitute the word left for right.

Exercise 5: Spiraling upward—left hand, return to standing

1   Initiate the movement in the lower body. The movement is supported by the breath and is initiated by the tailbone. It sequences through the pelvis, belly, chest, shoulder blade and out through the arm and hand. Follow the steps as described in Exercise 2. Simply substitute the word left for right.

Exercise 6: Left hand spiral downward and upward

1   Repeat the steps in Exercises 1 and 2, spiraling down and back up five times.

2   Make adjustments to maintain balance and alignment. Use spatial intent. Simply substitute the word left for right.

Foundational movement principles in the spiral

In this section I'll introduce specific Foundational Principles of Movement and show you how and where they appear in the spiral exercise, and how they support the movement sequences. The principles are:

Breath support

The manner in which the breath initiates and supports the dynamics of movement. Breath affects and is affected by the mover's inner psychological, emotional, and physical states, and by the nature of the outside world. Restriction of breath can create restriction of movement, emotion, and thought.

Spiral: The breath changes the shape of the torso—first allowing the body to sink as the lungs empty, the ribs narrow, and the diaphragm rises to make room in the belly. To stand, the breath begins filling the lower lungs. As more breath is drawn in, the lungs expand in three dimensions and the upper torso lengthens and widens. This supports the rise and uncurling of the body.

Initiation

The source of the movement. While the terms below identify broader regions of the body where movement may originate, it can begin in any part of the body.

- Core—the torso or trunk of the body.
- Proximal—the shoulder and hip joints
- Mid-limb—elbow, wrist, knee, ankle.
- Distal—the extremities: hands, fingers, feet, toes, head.
- Upper body—the torso, arms, head.
- Lower body—pelvis, legs, feet, toes.

Spiral: On the way down, the movement begins distally (the hand). To rise, the core initiates, pressing the tailbone downward.

Sequencing

The manner in which movement transitions through the body. Lack of sequencing usually reveals a holding pattern or lack of awareness in the body. For the purposes of this chapter, the terms below will be used.

- Successive—adjacent body parts move one after another (fingers fold, then hand, wrist).
- Simultaneous—all active body parts move at the same time.

Spiral: The sequencing is successive, flowing down through the body from hand to foot. The hand initiates, the eyes follow and take the spine into a curve. When crossing the midline of the body, the hip joint is engaged and, as it turns, the legs must respond all the way down to the rotation on the ball of the foot. To return to standing the tailbone initiates; the movement sequences downward as the quadriceps muscles engage, the knees and ankles unbend, and the foot rotates. At the same time, the movement sequences through the hip joints and upward through the torso, shoulder, and out through the arm to the hand.

Grounding

Grounding refers to the physical relationship one has with the earth in order to provide stability. The degree of grounding may be very rooted, stable, and consistent, or tentative, unstable, and inconsistent. Grounding is related to the center of weight and center of gravity (see below).

Spiral: The body is grounded through the feet to the earth, even when on the balls of the feet. As you twist and descend through the spiral, the center of weight must be directly over the feet in order to maintain the stability needed to descend and rise again.

Dynamic alignment and connections

This is the *dynamic* alignment and connection of the skeleton. It's not simply the structures themselves (leg bones, etc.). It is the relationships between the structures and how they work together that supports weight bearing, efficient movement, and fulfillment of one's intention in moving. Key connections are:

- Head to tailbone (spinal): Connects upper and lower body. It provides a sense of alignment and the vertical axis within us. A break in this connection can restrict breath support and create unneeded tension. The head thrust forward might, for example, imply the intelligence leading, or a reaching forward for approval.
- Scapula to fingertip: Connects from core to distal (torso

to hand). This connection allows for an extension into the surrounding space and is related to relationships. Developmentally, as the infant discovers and uses the hands, a differentiation is made between the torso and hand. The body becomes "this" and the hand becomes "that." This develops into the sense of me (here) and the hand (there). The differentiation later develops into me and you.

- Sit bone to heel: Connects the pelvis to the ground. This connection promotes stability for exploring mobility. It is a solid physical foundation for strength and for exploration of the world. One's relationship to the ground is reflective of one's psychology: "he can't stand his ground," or "stakes out his territory."

Spiral: These connections are vital to moving through the spiral. The heel–sit bone connection grounds the body and levers it up and down. The relationship between the heel and sit bone remains connected even when the knees and hip joints are bent. The head–tail (spine) becomes engaged when the eyes track the hand through the space. That engages the head, which in turn engages the spine. So there is a dynamic alignment; the spine maintains its connectivity and sequencing even as it twists. And the connection between scapula and hand is the bridge that then connects the body to the space.

Body organization

This refers to various ways the body can be organized to prepare for and engage in movement.

- Breath—use of breath as a somatic element to sense and organize the body as a whole.
- Spinal—a way of organizing via the dynamic head–tail connection.
- Upper/Lower—organizing via the relationship between the upper and lower body—the way they are connected and yet distinct. There is a focus on accessing space with the upper and shifting weight in the lower.

- Body Half—organizing the body bilaterally to allow one side to move and one side to remain stable. When the movement of the right and left sides of the body are separated the midline of the body is established.

- Cross Lateral—organizing the body via a diagonal that runs from the arm through the body to the opposite leg. Crossing the midline of the body offers more movement choices and greater range of movement. It parallels the crossing that occurs developmentally between the right and left cortexes of the brain. Both crossings result in more skills and more choices.

Spiral: The spiral is naturally three-dimensional. As such, the body must be organized in a complex three-dimensional manner to ride the spiral through space. Cross-lateral movement is the most complex organization and in this case encompasses both breath and spinal organization.

Center of weight

The center of weight is located in the lower belly and provides a center of gravity when the body is in an upright balanced stance. However, the center of gravity changes each time a person moves. Both centers relate to balance, stability, and mobility. They are used as a focal point for breathing and vocal support. Some cultures believe it to be a center of life force.

Spiral: To spiral, the center of gravity must be maintained over the supporting structures (legs and feet) even as you turn and fold and sink. Otherwise, as you may have experienced, the weight pitches one way or another and balance and stability are lost.

Weight shifts

Weight shifts are the transfer of weight between supporting body parts. A lunge in fencing would be a functional shift. A constant side-to-side shift from foot to foot might be an expressive movement that indicates nervousness.

Spiral: A portion of the weight shifts subtly to one foot to allow the other to rotate on the ball.

Spatial intent

Bartenieff found that when her polio patients had an intention in space, the intention was far more effective in rehabilitation than rote repetitions of movement. Physical action in life and on stage results from need, motivation, and striving for values. Intention focuses that physical action. If I am thirsty, I intend to pick up a glass of juice to quench that thirst. That intention organizes my body's capabilities to complete the task, to reach into space for the glass.

Spiral: There is a destination and a path when moving in the spiral. Your goal is to reach the destination (foot); your intention is to follow the path of the spiral to that foot. The eyes focus on the hand as you reach out to ride the path of the spiral through space. As it does, the head, spine, arms, hips, legs, and feet organize to remain on the path and reach the destination. They must remain organized in order to find stability when stopped at the bottom of the spiral. To return to standing, follow the same process moving outward and upward. You'll notice here that there is a need for a push into the earth to rise.

Relating movement principles to character history and traits

This is a simple example of how Foundational Principles of Movement might be aligned with the information gleaned from dramaturgy and script analysis.

Othello: As a leader of his people and his army, Othello would not only possess strength, but project it as well. To do so he would need strong *breath support, grounding,* and *dynamic connections* throughout the body. Initiating with *core support* creates *stability* and strength. *Simultaneous sequencing* would best serve a man of immediacy and action. Organizing the body via upper-lower generates both stability and mobility. *Cross-lateral* movement would also be present from his weapons training, particularly the sword.

Iago: A creature of deception, false subservience, and degradation is expressed quite differently. To organize his body *bilaterally* would create a physical dichotomy, allowing him to present and express his false loyalty to Othello with one half of his body, while turning and hiding the other half, thus hiding his devious hatred and lies. Using more *shifts of weight* would make him harder to read, to pin down. *Successive sequencing* could hint at the movement and rhythm of a snake. A shallow and seemingly weak *breath support* could convey his subservience when with Othello, yet be replaced with strong support as he takes his asides to the audience, revealing the true nature and power of his plans.

The Bartenieff Fundamentals

Bartenieff states: "There are six basic exercises … The six are considered basic because they are applicable to all activity. They are concerned with the internal support of the body as it develops into uprightness. In that sense, they are concerned with centering. That means being able to connect with the source of one's strength, even when in motion so that balance is maintained" (Bartenieff 1980: 20).

In the following section, I describe the "Basic Six" BF exercises. At times, they are supplemented with other exercises of my own or those created by others. Each of the exercises reinforces some aspect of the Foundational Principles of Movement inherent in the BF.

The basic six Bartenieff Fundamentals

1 Thigh Lift
2 Pelvic Forward Shift
3 Pelvic Lateral Shift
4 Body Half

5 Diagonal Knee Drop

6 Arm Circle/Sit-up

The foundational movement principles described earlier (p. 17) are inherent in the six BF. See if you recognize them as you explore these exercises.

Bartenieff Fundamentals: The Thigh Lift

The Thigh Lift is a simple exercise in which you lift your bent leg while lying on the floor on your back, your knees up, and feet flat on the floor. It engages the iliopsoas muscles, a set of deep postural support muscles, the strongest of the hip flexors. They are connected to the front side of the lumbar vertebra of the spine and run forward and deep through the hip joint to the top and front of the femur leg bone. So they connect the upper and lower body, and the front and back of the body. This provides greater stability in the core to mobilize, and greater support for hip movements in multiple directions.

In my opinion, when actors have a kinesthetic sense of their deep core, they then have a concrete physical experience to relate to their vocal and character work. Things such as three-dimensional breath or access to the lower resonators is no longer an idea, but a visceral experience. Having a felt sense of the body also offers the actor the opportunity to physically center a character in, for example, that low belly.

The support for the Thigh Lift is initiated from deep in the core at the iliopsoas muscle and flows outward. Partway through the lift, the quadriceps will begin working; however, the quadriceps should not initiate the movement, only carry it on. If there is unnecessary tension in the musculature, this sequencing may be restricted. In that case, choose one of the tension release exercises explored earlier and then return to the Thigh Lift.

See: 2 Demonstration of the Thigh Lift
https://vimeo.com/channels/thelabanworkbook/199996287

Exercise 1: The Thigh Lift

In learning the Thigh Lift it is helpful to name the different processes within the sequence. Although the processes overlap and intertwine, each can serve as a marker along the sequence of movement. This serves as a simple guide for a complex movement. It also allows you to work on any section independently, and then place it back in the context of the full sequence.

1 *Start*—lie on your back with knees up and feet flat on the floor.

2 *Breathe*—inhale through the nose, filling the torso in a relaxed way.

3 *Release*—exhale through the mouth; allow a full release like a slow sigh. The release sequences through the chest, and the chest softens and falls toward the floor.

4 *Hollow*—the release and sequencing continues into the abdomen. As the breath is exhaled, the diaphragm pulls up and the belly falls toward the floor. The abdomen looks and feels hollowed.

5 *Lengthen*—the spine lengthens as a result of the exhalation, the hollowing, and the iliopsoas lengthening. The muscles of the low back relax and lengthen, releasing the sacrum to the floor, and the tailbone tips up slightly. The lengthening also travels head-ward, but for now, we'll focus on foot-ward.

6 *Initiate the lift*—the psoas initiates the lifting of the leg, then the quadriceps engage, both working to lift the leg. The knee remains bent, taking the foot in an arc upward. When the lower leg is parallel to the floor, take a breath in.

7 *Lower the leg*—as you exhale, release the spine to lengthen and lower the leg slowly.

8 *Hands-on reinforcement*—repeat the sequence, this time using your hands to trace its path. Place your hands on your chest and as you exhale and it softens, slide your hands down the ribs toward the belly. As the belly hollows, let your hands continue sliding down into the hollowing and then each one

toward the hip sockets. This last part traces the path of the psoas muscle.

A hands-on approach like this will speed your learning of the sequence. By placing your hands on your body and moving them along the progression of the *breathe–release–hollow–lengthen–initiate* sequence, you stimulate mechanoreceptors. They send signals to the brain that senses that particular part of the body. The brain uses the input to make a body map, a kind of virtual body part. So the more you stimulate the receptors and move, the more detailed the map becomes and the more efficient the movement.

Bartenieff Fundamentals: Pelvic Forward Shift

The pelvic forward shift is performed while lying on the floor. It's called a forward shift because although the pelvis is moving upward in the space, it is moving forward in relationship to the body-self (Casciero 1998: 114).

Use the *breathe–release–hollow–lengthen–initiate* sequence for this movement.

1 *Start*—lie on your back with knees up and feet flat on the floor.

2 *Breathe*—inhale through the nose, filling the torso in a relaxed way.

3 *Release*—exhale through the mouth; allow a full release like a sigh. The release and sequencing soften the chest, the abdomen hollows, the spine lengthens, and you raise the pelvis.

4 *Lengthen*—the spine lengthens as a result of the exhalation, the hollowing and the iliopsoas lengthening. The lengthening can be felt moving along the spine upward and downward. The muscles of the low back lengthen, releasing the sacrum to the floor, and the tailbone tips up slightly.

5 *Initiate the lift*—follow the lengthening of the iliopsoas and the tilt of the tip of the tailbone upward and lift the pelvis, pressing the feet firmly into the floor on your exhale.

6   The pelvis is raised and the center of weight shifts forward until a straight line is formed from the shoulder to the knee. The head–tail and sit bone–heel connections are engaged. The feet are grounded and supporting weight.

7   While in the lifted position, allow the breath to be free. Notice if there is any unneeded muscular tension and release it on a breath.

8   Settle the pelvis to the floor by focusing on and deepening hip joint.

9   Repeat the sequence five times.

Application: C-curve Squat

Arthur Lessac's C-curve Squat includes a Pelvic Forward Shift and so it engages many of the same movement principles, although done from a standing position.

See: 3 Demonstration of the C-curve Squat
https://vimeo.com/channels/thelabanworkbook/199987680

Exercise 1: Standing to squatting down

1   Use the *breathe–release–hollow–lengthen–initiate* sequence.

2   Begin in standing position, arms at sides, feet apart, and balanced. *Inhale* through nose.

3   *Exhale* through the mouth throughout the movement.

4   At *initiation*, tilt the tailbone forward and let the pelvis follow the tailbone forward and downward into a squat. The whole spine follows the curve in a *successive sequence* and at the bottom takes the shape of a "C curve" (Lessac 1978: 176). The spine is curved, but fully aligned from *tailbone to head*. Ideally, the feet are flat on the floor. However, everyone is built differently, so some must remain on the balls of the feet.

5   As the *breath* is exhaled there is more room for the body to change shape and condense. It is important to allow the hip joint to *flex* and *deepen*.

Exercise 2: Squatting to standing up

1 To rise to standing, *inhale* starting at the *tailbone* and imagine the breath traveling all the way up the front side of the spine. At the same time as you begin, press into the earth with the feet and legs and engage the deep support muscles. Allow all of this to lift the body up. It starts in the C-curve and then unfolds on the way to standing

2 Repeat the squat and stand sequence five times.

3 Walk through the room and note any changes in your walk, rhythm, or awareness.

Exercise 3: Adding the arms—standing to squatting down

1 Before moving, let the elbows be at your sides, the arm bent 90 degrees, and the palms facing up.

2 As you inhale, pull the elbows straight back until the hands are near your ribs.

3 When you exhale, scoop the arms forward and downward in an arc. This happens at the same time that you are scooping the tailbone down and forward. The arms trace the same curved path of the tailbone, ending in a "U" or C-curve on it's back.

4 You arrive in the squat in a curved position, the shape of a "C." The spine is a curved line from head to tailbone. The head/neck are a part of the curve, not tilted backward.

Exercise 4: Adding the arms—squatting to standing up

1 Pull the elbows back on your *exhale*.

2 To rise to standing, *inhale* starting at the *tailbone* and imagine the breath traveling all the way up the front side of the spine.

3 At the same time press into the earth with the feet and legs

and engage the deep support muscles. Allow all of this to lift the body up. It starts in the C-curve and then unfolds on the way to standing.

4 As you *inhale*, the hands come together at the navel and travel up the midline of the body, following the breath upward. At the top they spout like a whale and fall in an arc to your sides

5 Walk through the room and note any changes in your walk, rhythm, or awareness.

Exercise 5: The Standing Thigh Lift

1 Return to the Thigh Lift on the floor and do five lifts with each leg. Use the *breathe–release–hollow–lengthen–initiate* sequence.

2 Come to standing with the feet slightly apart. Lift one knee up and balance on the other leg. Repeat with the other knee and leg. Notice the subtle *weight shift*.

3 Now do the Thigh Lift from the standing position. The sequence plays an important role here because you are negotiating with gravity.

4 Follow the breath down through the hollowing and initiate with the tailbone, dipping it forward like the beginning of the squat. Let that initiate the lifting of the knee and allow the torso to come forward a bit into a slight C-curve. Let the leg down slowly as you lengthen and straighten the spine.

5 Repeat three times on each side. Notice the lateral shift of your pelvis as you shift your weight on each standing thigh lift, because that's what is coming up next!

Bartenieff Fundamentals: Pelvic Lateral Shift

This BF is a lateral shift of the pelvis in a pure side-to-side movement while on your back on the floor. Its goal is to engage the pelvic floor muscles (while standing, imagine a diaphragm like the one used for breathing, except at the bottom of the bowl of your pelvis). It becomes more engaged in forward weight shifts, walking, and rotating the thighs. It creates more stability for locomotion and changing direction. By increasing core support, the surface muscles can be used less, often resulting in less tension. And that means freer breath, freer movement, and freer voice.

Exercise 1: Pelvic Lift and Shift

1 *Start*—lie on your back with knees up and feet flat on the floor.

2 *Breathe*—inhale, filling the torso in a relaxed way.

3 *Release, hollow, and lengthen*—exhale, allow a full release that sequences through the chest and continues into the abdomen to create the hollowing and lengthening.

4 *Initiate* the lift—tilt of the tip of the tailbone upward and lift the pelvis, pressing the feet firmly into the floor.

5 *Shift* the pelvis to the right in a direct line. Let the bone that sticks out at the hip (trochanter) lead the way. Keep the pelvis level the whole time. Set the pelvis down.

6 Repeat the sequence—lift the pelvis by *initiating* with the tailbone. *Shift* the pelvis back to the center by leading with large hipbone. Then lower the pelvis to the floor.

7 Repeat the sequence to the other side.

8 Now lift and shift the pelvis to the right and set it down, lift and shift to the center and set it down, lift and shift to the left and set it down, and then lift and shift back to the center and set it down. Repeat this progression five times.

Bartenieff Fundamentals: Body Half—homo-lateral connection

The Body Half experience delineates the right and left sides of the body, establishing the midline of the body. For example, the torso and limbs on the right side of the body move together (homo-lateral). The initiation for this exercise is normally elbow and knee (*mid-limb initiation*). I also included a variation (Exercise 2) that uses *core initiation*, providing an experience of the differences between core and mid-limb initiation.

Note *breath support* and *head–tail, heel–sit bones,* and *scapula–hand* skeletal connections.

Exercise 1: Body Half—mid-limb initiation

1 Lie on the back with the body in an X position. Stay as flat as possible throughout.

2 *Exhale* at the same time that you draw the right elbow and knee (*mid-limb initiation*) together on the floor at mid-waist level. The spine (*head–tail*) will bend in that direction, shortening the right side. Let the head roll that way also.

3 Keep the left side of the body on the floor while the right side is in motion. It must remain *stable* and *grounded* while the right side is *mobile*. If the left hip does leave the floor, don't bring the right elbow and knee as closely together.

4 *Inhale* at the same time that you *initiate mid-limb*, extending the arm and leg to the return the original X position. The *breath* changes the shape of the torso, supporting the movement.

5 Repeat five times on each side.

Exercise 2: Variation on Body Half with core initiation

1 Lie on your back in an X position.

2 On an *exhalation*, *initiate* from the *core*, drawing the ribs and the curved crest of the hipbone closer together on the right side.

3 This will curve the spine to that side and let your elbow and knee draw together. Continue by engaging your arm and leg to complete the movement.

4 Keep the left side of the body *stable* and *grounded* while the right side is in motion.

5 *Inhale*, filling the torso on the right side and opening the space

between the ribs and crest of the hip. Use it to initiate the return of the arm and leg to the original X position.

6   Repeat five times on each side.

Exercise 3: Condensing to fetal

You've worked one side of the body (bilateral) in the two previous exercises. Here you will extend the movement and engage the other half of the body, connecting *upper/lower* and condensing into the fetal position. Start on your back, limbs arranged in X position.

- Imagine yourself in a circle, like da Vinci's Vetruvian Man.

- Repeat Exercise 1, *exhale* and condense the *right side* of the body by bringing the elbow and knee together. You now have one side of the body condensed and one side open.

- As the open side of the torso reaches the end of its ability to stretch, extend the movement by sweeping the left hand upward and around the circle to the right. The left foot sweeps downward and around the circle to the right. Keep them on the floor.

- To engage the muscles of the torso to connect the *upper/ lower*, it's necessary to keep the arm straight and *the whole* leg straight as you swing it from the hip joint. The strength and *stability* needed to do so engages the core.

- Wait until your arm is at 10 o'clock and leg at 8 o'clock to fold into the fetal position.

- To unfold, inhale to support the changes in the torso as you slide the left hand up and left foot down until the limbs straighten, and the torso unfolds, and you roll over on your back.

- Return to the X position by adjusting the arms and legs.

- Repeat five times on each side of the body.

- With a partner, use hands-on guidance to map the proper form and the pathways.

Exercise 4: The Book—bilateral folding

This helps to further establish the midline of the body. It's called "The Book" because it mimics the opening and closing of a book.

1 Begin in the fetal position on your right side.

2 Imagine that you are a book. Keep the left elbow and left knee in the same plane, and the right elbow and right knee in the same plane, as if they are the front and back covers of the book.

3 Lift your left side off the floor and open it like you would a book cover. If you continue to open, it should take you onto your back, bringing the right elbow and knee (the back cover of the book) off the floor a bit. You will end up on your back with both sets of your arms and legs forming a V.

4 Now close the back cover of the book by folding the right side (elbow/knee) to the floor on the left. You'll again be in the fetal position, but on your left side.

5 Repeat to the right by reversing the procedure.

6 Repeat the entire set—left/right—five times.

7 Bring yourself to standing. Notice yourself physically. Don't alter anything, just notice. Begin walking and again notice how you feel and move.

Bartenieff Fundamentals: The Diagonal Knee Drop—the contralateral connection

Contralateral movement occurs when you reach across the mid-line of the body, taking you into three-dimensional movement. It is also a way to organize movement via the diagonal in the body. Developmentally, this crossover parallels the crossover that occurs between the right and left hemispheres of the brain. Both result in new perspectives and abilities. Exercise 1 is an adaptation of the Heel Rock introduced earlier. Exercise 2 is often taught in the Laban Certification training. I've included them because they are effective in delivering the experience of the diagonal in the body and of contralateral body organization.

Preparation Exercise 1: Diagonal Heel Rock

The Diagonal Heel Rock offers a somatic experience of the *diagonal* in the body. It engages *breath support, grounding, sequencing*, and *skeletal connections*, and reveals holding patterns in the diagonal.

1 To prepare, work with a partner and repeat the Heel Rock exercise from the Tension Release section. Consciously use your inhalations and exhalations to soften and allow the sequencing of the rocking to flow from your heel to your head. Partner A is on the floor, Partner B is attending.

2 Now move to the diagonal version of the Heel Rock.

3 Partner A slides the arms and legs out until the limbs and body form an easy X position.

4 Partner B sits at the end of Partner A's right arm, and looks down the diagonal from the arm through torso and down the left leg. Partner B adjusts the arm or leg as needed so it is in line with the diagonal.

5 Partner B grasps A's wrist with right hand and encircles it with the thumb and forefinger of one hand (like a bracelet). The left hand holds the fleshy part of A's upper forearm just above the elbow.

6 Partner B gently pulls the arm (without lifting) until the diagonal in the body—right wrist to left foot—is engaged and stretched. Hold the stretch for 20 seconds, then release. Repeat.

7 Partner A—initiate a Heel Rock using just your right foot, this time it sequences up the diagonal to the left hand. Rest.

8 Partner B grasps the wrist of the right arm as before and pulls hard enough to rock the skeleton in time with Partner A's rocking. It is a gentle pull and release.

9 Repeat on the other diagonal.

10 Repeat with Partner B on the floor.

Exercise 2: The Diagonal Knee Drop

This engages *breath, initiation, sequencing, grounding,* and *cross-lateral organization.*

1 Lie flat on the back with knees up and feet flat on the floor. Slide your left arm along the floor until it is in the X position, as it was in the Diagonal Heel Rock. This will allow the movement to sequence all the way up the diagonal from the knees.

2 With a release of breath, *allow* the knees to fall to the right side. Keep the *head–tail* aligned as you *allow* the torso to twist. Let the movement *sequence* from the knees through the torso and into the left shoulder. Allow the head to roll to the left also.

3 Engage the psoas, and use your *core* and *breath support* to return the legs to the original position. *Inhale* as if sucking through a straw. Imagine the *breath* filling the pelvis and as it fills, it presses the whole sacrum to the floor. This allows the return of the bent legs to their original upright position.

4 Repeat above five times on each side.

Exercise 3: Application—the Sitting Knee Drop or "swimsuit pose"

The Sitting Knee Drop offers a somatic (physical) experience of the diagonal in the body. *Sequencing* from knees to shoulders it engages *breath support*, and a *dynamic head–tail connection* as the upper body twists against the lower.

1 Sit on the floor with the knees up in front of the torso and feet flat on the floor.

2 With a release of *breath*, *allow* the knees to fall to the right side. Keep the *head–tail aligned* as you *allow* the torso to twist. Allow the movement to *sequence* from the knees through the torso and into the shoulder and head. The resulting posture is reminiscent of the poses used in swimsuit advertisements.

3 This time, the sacrum will *initiate* the movement and the psoas will be engaged to lift the knees. Fill the torso with *breath*,

imagining that as it fills, it presses the *tailbone* to the floor, which allows the return of the legs. Allow the hip joints to soften and deepen as the knees rise.

4   Repeat above five times on each side.

5   Variation 1: Adding sound:

   a   As a result of the deep in-breath and deep flexion of the hip joints, there is a somatic experience of depth in the body. It is an opportunity to connect breath and sound to a deep source.

   b   Drop knees as before. On the return inhale as if through a straw.

   c   When the knees have returned to the upright position and you are once again sitting, the lungs will be full. Initiate sound from the deep source. Speak the word "darling" from the pelvic bowl. Take advantage of the release of the tongue on the "D" sound into the wide vowel "Ah."

   d   Repeat three times on each side.

   e   You may also explore and extend the sounds "oo," "o," "ah," and "ee." Shape the vowels correctly to get the best placement and resonance.

Bartenieff Fundamental: The Arm Circle and Arm Circle Sit-up

Preparation Exercise 1: Connecting and releasing the shoulder blade (scapula)

Tension in the chest and back is fairly common, affecting *breath support, sequencing*, and *core stability*. The next two preparatory exercises soften and fold the chest and open the back, mobilize the scapula, and increase awareness and allow a release of the torso, neck, and shoulder joints. I chose the exercises because all of the elements above are needed to be effective in doing the Arm Circle and Arm Circle Sit-up. Also, a released body has more potential for expressing physical and vocal nuance, for communicating the inner life of the character.

1 Lie on the left side with arms extended forward, at shoulder level and perpendicular to the torso. The palms are facing one another. The knees are bent and pulled slightly into the fetal position for stability. The thighs are stacked one on top the other.

2 Keeping the right elbow straight, slide the right hand away from the torso and across the lower hand until fingertips touch the lower wrist. Then slide it backwards until the upper fingertips touch the lower wrist.

3 Repeat this movement as if washing your hands. Continue for a few minutes and then roll onto your back and rest.

4 Repeat the above process while lying on the right side. Rest again.

5 Slowly roll over, get to your knees, and come to a standing position. Begin walking. Avoid changing your posture or returning to a habitual way of walking or standing.

6 Notice any differences in the breath, chest, hip joints, etc.

Preparation Exercise 2: Softening the chest and ribs

This exercise is breath-based, and centered on the sensations in the body. It continues to release and activate the scapulae, and adds shoulder joint, spine, and pelvis. It all adds up when you get to the Arm Circle Sit-up.

1 Start on loft side, facing left. Imagine that you are lying on a clock and your arms are at 3 o'clock. Repeat Exercise 1.

2 Now slide the right arm down to what would be 5 o'clock. Extend and retract the straight arm as you did above. Allow the chest to soften and the ribs to sink. After a few minutes, roll onto the back and rest.

3 Return to the original position on the left side. Slide the right arm out behind you to what would be 8 o'clock. Extend and retract the straight arm as you just did. The shoulder will roll back and forward. Be aware of the widening through the torso and the breath support needed. After a few minutes, roll onto the back and rest.

4 Return to the original position. Slide the right arm up to what would be 12 o'clock. Extend and retract the straight arm as done before.

5 Allow the ribs and pelvis to move away from each other as you extend, and then back toward each other, as the hand slides back. (You did this in the Body Half section, Exercise 2: Body Half with core initiation.)

6 After a few minutes, roll onto the back and rest.

7 Return to the original position on the left side. Extend and retract the arm three times in each of the positions as done above (3, 5, 8, and 12 o'clock).

8 Extend and retract the arm once in each of the four positions.

Bartenieff Fundamental: The Arm Circle and Arm Circle Sit-up

See: 4 Demonstration Arm Circle Sit-up
https://vimeo.com/channels/thelabanworkbook/199987606

Exercise 1: The Arm Circle

1 Begin on your back with the knees up and the feet flat on the floor.

2 Drop knees to the left. As in the Knee Drop done earlier, the pelvis, which is passive, is affected. As it twists, its pull will *sequence* up the spine and out through the right arm, taking it into the *diagonal*. Allow the head to be affected, releasing to the right.

3 Imagine again that you are lying on a clock. Rotate the right arm clockwise over your head and toward the dropped knees and then complete the circle. Repeat five times.

4 Actively use the *breath* to support the movement by *exhaling* and *condensing* as the arm moves across the body from 12 (at top of head) to 6 o'clock (at feet). Then *inhale* and *expand* as it moves from 6 to 12 o'clock.

5   Now track the hand all the way around the circle with your
    eyes. This *spatial intent* will help to *organize* the body and
    support the movement just as it did in the spiral. *Tracking* will
    engage the head and spine, so as the arm moves from 3 to
    9 o'clock the head lifts slightly, engaging the core for support.
    Both shoulders rise slightly off the ground.

6   Use your experience from Preparation Exercise 2 and allow the
    torso to *narrow* and *sink* as it moves from 12 to 6 o'clock, and
    widen, then *lengthen* from 6 to 9 o'clock.

7   Repeat five times. Rest.

Exercise 2: Arm Circle Sit-up

1   Begin with the right hand again, circling three times. Track the
    hand. As your arm crosses your head, exhale to begin the
    fourth circle. Keep the spine long as you reach out as far as
    you can into the space to the left. You must reach out to go up.

2   Continue reaching outward as you circle, tracking will ensure
    the head and torso will follow. At 5 o'clock the torso crosses
    the knees and the circle begins to rise slightly and become a
    spiral. Now begin inhaling, filling the trunk to support the rest of
    the lift.

3   As you continue rising through 6 to 7 o'clock, let the right leg
    unfold and slide to the right.

4   Continue tracking the hand as it reaches outward and begins
    rising as you move toward 9 o'clock. This will take you into a
    sitting position.

5   When combined effectively, these components create a feeling
    of "falling up" into the sitting position.

6   Left hand: Repeat Exercises 1–2, this time drop the knees to
    the right and use the left arm

7   Note: it's possible to continue the Arm Circle Sit-up in a way
    that takes you right into the spiral going up into standing. And
    there is a way to spiral all the way down into the Arm Circle to
    the floor.

Exercise 3: Reversing the process

1   To return to your back, watch the right hand as it spirals
    outward and down to the left, tracking it back to its starting
    point on the ground.

2   In order to ride the spiral and avoid plopping the torso on the
    ground (it hurts), reach outward to get down. This reaching
    out folds the torso, taking it closer to the ground so the left
    shoulder just rolls onto the floor (and doesn't hurt).

Identifying foundational movement principles in the Arm Circle Sit-up

Work with the mechanics of the Arm Circle Sit-up until you understand and can perform it. Then challenge yourself to identify the
various foundational concepts and principles that you've explored in
this chapter as they operate in this exercise. Use your experience of
doing them and of observing others doing them to help to name the
principles. I led you through the same process at the beginning of the
chapter when identifying the foundational elements used in the spiral.
Now it's your turn to do the same here.

Foundational movement principles

- **Breath support**
- **Initiation:**
    - Core   – Mid-limb   – Distal
- **Sequencing**
    - Successive   – Simultaneous
- **Dynamic alignment/connections**
    - Head–tail
    - Scapula–hand
    - Sit bones–heel

- **Body organization**
  - – Upper/Lower
  - – Bilateral/Body Half
  - – Contralateral/Diagonal
- **Grounding**
- **Weight shifts**
- **Spatial intent**

Some final fun: Ride the spiral!

Return to the spiral and repeat those exercises. Feel each of the principles as you ride the spiral down and up again. Notice any differences between the first time doing spirals and this time. Articulate them in a journal or with your classmates, studio members, or colleagues.

Creating physical characters with movement principles

Exploration 1: Creating a physical character

1 Choose one set of the foundational principles drawn from the above list. If needed, you can find their definitions in the section on foundational movement principles in the spiral.

- Core initiation/strong breath support/body organized upper/lower

- Initiate with the hands (distal)/shift weight a lot/weak grounding

- Cross-lateral organization/successive sequencing/dynamic posture

- Bilateral organization/simultaneous sequencing/initiate mid-limb (elbow, knee)

- Head–tailbone connection is broken (head forward), only upper body expressive

2   Bring a character to life based on your set of choices. Explore each of the movement principles separately and note the physicality it promotes in you.

3   Combine the concepts/principles and notice how this changes the character's rhythm, speed, perception, and choices. Does a synergy arise? Does a shape or rhythm develop? Is an age or outlook on life suggested? Are there feelings or emotions it stimulates? Do you associate it with a particular kind of person, place, or event?

4   Choose a physical action that has a beginning, middle, and end. Example: walk to the other side of the room and sit down. Play that action via this physical character. Create two more of these physical actions for your character.

5   What have you noticed about the way this character looks at and relates to the world around her or him? What "worldview" arises from her or his physicality?

Exploration 2: Improvising in physical character

Continue working with the character created in Exploration 1.

1   Form small groups of 3–5. Each group chooses one of the following:

- Three characters are walking their dogs. Dogs, leashes, people become tangled.
- Five characters build a rain shelter out of whatever they can find in the room.
- Two characters are digging a grave.
- Four characters are planning a bank robbery.
- Create additional scenarios as needed.

Strive to maintain the physical nature of the character while interacting with others. The key is to respond from the worldview of the character that developed from your explorations of the various movement principles and concepts.

2   How did this physicality influence the way you related to others? What did you discover about your character's movement preferences (and your own) once you began interacting with others in the improvisation?

Exploration 3: Adding text—open scenes

1   Choose a partner and one of the open scenes from the chart on the following pages.

2   Use the character you have developed in the above explorations.

3   Rehearse and perform the open scenes.

4   Variation 1: Choose a well-known person (president, movie star, etc.) and note the foundational concepts and principles he or she prefers to use. Use those foundational movement principles and create a character based on that person.

5   Variation 2: Choose someone in your class or acting studio. Study and rehearse their foundational movement concepts and principles for several days. Then perform in the open scene as that person.

Open scenes

Scene 1	Scene 2
A. Hi.	A. Back again?
B. Hello.	B. Yeah.
A. Been waiting long?	A. Why?
B. No, not really.	B. Missed the place.
A. Sorry I'm late.	A. They always come back.
B. No problem.	B. I didn't think I would.
A. Are you sure?	A. No?
B. Yeah.	B. Something told me to … a dream.
A. Ok, well we should go.	A. Dreams don't mean anything.
B. Yes.	B. This one does.

Scene 3	Scene 3 A (variation)
A. Here, let me help you.	A. Here, let me help you.
B. No, I'm fine.	B. No, I'm fine.
A. I insist.	A. I insist.
B. No need.	B. I said no.
A. I'll just take this one.	A. No reason to bite my head off.
B. Please, not that one.	B. Get out of my way.
A. Why not?	A. No, I will not get out of your way.
B. It's the only one of its kind.	B. I'm warning you …
A. Oh, I see now.	A. Don't. Please don't. Please …
B. Thank you.	B. I told you once … now it's too late.

Scene 4	Scene 4 A (variation)
A. Can I come in?	A. Can I come in?
B. Who is it?	B. Who is it?
A. It's me.	A. It's me.
B. Oh … oh … of course it is.	B. Oh … oh … of course it is.
A. Who else could it be?	A. Who else could it be?
B. No one … just a moment.	B. No one … just a moment.
A. Were you expecting someone else?	A. Were you expecting someone else?
B. Why would I be expecting someone else?	B. Why would I be expecting someone else?
A. It just seems odd the way you …	A. It just seems odd the way you …
B. Are you accusing me of something?	B. I what?
A. No, I just … I'm sorry.	A. Took so much time.
	B. What are you saying?
	A. That something's not right.
	B. Are you accusing me of something?
	A. Yes … I mean no. I'm sorry.

Exploration 4: Adding text—short monologues

1 Perform one of the shorter, well-rehearsed monologues in your repertoire.

2 Now perform it as the physical characters you developed in Exercise 1.

3 How does this affect the way that you deliver the monologue? How might the worldview have changed? Are the tactics different?

4 Perform a different monologue, use the physical character developed in Exercise 3.

5 In subsequent classes or rehearsals, experiment with a different set of foundational principles to create a new character. Then perform your monologues as that physical character. You may

find that this exercise reaffirms or informs character choices that you've made in creating the original character from the play, but also what choices are definitely not justified.

It's all yours now ...

Engaging the foundational movement principles via the Bartenieff Fundamentals or any other exercise is empowering and highly useful. I encourage you to work with this material and over time you will find your awareness and abilities changing. Yet each of us works in a slightly different way to achieve our goals as an artist, on stage and in life. So feel free to take the principles, ideas, and exercises and adapt them, build on them, and cross-pollinate them in ways that serve you and others. All I insist on is that you have fun doing it! Cheers.

Summary

The Bartenieff Fundamentals offer the theater practitioner the tools to expand physical awareness and presence. They build new skill sets and provide more choices, specificity, and clarity in developing character and physical action. They yield insight into the relationship between the inner life—the psychology of a character—and the manner in which that is expressed.

Laban Movement training and the BF clarify the movement preferences of the actor and the character. The actor first comes to know and understand the movement principles and vocabulary by applying them to herself. In this way, she comes to learn to recognize her own movement habits, biases, or preferences. For we all express ourselves in patterned and habitual ways that have roots in our life history and values. We do so without being aware of them, we are "just us."

Working with the Bartenieff Fundamentals is an effective way to increase self-awareness in the actor. The BF requires concentration on the breath, the body, and movement. There is an inward focus and bodily sensation and feelings are heightened. By bringing the energy of conscious awareness into the body, one becomes "embodied."

As actors become more attuned to their bodies and physical behavior, they notice *how* they do things, revealing their own habitual patterns of movement. Then they begin to glean *why* they behave and move in the ways they do, revealing the underlying values and psychological processes associated with their movement. Self-knowledge like this gives them insight into their own psychology and how it is manifest in their physical behavior. More importantly, this leads to an understanding of a character's psychology and its expression in movement.

The BF not only increase actors' awareness of their movement preferences, they also support them in expanding the range and depth of their expressivity. Perceptual-motor patterns like those found in the BF are tied to habitual thought and emotional patterns, some of which may affect the actor and his process in detrimental ways. Liz Shipman notes that "Actors reflect in their work the strengths and limitations that they experience in life" (Shipman 1985: 191). Somatic processes like the BF can release tension, and introduce new movement patterns and neural pathways. This is one way to change limiting patterns and with it a new way of sensing, feeling, and taking action becomes available to the actor.

The actor learns to increase her range of movement and expressivity and to develop a specific vocabulary to describe and reproduce movement. Equipped with that knowledge, she is able to make conscious choices to use her own preferences effectively or to call on her training to discover new movement patterns that are more authentic for the character's history and circumstances. In all, she has more physical tools to express the work of her imagination and the intention of the playwright.

That sounds like a fine foundation for any actor, auteur, or creative artist.

Acknowledgments

I'm grateful to Katya Bloom for her generous invitation to join this group of fine artists-educators and for her insights into my chapter. My thanks to Barbara Adrian for support in a difficult time, to Claire Porter for her humor and many question marks, and to Jennifer Mizenko for leading by example. Thanks also to the men in my NW group. I'm most indebted to my wife, Meliss, who has been ever supportive.

Further reading

Bartenieff, Irmgard, with Dori Lewis (1980). *Body Movement: Coping with the Environment*. New York: Gordon and Breach, Appendix B.

Goldman, Ellen (1994). *As Others See Us: Body Movement and the Art of Successful Communication*. Luasanne, Switzerland: Gordon and Breach.

Goldman, Ellen (1994). "Perceiving Movement," in *As Others See Us: Body Movement and the Art of Successful Communication*. Luasanne, Switzerland: Gordon and Breach, 1–3.

Goldman, Ellen (1994). "Reflections," in *As Others See Us: Body Movement and the Art of Successful Communication*. Luasanne, Switzerland: Gordon and Breach, 169–70.

Goldman, Ellen (1994). "The Evolution of Our Movement, in *As Others See Us: Body Movement and the Art of Successful Communication*. Luasanne, Switzerland: Gordon and Breach, 127–9.

Hodgson, John and Valerie Preston Dunlop (1990). *Rudolf Laban: An Introduction to his Work and Influence*. Plymouth: Norcote House Publishers Ltd.

Hodgson, John and Valerie Preston Dunlop (1990). "His Approach to the Training the Actor," in *Rudolf Laban: An Introduction to his Work and Influence*. Plymouth: Norcote House Publishers Ltd, 39–43.

Hodgson, John and Valerie Preston Dunlop (1990). "His Innovations in the Theatre," in *Rudolf Laban: An Introduction to his Work and Influence*. Plymouth: Norcote House Publishers Ltd, 25–30.

Hodgson, John and Valerie Preston Dunlop (1990). "Laban's Ideas on Movement," in *Rudolf Laban: An Introduction to his Work and Influence*. Plymouth: Norcote House Publishers Ltd, 15–20.

Laban, Rudolf (1980). *The Mastery of Movement*. London: Macdonald and Evans Ltd.

Laban, Rudolf (1980). "Introduction," in *The Mastery of Movement*. London: Macdonald and Evans Ltd, 1–7.

Laban, Rudolf (1980). "The Significance of Movement," in *The Mastery of Movement*. London: Macdonald and Evans Ltd, 88–93.

Laban, Rudolf (1980). "The Study of Movement Expression," in *The Mastery of Movement*. London: Macdonald and Evans Ltd, 141–3.

2
MOVING INTO CHARACTER

Katya Bloom

You can have a physical movement that can give you your whole identity.

ROBERT DE NIRO, *NEW YORK TIMES*, NOVEMBER 18, 2012

As an actor, how do you create physically specific, believable, and dynamic characters that really come alive? By recognizing that your body and your mind are not separate entities, and your body is always speaking, you can tune in to your movement as one of your best creative resources.

Acting requires risk taking, stretching yourself beyond your personal qualities and comfort zones. It requires a willingness to expand your range of expression, to enter unknown territory with each new role, and discover new ways of experiencing the world.

In this chapter you will be introduced to many ways in which Laban Movement Analysis (LMA) can support you in that process. By offering a set of tools to explore and embody the physical, psychological, and imaginative realms simultaneously, LMA helps you reach beyond your own habits; it helps keep you from being typecast, and from repeatedly playing yourself.

When exploring a role via movement, you can uncover many layers of a character's being. You can gain new perspectives, and open a range of possibilities you may not otherwise have considered; and there is scope for greater depth and specificity in the choices you make.

Developing greater awareness of your body and its movement brings you into the here and now of space and time. It is often through physical explorations that the keys to unlocking difficult scenes can be discovered.

Rudolf Laban was quite definitive in his view on the subject:

> The average actor will admit only with reluctance that the enjoyment of his art by the public is based upon a subconscious analysis of his movement. The spectator derives his experiences from the artist's movements. ... meaning is conveyed by movement. (Laban 1950: 97)

Laban Movement Analysis, especially the Effort Theory of movement dynamics, which will be elaborated on in detail in this chapter, provides a systematic way of embodying a wide variety of psychological and emotional *States* and *Drives*, the range of which will stretch the boundaries of any individual's normal repertoire of responses. When actors are guided in Effort-based movement experiences, raw emotion can be given breathing space in a safe and contained way. Clear transitions from one State to another can be felt, as decisions are made from moment to moment.

I have organized the chapter in two segments, which I have titled **Tuning** and **Transforming**. All the exercises are improvisational; they are to be used as creative springboards for discovering and developing your own movement vocabulary. They can develop your capacity to observe, embody, and play.

Tuning means making contact with your own bodily instrument, and I suggest several tuning exercises to awaken your body and your senses. In the second and predominant part of the chapter, we progress to **Transforming.** There, I outline Laban's Effort Theory in detail and offer exercises for using his ideas and frameworks to create and embody rich and layered characters.

Tuning the bodily instrument

Ute Hagen writes:

> As an actor, in order to reveal what's at stake for the character on the deepest level and allow for pertinent communication with the audience, I must make myself, for ultimate expression, more vulnerable than in life. What you reveal and do when you are truly vulnerable is totally different from when, as in life, your purpose is, so often, to prove that you are invulnerable. (Hagen 1973: 214).

In order to find the pure vulnerability Hagan references, we find inspiration in exploring everyday movement, much like a baby or young child does. A child plays with and discovers movement, and through movement, discovers the world. In tuning our bodies, we develop our repertoire of lying, rolling, sitting, kneeling, crawling, walking, jumping, etc., finding new ways to give form to all these familiar actions. As we tune our bodies and our senses, we become more articulate and more open.

The tuning exercises are a practice for keeping multiple channels of communication open simultaneously, both within your own being and between you and the outside world. This kind of practice prepares you to fully embody the flow of changing circumstances.

In **tuning**, the emphasis is on being *receptive* to the body and basic qualities of movement as Laban defined them, as a prelude to *active* expression. The four Effort qualities are:

1 The sensation, and activation, of your body's **Weight**, exploring its relationship to gravity.
2 Your relationship to the outside world of **Space**, and the resulting awakening of your mind.
3 Your relationship to **Time**, your inner impulses and rhythms.
4 The **Flow** of your feelings, and the openings and closings of your flow of energy.

Tuning helps to:

- Develop and sustain a three-dimensional sense of being.

- Engage with the sensory–motoric language of the body.

- Gain recognition of personal habits that may limit your range.

- Develop awareness of self, others, and the environment simultaneously.

- Be flexible in changing psychophysical states.

- Develop an articulate body, and new movement vocabulary.

- Discover resonant physical forms and images.

- Develop more acuity in choosing the manner in which actions are executed.

- Recognize the relationship between your body's impulses and your thoughts.

- Become more open to being moved.

The tuning exercises offer processes for listening and responding to your experience and your context. There is a difference between a conceptual use of Laban categories and an embodied use. The intention of these exercises is to shift the emphasis from cognitive understanding or interpretation to a somatic and emotional structuring, via shapes/images/forms/positions/directions/phrasing. Although the tuning exercises may not always explicitly focus on Laban terminology, the Effort qualities of Weight, Space, Time, and Flow are always implicit.

Sometimes, when I'm sitting with a group of actors, before we do anything, I ask them to notice their physical positions, and, holding their positions, to look around the group. We immediately see that all of the bodies are "speaking"; everyone's "neutral" body conveys expression.

Tuning exercises

1. Body part warm-up

- Start walking; bring your attention to your feet. Take as much time as you need to feel the soles of your feet—the heels, arches, balls and toes … Perhaps stamp or swivel to activate your feet. As you enliven the sensations, notice the expression in your feet—the decision, the indecision, the intention, direction, speed …

- Once you are *in* your feet, bring your attention to your ankle joints, and explore your range of movement and sensations in each ankle joint. Progress to your knees … then your hips … really taking time to contact each specific joint. Then, sense all the leg joints at once, sensing your whole legs … Are the two legs different? Perhaps exaggerate the difference for a time.

- Then focus on your pelvis; let it take you to the floor and lead you in rolling slowly round, feeling all the pelvic bones and spaces, right to the bottom—tailbone, sitting bones, pubic bone …

- Move your awareness to your ribcage and continue rolling on the floor … slowly, opening the three-dimensional volume of space inside your torso. Then, as you roll, sense the volume of your neck … and of your skull as it contacts the floor … slowly rolling. Allow your breathing to be full and free.

- Pause and *re-member* your feet, legs, torso, and head …

- Move your awareness to your hands and fingers. As you move them, sense all the little joints.

- When your hands are in your awareness, connect them with your feet. Spread your attention, to mind your moving feet and hands at the same time. To find your feet again, it is helpful to put them back on the ground, and slowly come back to standing find your own organic way to do that. As you go on …

- Move your wrists … then feel their relationship to your ankles … Next sense each elbow—how do they move? Take your time … Then, how do elbows and knees relate? Now move your shoulders … followed by minding your hips at the same time—both are the nearest joints to the spine.

- When you have given attention to all the parts, then just go on moving, letting your attention shift from part to part. Let parts get to know each other. As the parts "speak," maybe your voice will want to join in!

- Find your own moments to pause, giving yourself time to stop, breathe, and recognize what you feel in your position … Or a leader can call "stop" periodically, so that you stop the flow of movement. Notice and embody your whole position, your breathing, your feeling, your imagination, possibly a sense of character … See the others from your position.

- If you are working on a play, you could bring the character to mind, and continue to improvise, making free choices in movement, allowing thoughts and feelings to arise and disappear as you move. You may imagine where you are, who you are with, what you dream about or long for; or lines from the play may simply come to mind.

2. Moving sculpture

- Begin either lying down or sitting in any relaxed position. Settle comfortably, feeling your three-dimensional form, as if you are a living sculpture. Notice, even emphasize, the large or small asymmetries; feel the resonant gesture and expression of your position. Feel your feet … your belly … your back … your sides … your face, etc. (If someone is guiding this exercise for a group, s/he can name body parts for the movers.)

- Then, let your body slowly change its shape, again and again, finding natural pathways from one "sculpture" to another. Stop in each place to fully embody your new sculptural form.

- Notice how your view of the space changes as you discover different levels, different angles with your movement.

- Feel the character of each sculptural form. Let each pause be a new beginning, as you transition into a new "story" or "character."

- Start alone, but if you are in a group, develop the exercise by becoming aware of being among others, as you move through the space. See and be seen.

- Then, make eye contact with one person—once established, keep going in a movement "dialogue" with a partner (or a small group). You need not hold onto eye contact to have a dialogue; explore the possibilities. Allow your body to discover the relationships and the story as you listen and speak through movement.

- Next, try adding sounds—perhaps feet or breath sounds first; then accompany your movement with vowels or punctuate it with consonants. Have a dialogue in moving gibberish.

- When you finish, chat with your partner(s) about your experiences.

3. On and off the wall

- Use the wall to enhance your feeling of three-dimensionality. Feel your back, your sides as you lean or press into the wall, and slowly ooze yourself against it. Imagine yourself as a moving sculptural relief.

- Then emerge from the wall; peel away from it and then lean back into it. Notice what it's like to be free-standing.

- Next, move through space to another wall. Can you be aware of the volume of your form as you move from wall to wall? Be in a wall story with others.

4. Your spot, your place, your space

- Imagine the room is a stage. Place yourself where you feel comfortable, a place that you feel is *your spot*. You can be in any position—lying, sitting, standing, etc. Notice yourself in relation to the walls, the windows the other people. Feel into your contact with the floor, or chair, or wall—whatever you are physically touching. Move slowly into another position, without leaving your spot. Go on, finding the many different positions and angles and levels in that one place. Does your attitude change from position to position?

- Now expand your sense of space to the area immediately around your spot. Your close quarters—this is *your place*. See it from your spot, and move in ways that refer to it; gesture with your arms and legs to help you feel at home in your place.

If your spot is like a small room, your place is like your house—imagine that you can see out through "windows" onto the rest of the space.

- Beyond your place is the space. Perhaps other people are in the space. See the space from your spot and from your place. Feel the moment when you leave your spot and your place and move into the space; does it support you to remember your place and your spot?

5. Measuring personal space

- How much space do you feel is "yours"? First feel your own skin, actually touch the outline of your body, feel your clothes as a second skin. Move through space with this awareness.

- Then extending your hands a few inches off your body, measure the small bubble of space all around you. Is it like a safety zone? Are you unconcerned with what lies outside? Or perhaps you feel oppressed by the outside world.

- Then extend your reach to elbow distance all around you, taking more space. How does your attitude change as you move through the room?

- Next, open your arms out all the way, feeling the tips of your fingers and toes defining the outline of your bubble of personal space. Laban calls this area that you can reach around your body your *kinesphere*. Does it affect your feeling of stature, and if you are with others, your status in a group?

- What's it like when your kinesphere overlaps with someone else's?

- Play around with changing the size of your kinesphere. Use your hands to guide your relationship to space and to others as you move through the room. Notice when you start to feel your space is too closed in, or too big and exposing, and adapt. Try imagining each size is a different color.

As an actor, how does the size of your kinesphere change in different roles, or scenes?

6. Mind your center

- Put your hand where you sense your own center is—the place where you feel your energy and attention are strongest in your body. Walk around and sense where in your body you are "coming from."

- Then, place your attention (and maybe your hand) on your low belly and breathe into the center of that space. Imagine a colored light there, radiating out in all directions. Let the sensation inform your whole being. As you take a walk, imagine "seeing" from your belly. Notice your attitude toward yourself and toward others. Perhaps share a few words with someone.

- Do the same, placing your attention in turn, at the center of your chest ... of your head ... and of your knees. Notice the different sensations and attitudes, and sense of personal space you feel with each.

- If you are in a group, watch half the group walking in the space. Observe who seems have the highest natural center, and who has the lowest. Reverse group halves.

- When you play a character, explore whether and how the character's center differs from your own.

7. Feet, feet, feet

- Feet are a great place to start to find the base for a character; but it's important to recognize your own preferences first. Stand and close your eyes. Notice how your weight falls through your two feet. Notice the difference left and right, front and back, noticing heels, toes, inside, outside of your feet. Imagine the feet like hands, sensing the ground.

- Next play around with what it feels like to bring your weight to the fronts of your feet. Take a walk like that. Then do the same placing the weight back on the heels ... then the inside ... the outside ... Notice how your body wants to adapt to the changing placements. Exaggerate the postures, and gestures that come to you. Imagine the characters you are creating and go whole hog with them. Then rein them in, until you feel only the emotional residue of the larger expression in more life-size characters.

8. Partner tuning: Dialogue of active and passive

(Thanks to Prapto Suryodarmo from whom I learned this exercise)[1]

This exercise for a group uses touch to initiate movement in a partner. It supports the skills of physical listening and nonverbal communication. (Group leaders may wish to confirm that participants are comfortable with touch, before guiding this exercise.)

- Partners A and B are both moving in proximity to each other; but partner B moves only from the exact place on her body that partner A touches. A gives a clear intention and direction with her touch. A watches the effect of the movement, and touches B again, somewhere else—perhaps to signal a change of direction or to facilitate B's making the next logical movement.

- The group leader will periodically say "change roles." The changes can come faster as the partners get accustomed to the exercise, so that it eventually becomes a dialogue of give and take, without anyone naming who is active or passive.

- The challenge for the active partner, the toucher, is to stay grounded, to see with her whole body, and not be "pulled out of herself" by attention to her partner. For the receptive partner, the challenge is to keep mentally and emotionally present to the changing experience, adapting to the different cues, without becoming an automaton.

The flexibility this exercise engenders breaks up assumptions and expectations of doing according to plan.

(Student response to this exercise, Royal Academy of Dramatic Art [RADA])

Summary of tuning

These fundamental tuning exercises support you in being present and responsive on stage. If you can be present in yourself, you can dare to deviate from your patterns and habits. The tuning work paves the way for transformation, opening yourself to listen and respond, once in character, to your fellow actors and your surroundings.

Being present in the Effort qualities Laban named as Weight, Space, Time, and Flow (to be elaborated on in the Transformation section) allows you to know more precisely who you are, where you are, and what the atmosphere is, as well as to more easily gauge your own and others' responses and rhythms from moment to moment. Let's dive in!

The art of transforming

Through *tuning* your body, you implicitly open the channels of all four Effort qualities, balancing your awareness of what is going on inside of you with what is outside. Now let's turn to *the art of transforming*, as approached from a movement perspective. Actors in both classroom and rehearsal settings consistently report discoveries and insights from Laban-based explorations:

It refreshed the text; I found different colors, different voices, bypassing the intellect.

I found the transitional moments, when inner rhythm, intention or feeling changed.

It opened up the text, the words express themselves.

I found aspects of character that don't get expressed in the play.
(Student responses to Laban classes, RADA)

First things first

Some of the simplest, most basic things to try in order to shift yourself off your own center—physically, psychologically, and emotionally—are suggested in the following four exercises:

1. How do you meet the world?

Sitting in a chair or standing, relax your body and sense the easy vertical axis of your spine. Now, consider your character's natural posture, and how it is similar to or different from your own.

The following options for exploring postural body attitudes relate to the three *dimensions*: **vertical** (up and down), **horizontal** (side to side) and **sagittal** (forward and back). The effect is both physical and emotional, as you will see.

Take time to experience the effect of each option. Breathe into each one, and, if in a group, feel your attitude and thoughts vis-à-vis others. Return to "neutral" between each change.

- Let your body spread and become wider. Widen your torso, your stance, your facial features. Find wide gestures. Then make your body and face narrow.
  Widening and narrowing are along the horizontal dimension.

- Move your torso forward, as if ahead of yourself; then retreating backward as if behind yourself. Explore advancing in parts of your spine or your head, while other parts retreat. Reverse the parts.
  Advancing and retreating are along the sagittal dimension.

- Try rising up above or sinking into gravity. Remember to let your facial expression join in.
  Rising and sinking are along the vertical dimension.

- What do different combinations of directions elicit? For example, try widening, advancing, and sinking all at the same time.

- Maybe the two sides of the body are different. What would that express about a character?

- Do the exercise in a heightened, exaggerated version first; then relax it a little, so you still feel the effect, not as a caricature, but as a naturalistic character.

2. Meeting others in a group

This is an exercise for exploring posture and body attitude in a group:

Each person receives a slip of paper with two of the six postural body attitudes: *rising, sinking, widening, narrowing, advancing, retreating*— for example, "rising and widening" or "sinking and advancing."

- Find this postural combination by finding the first quality and then adding the second—and let a character emerge.

- Then, embodying the character you've created, see each other. Who are you drawn to? Who repels or scares you?

- Someone suggest a situation—maybe a party or an audition. Mingle and improvise, nonverbally … then verbally … then again without words. Perhaps put on some music and dance with a partner.

3. Where is a character's weight on the feet and where is "center"?

These questions were in the Tuning section; but here you are working with transformation.

- Does your character's posture affect where your weight is on your feet? Or vice versa, does the placement of weight affect your posture? (Actors often get clues about characters from their shoes, so feel free to try this exercise with shoes on.)

- Where in your body do you feel you are coming from, physically and psychologically? Your chest? Belly? Head? Someplace else? Explore a range of possibilities.

Movement qualities: Laban's Effort Theory

Next, let's consider the Effort qualities of a character's movement, that is, their relationship to the elements of Weight, Space, Time, and Flow. How do the Effort characteristics of someone you are playing differ from your personal traits? Laban felt that discovering the character's discrete sequencing and rhythm of Effort choices was a key to fully embodying that character. (The notion of *rhythm*, in this context, is not only to do with the element of Time; it refers to the particular sequencing of a character's use of *all* the Effort qualities.) Laban seems to be aligned with actor Christopher Walken's instinctive approach to rhythm, though they express themselves differently. Here's what they had to say:

> In his first intuitive approach to his role, the actor ... might be unaware of the particular sequences of Effort qualities he chooses. Yet in the process of formulating his part, giving it shape and remembering it, he has consciously to select movement phrases, rhythms and patterns.
>
> (Laban 1950: 117)

> I'm essentially looking for a rhythm. For me, acting is all to do with rhythm. When I figure stuff out, it has to do with finding the rhythm. Always.
>
> (Interview with Christopher Walken, *Guardian*, December 2, 2012)

Some questions to ask yourself are:

- How is the person you are playing different from you in terms of how s/he engages with the world physically? Is a character's use of **Weight** stronger or lighter than your own?

- Does his/her mind work differently? How do you experience the **Space** around you? Is the character's way of thinking more focused, detailed, sharper, narrower than yours? Or is she able to let her mind wander and drift more freely? Is he someone who can see the big picture?

- Is the character more, or less, intuitive than you? Does she have a finger on the pulse of **Time**? Does he feel more rushed, or more leisurely, than you? Or is the character oblivious to the passing of time?

- How does s/he deal with emotions? Is she more controlled, more agitated or tense than you are, or more free and easy? How does his energy **Flow**?

You can answer these questions by analysis or imagining alone. But by playing around, engaging in physical explorations of Effort qualities and body shaping, you may stumble across some even more interesting, previously unthought-of options. By trying out a full range of possibilities, you can discover how characters change in their journeys through a play.

4. Playing around with walking

In this exercise we use the simple act of walking to begin exploring Laban's Effort qualities of Weight, Space, Time, and Flow. It's helpful if someone else gives you the prompts below; but if you are on your own, you can easily coach yourself.

This exercise can follow on from the Tuning exercise—"Body Part Warm-up" (p. 52), in which case you will already be sensing your whole body. Do this exercise with a character in mind. Or let characters and scenarios emerge and dissolve in your imagination as you explore.

- Start walking through the space. If you are in a group, make changes of direction, sensing your relationships with others, creating curved paths.

As you go on, make the following alterations, and note the emotional and psychological changes:

- Take bigger steps. Then, much bigger. Let your whole body become bigger.
- Take smaller steps. Then, even smaller. Contain your body to fit.
- Increase your speed. Then, even faster, as if you're on an urgent mission!
- Slow down and take it very leisurely. Savor time and relax your breathing.
- Plant your feet more firmly, hearing every step. Wake up your strong, muscular body.
- Make your steps soundless, lighter than air. Let that filter through so your whole body feels buoyant.

- Observe the smallest details of what's around you. Notice how this focuses your mind.

- Avoid the details, but, with relaxed eyes, take in the wide angle overview—note the different way of relating to space.

- Close your eyes and continue moving; notice how you adjust your energy flow, and where in your body caution resides.

- Now that you've tried these changes singly, try mixing two or three together. For example, make your movement bigger *and* faster; or smaller, lighter, *and* more closely focused on the details of your world.

This introduction should begin to give you a visceral sense of how changing your movement qualities changes your consciousness—your feelings, thought patterns and general mood. It might be a good idea to make some notes afterward to remind you of your various experiences and your associations to them.

The four Effort qualities—making the psychological links

Laban's Effort Theory is concerned with the expressive, qualitative aspect of movement. Effort pertains to *how* a movement is performed and is thus related to feeling more than form. It is therefore of utmost importance in considering the relationship between movement and psychological and emotional states.

Laban identified **Weight**, **Space**, **Time**, and **Flow** as the four Effort qualities which spark or motivate movement, in response to internal or external, conscious or unconscious impulses, even before any visible movement is made. He also named two qualities to define either end of a spectrum of possibilities in describing how each quality could be manifested.

He found the four Effort qualities corresponded with the four psychological types described by Carl Jung as *sensing, feeling, thinking*, and *intuiting* (Jung 1971). Laban co-opted these categories to augment the descriptions of each quality. I'll say more about this later.

First, I'll describe each of the Effort qualities, and name the two sides of the spectrum pertaining to each one. These are followed by an exercise or two for each quality. Keep in mind that it is really impossible to isolate just one Effort quality in one's movement. In fact, all four are present in all movement, but usually only two will be in the foreground. We'll get to that when we look at States of Mind.

Weight—the body of intention and sensation

The element of **Weight**, designated as **strong** or **light**, relates to the physical *sensation* of the body itself, the skin, the muscles, the literal, material substance, both surface and depth of the body, and the sense of touch. In bringing this aspect of experience to life, through making it conscious, Laban suggested that one develops an *intention* to do something with the body. Usually this something is done in relation to others, who are either available or not to one's intentions toward them.

STRONG WEIGHT: determination, impact, earthy
LIGHT WEIGHT: delicate, gentle, ethereal

5. Explore different sensations of Weight

- Activate your body by strong, powerful stretching. Work with the floor to push with strength, and/or reach into space, engaging your muscles.

- Then explore the more delicate sensation of lightness in sensing the air against your skin and your clothing on your body as you move.

- Notice what these different ways of animating your body offer.

- Also note that both strong and light are *active* uses of Weight. *Passive Weight*, when we completely give in to gravity, is not part of the spectrum of the Weight Effort. But it can be expressive nonetheless, as you can experience in the next two exercises.

6. Explore Weight with a partner

(Thanks to Adam Bradpiece for this exercise)[2]

- Walk while holding hands with a partner. One leads; the other keeps in sync with leader's tempo and direction as exactly as possible.

- Then, at a designated moment, the partner *actively* resists the leader.

- Next, the partner *passively* resists the leader—really let your body be limp and pulled along.

- After you have tried these variations, return to partners keeping in exact sync again. Notice if anything has changed.

- Repeat the exercise, changing roles. Then chat about what parts felt most comfortable—leading, being led, resisting, etc.

7. Hands and gesture

- Begin by sensing your hands. Take it slowly … Let them touch each other, touch your clothes. Keep them near you to begin. Touch your heart … your face … Notice how meaningful a gesture can be, how soothing. Then touch the air. Be on the lookout for gestures that feel natural and convey meaning for characters you are working on. Let your hands speak! If you are alert, you will discover gesture quite naturally—new gestures, different from your own.

- Explore the range from **strong** to **light** gestures, and let your whole being join in with the quality of the gesture.

- In a group, notice the gestures of others, and let them influence your own.

- Converse with a partner using only your hands. Perhaps add gibberish as you continue the "dialogue."

- Try doing practical activities with varying qualities of Weight—pack a bag, for example. Sense your hands and your gestures.

Space—the body of attention/thinking

The element of **Space** relates to one's *attention* to the outside world, one's perspective, one's particular point of view. Just as Weight is concerned with the realm of physical experience, Space is concerned with the realm of the mind, and the function of thinking.

DIRECT FOCUS IN SPACE: pinpointed, sharp focus, catching the details, honing in on an idea

FLEXIBLE (aka INDIRECT) FOCUS IN SPACE: the overview, the periphery, the range of possibilities, or thoughts available

8. Pointing

- Using the gesture of pointing to guide your attention, scan the space around you, including above, below, behind. Allow your body to change levels and shape as it follows your gaze. As you scan, register various points of focus, letting your attention sharpen—the spot on the ceiling, the car outside the window, the color of someone's socks … See these clearly, but don't fixate on any one point. Let your finger, your body, and your mind move on freely, as you scan from point to point.

- Now, stop at each point for a moment; relax your body and your eyes, and then move on until you stop at the next point of focus. Be present every moment!

Has this exercise helped to heighten the clarity of your attention to space? If you are exploring a character, what do you notice about the character's thinking?

9. Hands like a movie camera

- As you move, let your hands guide your point of view, panning, zooming, narrowing in, widening out. Let them guide you off-center, shaping your body into tilts and angles that give you alternate perspectives.

- Imagine other body parts as a film camera—seeing from your heart, belly, ankles, knees! Imagine the back of your head is a camera.

- Explore the range of how characters you are playing relate to space, and to others.

Time—the body of intuition/deciding

The element of **Time** is related to the impulses, decisions, rhythms, and phrasing of one's movement. The experience of time—within oneself, in the outside world, and interpersonally—is *inherently intuitive*, as is the recognition of the natural order of events and change. The experience of choices and transitions is linked with the element of Time.

QUICK (aka SUDDEN) TIME: accelerating, urgency

SUSTAINED TIME: decelerating, taking one's time

10. Exploring rhythm and pace

- With a character in mind, find your temporal range in walking, or performing a task, or moving in a freeform way. What is it like to move as slowly as possible, as fast as possible, and all degrees in between? What is it like to make instinctive decisions to vary your pace?

- Try moving in relationship with a partner, having a nonverbal dialogue, tuning in to each other's rhythms. Feel the melodic or percussive qualities, the starts and stops of phrasing. Hear the tempo of your inner thoughts. Your breath, your heartbeat. Be *in* time.

- Try adding sounds or gibberish. Or play with words or text.

11. Group body sounds

- Start walking, hearing your footsteps land on the ground. Hear the others' too. Be in the world of sound and time, as you accent your movement with vocal and body sounds, tapping, clapping, stomping, hissing, etc.

- Notice the interactions that occur in a group when you communicate through timing, even though your rhythms may be different. Notice that sometimes you are more involved in "speaking" and other times more in "listening."

Flow—the body of feeling/energy

The element of **Flow** highlights the degree of control or freedom of movement, and this corresponds to the degree of control or freedom of breath, energy, and feelings as expressed through the moving body. Of interest is how the flow of energy and feelings opens toward or closes away from relationship. Flow also speaks more practically of the degree of *precision* in movement.

FREE FLOW: carefree, reckless, generous, exuberant
BOUND FLOW: cautious, precise, withheld, sneaky

12. Eyes closed

- Close your eyes and notice your breathing. Notice the places in your body that are holding some tension. Try not to judge or change things. Gradually allow yourself to experience the emotional affect.

- Then slowly start to move, changing your position, or moving through space. If there are others in a group, you may inadvertently touch someone; if so, stay a moment and notice your feelings, thoughts, and sensations, before moving on. Notice the subtle openings and closings, bindings and freeings of energy and feelings.

Some people may find closing eyes in a group to be quite scary. If you do, you might find it helpful to be by a wall, for support. It is also helpful in a group if a teacher or director keeps an eye on the overview and intervenes if someone is in danger; but I have always found that people will instinctively take their time and control their flow.

13. Playing with proportion

- With a character in mind, play with how big or small you make your body shape as you move. Pause in different positions, and notice when your energy opens out toward the world (*Free Flow*), and when it flows inward toward yourself (*Bound Flow*). Recognize when you feel cramped, hidden, or claustrophobic, and when you feel you are overextending yourself, beyond your comfort zone.

- Try unusual affinities: Can you be small and feel free? Be big and feel bound?

- Discover the proportion that feels right for a specific character, and gives you appropriate breathing space. It may be helpful to consider the degrees of intensity from 0 (extremely bound) to 10 (extremely free).

- How permeable do you feel? Do you find any gestures or postures that make sense for the character? Can you recognize how these questions relate to Flow?

14. Fighting and indulging Effort qualities

Note that the Effort qualities that resist or condense energy are referred to as the **Fighting Efforts**: Strong Weight, Direct Space, Quick Time, Bound Flow. Those that allow the energy to expand are called **Indulging Efforts**: Light Weight, Flexible Space, Sustained Time, Free Flow.

- As you explore a character, try focusing on your selection of Fighting or Indulging Effort qualities. Which qualities does the character resist with, and which does the character indulge in? What prompts a change from one to the other? When might a character fight/resist in one Effort and indulge in another Effort at the same time?

Laban's States of Mind: Combining two Effort qualities

I've always been impressed by the fact that upon entering a room full of people, you find them saying one thing, doing another and wishing they were doing a third. The words are secondary and the secrets are primary. That's what interests me most. (Mike Nichols, *New York Times*, November 20, 2014; article by Bruce Weber)

As Mike Nichols suggests, in theater as in life, the subtext is often the primary form of communication. In this section, I introduce Laban's six States, which I refer to as States of Mind. These specific moods, or "Inner Attitudes," as Laban called them, support you in making the layers of subtext tangible.

Exploring movement in the different States provides the opportunity to discover different aspects of a character, enabling you to see the character from different angles; it evokes associations you won't have thought of before. You can access the nuances of a character's predominant State, as well as the kaleidoscopic changes a character makes from scene to scene and moment to moment, as circumstances change.

Exploring States of Mind through movement can reveal the "secrets" Nichols refers to—the conflicts, needs, desires, hopes, and passions of characters. Both conscious and unconscious impulses and motivations are clarified through these explorations.

A **State of Mind** is created when two of the four Effort qualities motivate a character at once, while the other two remain in the background. These two active qualities create a mood, or State—for example, Weight and Flow create Dream State; Time and Space create its opposite, Awake State. You will notice there are three pairs of opposite States, listed in these pairs in the table below:

Table 1.1 States of Mind

Dream	Weight	Flow
Awake	Time	Space
Near	Weight	Time
Remote	Space	Flow
Mobile	Time	Flow
Stable	Weight	Space

The States of Mind advance the exploration of movement qualities from the four "primary colors"—Weight, Space, Time, and Flow—to the six "secondary colors," or combinations of two qualities. Additionally, within each of those six States, there are four possible "shades." Each gives a different way of experiencing or expressing the State. For example, in Near (aka Rhythm) State, the four possible combinations of Time and Weight are: *strong and quick, strong and sustained, light and quick, light and sustained.*

The metaphor of color provides a useful image. We get purple from mixing blue and red. There is no green, no yellow—equivalent in the Near State to the absence, as motivating factors, of Flow and Space. But within the realm of blues and reds (Time and Weight in the Near State), we can explore different variations within the State.

It is paradoxical to think that by limiting your expression, you increase your range, but that is exactly what happens. Why? Because you discover how to get outside of your comfort zone, and thereby deepen and vary your experience.

The widely divergent kinds of exercises to elicit the different States that follow are designed to both focus and free your imagination. Obviously, exploring the exercises in movement will help you understand them experientially, in the way that reading about them alone cannot.

The six States: Descriptions and exercises

After describing the nature of each State, I provide an exercise that will help you experience that State. I also note the four possible combinations of Effort qualities within each State, so that you can be mindful of them in the exercises. For example, in Dream State, combining Weight and Flow, the four ways of expressing this State are *strong and free, strong and bound, light and free, light and bound.* These are very different, one from another, but all are within the Dream State. Try to move naturally from one to another to another combination within each State. If it doesn't happen naturally, use a little discipline to explore all four!

It will be useful to write down impressions and associations after you experience each State, both general responses, and particular responses for a character.

Relevant questions for your investigation are:

- What States are present in the character(s) throughout the course of a play?

- What States may be there before the play begins or after the play ends?

- What States are never expressed by the character(s), except perhaps in dreams?

I present the States in no particular order; but I do present them in pairs of opposites: *Dream and Awake*; *Remote and Near*; *Mobile and Stable*. Suggestions for music to support the States are on page 79.

Dream State: Weight and Flow—sensations and feelings

A less conscious attitude, focused on the inner world of body and emotion; it lacks the mental reflection associated with Space and the decision-making associated with Time. Possible combinations are:

Light and Bound   Light and Free
Strong and Bound   Strong and Free

15. Dream State Exercise: Starfish

(This exercise comes from Bonnie Cohen's Body Mind Centering®)[3]

- Lie on the floor, eyes closed, and imagine yourself as a six-pointed starfish: arms, legs, head and tailbone, all radiating out from center at your navel. Breathe into your hands atop your navel. Give up the "control center" in your head.

- Slowly explore moving each limb, visualizing its connection to the navel. Then try moving any two limbs, visualizing their connection *through* the navel. Allow your *feelings and sensations* to stimulate your imagination. Discover moving along the floor and out of the floor toward standing and back down again, always centered at the navel. Take note of your mood when you finish.

- Bring a character to mind, and, with eyes only partly opened, experience the person in the private, physical, and emotional realm of Dream State. You may discover something that *in-forms* your understanding of the character's inner life.

Awake State: Space and Time—thoughts and intuition

A practical, alert attitude; it lacks the sense of embodiment associated with Weight, and the emotionality associated with Flow. The Awake State sharpens your mind and intuition, your thoughts and decisions. Possible combinations are:

Direct and Quick   Direct and Sustained
Flexible and Quick   Flexible and Sustained

16. Awake State Exercise 1: Party Time

- In a group, mingling freely in the space, imagine a lively party, or the opening of an art exhibition. Then, secretly keep someone in view—you always want to know where that person is, but you don't want her to know you are watching.

- There is also someone you want to avoid. Do all you can to keep from seeing that one, while not letting the first one out of your sight. When you stop the exercise, be sure to take note of your state of mind. (You can end the exercise by asking everyone to touch both people.)

17. Awake State Exercise 2: Ball Name Game

Using some very fast and furious background music, a group plays a ball game, throwing the ball(s) from person to person without much hesitation, as everyone walks or runs freely in the space. Just before the ball is thrown, call the name of the person who is meant to catch it. After several minutes, lose the music and the ball(s); but keep going with the mood that has been created, taking up exploration of characters, text and relationship.

Remote State: Space and Flow—thoughts and feelings

This State has an abstract, detached quality, though one is thoughtful and in touch with feelings; it lacks the vitality and presence associated with Weight and Time.

Possible combinations are:

Direct and Free	Flexible and Free
Direct and Bound	Flexible and Bound

18. Remote State Exercise: Look But Don't Touch

Imagine there is someone or something in the room that you are longing for. You see it and have feelings about it, but you know that you cannot touch it. As you experience your thoughts, your feelings and the room itself, notice your State. Time and Weight are *not* motivating you at all. If you are in a group, choose someone to represent the object of your longing. Perhaps personalize the figure as someone you know. Explore your spatial relationship to that person. But do *not* touch them. Be sensitive to the emotional pulls you feel from your own inner thoughts and feelings and to outer people and objects in the space. Try emotionally "pulling" others to you, but remember, no touching! (Touch brings in physical sensation, which would change the State.)

Near (aka Rhythm) State: Weight and Time— sensations and intuition

This State has a rhythmical, earthy attitude of embodied physical intention and agency; it lacks the emotional quality associated with Flow and the perspective associated with Space. Possible combinations are:

Strong and Quick	Strong and Sustained
Light and Quick	Light and Sustained

19. Near State Exercise: Ho-down

(Thanks to Susanka Christman for this exercise)[4]

- Begin by bouncing one foot on the floor as you balance on the other leg. Bounce it lightly like a ball, as if a puppeteer's string is attached to your knee. Bounce a few times on one leg, and then switch to the other leg.

- Then take two bounces on one leg, two on the other ... Then in singles, bounce left, right, left, right ... Then start walking through the space with this same bouncing rhythm. Let your whole body really join in. Like a ho-down.

- If you are in a group, make a big circle to start. Half the group enter the space, maybe the men first, while the women clap, supporting them ho-down style; then reverse, women in, men clap.

- Finish with everyone in, dancing a leg-stomping, arm-flinging ho-down. Find your own counterpointed and syncopated rhythms. Whoop it up! When you stop, take on a character; see how you feel and what you want to do.

Mobile State: Time and Flow—intuition and feeling

An emotionally adaptable, changeable, impulsive, spontaneous State, it lacks the embodied intention associated with Weight and the thoughtfulness associated with Space. Possible combinations are:

Quick and Free   Quick and Bound
Sustained and Free   Sustained and Bound

20. Mobile State Exercise: Let Your Head Go

- This is a quirky, playful, impulsive State of Mind. Riding the waves of impulse, let the flow of time and feelings be your guide. Play with hearing an internal melody as you move.

- First just move your head and shoulders. Then let your whole body join in, making sounds as you move, to punctuate your movements, like a young child—staccato, legato—finding varieties of phrasing and melodious gibberish. Be sure to let your head go as you move to an internal, non-logical, flow through time—speeding up or slowing down at will. The specific emotions you feel may change, but changeability is your essence. This is the rhythm, not of a weighted bass line, but, rather, the flitting directionlessness of a butterfly. After the exercise, notice your mood, and how you relate to others in this State.

Stable State: Weight and Space—sensations and thoughts

A steady, steadfast attitude; a sense of physical presence and awareness of outside space. It lacks the changeability and emotionality associated with Time and Flow.

Possible combinations are:

Direct and Light   Direct and Strong
Flexible and Light   Flexible and Strong

21. Stable State Exercise: Handle-an-Object Ritual

- Begin by letting gravity affect you in whatever position you start in. Feel your three-dimensionality. Feel the breath as it shapes your torso.

- Without losing this sense of your body, slowly touch or handle an object—a light chair, perhaps, or an article of clothing, a suitcase, a teacup … any object will do.

- Now, with steady pace and thoughtful presence, begin to move with the object—this has a timeless, ritualistic quality. From one position to another, to another, without speeding up—always present in body, mind, and space.

- In a group ritual, one person at a time, mindfully place your object to create an installation or group sculpture. This can be

nicely done with chairs, for example. Remember to notice your
State of Mind afterward.

Determining your primary State

- A good way to determine your primary State is to notice which
State feels the most alien and awkward. Usually, its opposite
will be your preferred or primary State.

- Having gone through all the States, can you recognize your
primary State? Can you do the same for a character you're
working on?

- Next ask yourself which of the two Effort qualities making up
your primary State is your more preferred of the two; which are
you most strongly motivated by? If, for example, your primary
State is Awake, are you more motivated by (or based in) Space
or Time? Suppose you decide you have more affinity with
Space than Time. You can assume that through your affinity
with the Space Effort, you will also have easy access to the
other States with Space, namely Remote and Stable. Of course,
you may also feel that neither Effort quality is predominant.

- This kind of analysis is very helpful in ascertaining the primary
States of characters. You may also consider inherited
family States. Remember to base your choices on physical
explorations.

This process may sound formulaic, but I've asked many groups of
students to assess their own and their classmates' primary States.
There is almost always a consensus for each person. Colleague Juliet
Chambers finds that there is an *atmosphere* surrounding a character,
or even a group, that can be described as a State.[5]

Mapping changes from State to State

There will be key moments in a script that initiate a new thought, a new
attitude for a character—something another character does or says, or
an inner thought or impulse that can no longer be submerged. These

conscious or unconscious moments for a character usually signal a State change. They mark new beats in the text. Locating specific changes in State can identify landmarks for freely inhabiting a role, helping you to uncover the broad map of a character's journey.

- Improvise with one or more States, in the context of rehearsing a play. Don't let your fellow actors know which State(s) you choose. You can also set this up by asking each actor rehearsing a scene to randomly choose a slip of paper with a State written on it. Each actor plays the scene in the chosen State. Afterward, share thoughts and discoveries about the characters, the scene, and/or the play.

- Make sure that characters exploring different States are not unconsciously pulled into each other's State.

- Explore and discuss each character's primary State—in the whole play, and in specific scenes.

- Plot your character's journey through a scene or a play as defined by States.

Most rehearsals, most directors work with text and motivation to gain an intellectual understanding. There isn't time for play with movement. There's usually a rush to get a show up and running … In each scene there's usually a key to unlock the meaning. You can go over and over it in words and not find the key. I found keys in the movement classes.

(Student response, RADA)

Music to evoke the States

I encourage you to discover your own music to evoke the different States. Keep a running list of supportive music. Here are some of the ones I settled on over time. Remember that the music itself has a specific quality that will not usually conjure up all four combinations of the Effort qualities within a State. So you have to remind yourself, or your actors, to try them all, even if they go against the music. If you are guiding the exercises, you may want to suggest changes from to one combination to another.

Dream: Stephen Micus's album *Listen to the Rain* has many Dream State pieces, with a sensory and emotional quality. I like "For Abai and Togsham" in particular, for about the first 8 minutes; then the element of time becomes more rhythmic and prominent. I also like Eberhard Schoener's album *Meditation*.

Awake: Johann Strauss, *Knall und Fall Op. 132*, or Brahms, *Hungarian Dance No.5*—both accentuate the fast and furious side of Awake State.

Remote: The soundtrack to the Russian film, *Ulysses' Gaze* has a lonely, weightless, timelessness that works well with Remote State.

Mobile: Oregon's album *Crossing* has a particular track called "Pepe Linque." It's perfectly, playfully Mobile.

Near: Tina Turner—I like her track "Show Some Respect." It's so physical!

Stable: I use no music for the thoughtful, embodied Stable State, but you may feel differently. You could perhaps use something timeless like sounds from nature.

22. Draw the States to music

- Supply materials for drawing, and play music that conjures up each of the six States. Participants should try to draw *in* the States, being mindful of which two Effort qualities make up the State they are inhabiting, and which two are absent. Don't allow the absent qualities to creep in.

- Take a minute after each drawing to feel the effect, in your movement, your relationship to others, and your mood. Take time after the exercise to discuss the experiences; refer to your drawings. Share as a group or in pairs.

- If you are working on a play, try drawing in character, and after you draw, write your thoughts or improvise a scene.

Changing from one State to another

Once you (or your students) are quite familiar with the atmosphere of each State, explore changing from one State to another one. Here are a couple of exercises, one in which *one* Effort quality stays the same, but the other quality changes; and another example in which *both* Effort qualities change from one State to the other.

23. From Dream to Remote

What these two States have in common is the absence of Time and the inclusion of Flow. The first combines Flow and Weight, and the second, Flow and Space.

- Start sitting back to back with a partner, eyes closed. Start to sense and then physically explore the contact with each other's backs, as you slowly find what feels good. Let this gradually grow to include more of your back. Opening and stretching your body while including your feelings; breathe into your heart. See where this takes you … As you go on, keeping the contact and your eyes closed, let images arise, as if you are in a dream.

- To transition to Remote State, pause sitting back-to-back, open your eyes, and very gradually move forward, separating from contact with your partner. Let your eyes take in your surroundings. Take your time to bring yourself to standing, and continue to explore the space. Be aware of your partner and any feelings and thoughts that arise. You may come near each other, but don't touch. Don't touch anything at all. Notice your thoughts and feelings.

24. Exploring presence—from Near to Remote

Explore these *opposite* States to play with the idea of "presence."

- Start with Near State, accentuating the rhythms created by Time and Weight (decisions and sensations). Have the intention to make yourself more concretely present in your body, more down-to-earth and visible.

- Then transition to Remote State, as you give up Time and Weight, in favor of attention to Space and Flow (thoughts and feelings). Have the intention to become less visible, as if withdrawing from being present in your body, but being more present in your outward attention and your feelings.

- In a group, after everyone tries both States, let half the group watch the other half freely explore their relationship to *presence* based on these two States. The audience can give feedback.

Orientation to space: Dimensions and planes

In the first Transformation exercise, p. 60, "How do you meet the world?" we explored adapting the body's shape into three different dimensions:

Rising and *sinking* along the **vertical** dimension
Widening and *narrowing* along the **horizontal** dimension
Advancing and *retreating* along the **sagittal** dimension

Here, I would like to add that each dimension has an affinity with an Effort quality, as follows:

The **vertical** dimension has an affinity with the element of **Weight**, through the relationship to gravity.
The **sagittal** dimension has an affinity with the element of **Time**, in traversing forward or backward.

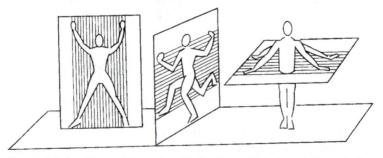

Figure 2.1 Spatial orientation related to the three dimensions: height, depth, and width. (Source: Maletic 1987)[6]

The **horizontal** dimension has an affinity with the element of **Space**, with a widening or narrowing of one's perspective.

The two-dimensional forms, or **planes**, are commonly nicknamed as follows:

Door plane—primary dimension is vertical, with its affinity with Weight; the secondary dimension is horizontal, with its affinity with Space.

Wheel plane—primary dimension is sagittal, with its affinity with Time; the secondary dimension is vertical, with its affinity with Weight.

Table plane—primary dimension is horizontal, with its affinity with Space; secondary dimension is sagittal, with its affinity with Time.

We can recognize that three of the States, those without Flow, have particular affinities with the planes.

25. Non-Flow State and plane affinities

Feel the State as you inhabit the planes, using Figure 1 as a guide. You may want to refer back to the exercise for each State:

- Stable State—Weight and Space, has an affinity with the Door plane.
- Near State—Weight and Time, has an affinity with the Wheel plane.
- Awake State—Time and Space, has an affinity with the Table plane.

I mention these affinities, because you can feel supported by relating to the spatial dimensions in these three States. And equally, it is helpful to recognize which dimension is missing from each of these States.

- Explore the three planes with the related States in mind; remember there are four variations within each State.
- Try it again with a character in mind.
- Just for fun, explore *dis-affinities*. For example, try Awake State

in Door plane. How does that affect you? Make some notes about your discoveries.

26. Pick a card

- Each person in a group chooses a slip of paper, on which is written two Effort elements—for example "light Weight and sustained Time." Embody these elements; first embody one, then add the other. Feel your mood and attitude, and imagine your situation. Recognize which State this combination is part of—in this case Near State—with elements of Weight and Time. Make sure that the other categories—in this case, Space and Flow—are *not* motivating you.

- Then, two people or more enter the space together. Feel each other's different attitudes, in silence first. Don't be pulled out of your State into someone else's.

- Add words as you improvise a scene; then return to no words. Others may wish to suggest a relationship and/or situation—for example: speed-dating; therapist and client; learning a dance; waiting for an audition; siblings; a panel discussion.

27. Interview

As in the exercise above, everyone chooses a slip of paper with two Effort elements and embodies the emerging characters. One by one, characters are interviewed by the group. Someone in the audience may give the interviewee a profession after seeing them enter the space. They are interviewed about their profession, while maintaining their State.

28. I'm in a State

- Each person chooses a slip of paper which names one of the six States. Take time for everyone to embody their own State, by engaging in the two Effort qualities that are present in that State, and making sure the other two qualities are not in the foreground. Play with the various possibilities of qualities within the State. Once everyone feels the State they are in, actors enter the space one by one or in pairs, and improvise a scene. The group then guesses the State(s).

- This can be a more in-depth project in which students develop short solo scenes, in which they present a character in one specific State.

Drives: Three Effort qualities at once

Drives combine three active Effort qualities at once. Drives therefore have greater intensity than States of Mind. This usually means being more invested in one's activity as a heightened externalized expression. There are four Drives, each very different from the others.

We take note of the Effort quality that is absent as much as we take account of the three that are present. The **Action Drive** is flowless; **Spell Drive** is timeless; **Passion Drive** is spaceless; **Vision Drive** is weightless.

There are eight possible ways of combining Effort elements in each Drive.

For the Action Drive, which has the distinction of not containing the element of Flow, Laban gave a name to each of the eight Actions. These are of great use to actors. The other three Drives are referred to as *transformations* of the Action Drive, in which Flow replaces either Weight, Space, or Time. Let's look at Action Drive first.

Action Drive and the eight Effort Actions

In the Action Drive, the Effort qualities of Weight, Time, and Space are all active. The missing element is Flow. Laban named the eight Effort Actions as follows:

Table 2.1 Effort Actions

Action	Weight	Space	Time
Float →	Light	Flexible[7]	Sustained
Punch →	Strong	Direct	Quick
Glide →	Light	Direct	Sustained
Slash →	Strong	Flexible	Quick
Wring →	Strong	Flexible	Sustained
Dab →	Light	Direct	Quick
Flick →	Light	Flexible	Quick
Press →	Strong	Direct	Sustained

The Effort Actions are useful in many ways. They are especially good for achieving the *visceral experience* of conflicting inner and outer characteristics, emotions, needs, or obstacles. They help actors discover and vividly convey the subtext even when no words are spoken. Effort Actions can also describe the overall personality of a character in broad brush strokes, lending specificity to gestures, actions, and qualities of speech.

How to embody each Action

To fully embody each Effort Action, rather than giving a generalized idea of each, you need to methodically embody each of the three Effort elements one by one, until you can experience all three simultaneously. You will feel it when the action crystalizes and is fully embodied.

For example, to **Punch**:

- Walk in the space, taking larger than normal steps that engage your leg muscles, and then activate your upper body as well with strong reaching stretches that really work your muscles. When you feel you are engaging Strong Weight throughout your body …

- Add Direct focus in Space, by catching a sharp point of focus with each step. Feel those two elements click in—Strong and Direct.

- Then, add Quickness in Time. To capture a moment of all three elements at once—from your walking, use your arm to literally Punch! Make sure the movement is well supported by your lower body, and catch a point of focus as you do the action. Stay for a moment and feel the intensity. Don't let your arm rebound, or your focus bounce away. Let out a low, supported sound—"Huh"—as you Punch.

- Feel that intensity for a moment, and then walk on, and gather your energy to Punch again. Do this several times. Then feel the effect on your breathing, your attitude, your thought pattern.

Practice each Effort Action this way. Refer to Table 2.1. Begin with one element; weave in the second, and then the third. Let your breath and your voice support and reflect your experience of each Action. If you are exploring Effort Actions for a play, spend time exploring each of them. Don't discard any of them as inappropriate. Some may not be expressed in the play, but may represent aspects the character no longer accesses, or qualities he only dreams of expressing. See what your imagination does with each of them, and keep notes of what you discover. Here are some suggested exercises.

29. Directing with Effort Actions

Let someone call out different Actions, as you apply them to text, or improvise in character. Let the Actions you are given affect your behavior and activities as well as your speech. If you are on your own, be your own director. Afterward go back and analyze the connections between Effort Actions, thoughts, and the physical actions of your character. Are there any that give you a new understanding or new interpretation? Are there choices you want to embed in your work?

30. Opposing sides of a character

Play with taking two Effort Actions, and moving between them, being clear about changing, as you work with a text, or just improvise movement in a scene. These Actions might be opposites, like Press and Flick; or those that only change one element, like Press and Glide (only changing the Weight element). Note how and when you change from one to the other, and what each represents for the character.

31. Divide the room into quarters

(Thanks to Juliet Chambers for this exercise)[8]

Divide the room in quarters, using tape on the floor. Assign each quarter an Effort Action. Move through the room in character, with or without text in mind, with or without speaking aloud. Notice the borders between quadrants, where you may feel two Actions pulling you at once. Notice interactions with others when you are in the same quadrant, and neighboring quadrants.

32. Effort Actions and activities

Use Effort Actions to inspire different ways of handling objects or different ways of carrying out activities. Let these different physical actions inform you psychologically and emotionally, and let your thoughts and feelings inform your choice of Effort Actions. Notice how the residual effects of an Effort Action stick around inside, even after you have moved on to another Action or State. In this way you can feel the complexity of a character, the layers of thoughts and feelings.

33. Effort Actions as inners and outers

It can be effective to choose an Effort Action to represent an inner emotional quality. By that I mean something a character feels inside, but doesn't want to, or cannot, show; she may not even know about that part of herself!

- Try this with Wring, for example. First, move in space embodying each element of Wring in turn. The strong muscular movement, the flexibility of no sharp focus in space, the lingering sustainment in time. Externalize these with sound—a deep, groaning "ugh," perhaps, as you do the action, like wringing out a towel with your whole body. Then use a word in place of the sound—"no" or "yes" ("no-o-o-" or "ye-e-es") are always good to explore; or try words from a script.

- Then internalize this feeling and quality of breathing, without doing the movement. If you have really externalized it, you will feel it inside.

- Next choose another Action as your "outer"; perhaps choose Dab, the opposite of Wring. Once you achieve Dab, accumulating one element at a time until you have all three at once—feel the pull between the inner and the outer actions of Wring and Dab.

- Try some text. Allow the underlying feeling of Wring to bleed through the Dabbing exterior at times, not only in your speech, but in your gestures.

- Play this way with different internal and external Actions. Play with partners, and groups, improvising or using text.

34. Political speeches with Effort Actions

- Political speeches are especially well suited to using Effort Actions with text. (You can use an impassioned speech from any period in history, about any issue—in other words it need not be restricted specifically to politicians.) Choose a speech and read it through several times, trying various Effort Actions to express an idea or a word.

- Then, in pairs, let one person direct the other, calling out changes in Effort Actions almost randomly. In this way, you will find new meaning, new rhythms, and new vitality in your communication. It would be advisable to have practiced embodying each action fully before you begin, so that the mere word "Float," for example, will create a full-bodied response that alters your entire being.

When you observe politicians, take note of the way Effort Actions can be said to define someone's personal style.

35. Silent movie acting

This exercise works best with small groups of three or four people. Among yourselves, dream up a highly dramatic silent movie scenario.

The hero, the villain, the damsel in distress, etc.—create your own modern versions of the old stories. Each character chooses a repertoire of one or two Effort Actions. Rehearse and then perform the dramas for the class, using some silent movie style music in the background.

36. Leaving or staying

This is a partner exercise. One person wants to leave; the other wants to stay. Improvise a scene, integrating body and speech, in which you use Effort Actions to explore various tactics, ways of playing your objective—to get your partner to go with you or stay with you. The Effort Actions should help you explore a wide emotional range.

The three Transformation Drives: How do you express the peak moments in a play?

Table 2.2: Transformation Drives

Drive	Defining characteristic
Spell	Timeless (Weight/Space/Flow)
Vision	Weightless (Time/Space/Flow)
Passion	Spaceless (Weight/Time/Flow)

By exchanging Flow for one of the components of the Action Drive, there is an intensification of the two remaining Effort qualities, to which Flow adds a heightened emotional quality. Like the Action Drive, there are also eight ways of embodying the three Effort qualities that make up each of the Transformation Drives, though these are unnamed.

You can explore these Drives by starting with one of the related States (listed in the descriptions below), and then adding the third Effort quality. You can also make a list of the eight possible combinations within each Transformation Drive; try out each one, and make notes afterward.

Because the Transformation Drives include the emotional element of Flow, they can characterize the most heightened emotional moments in a play. When there is a heightened emotional moment or scene, does the character lose touch with Weight, Space, or Time, while investing every-thing in the other qualities? The three Transformation Drives are as follows.

Passion Drive

Includes Time, Weight, and Flow (excludes Space)

This Drive is detached from the mental reflection associated with the element of Space. It is characterized by uncensored emotional and physical expression. The ability to reflect, associated with Space, is absent. A tantrum, for example.

Related States: Dream, Near, Mobile

Spell Drive

Includes Weight, Space, and Flow (excludes Time)

This Drive has a steadfastness which creates a spell-like intensity. It can characterize a way of exerting control over others, or of being controlled or entranced. A witch casting a spell, someone in a trance, for example.

Related States: Remote, Dream, Stable

Vision Drive

Includes Time, Space, and Flow (excludes Weight)

Without the physical sensation of Weight, this Drive can have a disembodied quality. It can characterize someone who is carried away by her emotional, imaginative excitement. A rousing preacher at the denouement of a sermon, or someone who expresses deep longing to be elsewhere, for example.

Related States: Mobile, Awake, Remote

37. Adding and subtracting elements

Play with adding and subtracting elements, changing back and forth between Drives and the States that make them up. Do this somewhat randomly—you can think about what you did afterward, and figure out what State or Drive you were in. If you are working on a play, find changes for every new beat or new thought.

38. Playing an Action using a Drive

- Give one person in a pair a slip of paper, on which an action word is written—for example: "to convince," "to berate," "to woo," "to encourage." Also on the slip is the name of a Drive. If it is Action Drive, write a specific action. Examples might be: "to convince" in Spell, "to berate" in Vision, "to woo" in Passion, or "to encourage" using Float. You may also give three specific elements within a Drive—for example: "to threaten" in Spell, using Direct, Light, and Bound.

- Try finding your own choices of Effort Actions or Transformation Drives to play other actions: to accuse, to confuse, to flatter, to inquire, etc. Try playing the same action in several different ways; don't be content with what at first seems the obvious choice. Surprise yourself!

39. Mapping movement through a play

Both actors and directors may find it useful to map the movement through the play using LMA. Make drawings or graphs to indicate the atmospheres of the beginning, middle and end, to describe each scene and/or the major events in a play. Plot the journeys of the different characters, or focus specifically on *your* character. Describe the progressive shifts of the Effort life, and the changing relationships to space using the LMA vocabulary.

Practicing Observation

Observation of fellow human (and non-human) beings in the outside world is an endless creative resource. As an actor, you may already have strong instincts when it comes to mimicry and empathy. You may intuitively know what it's like to get inside someone else's skin. But when you augment that instinct with understanding and naming of qualities, with reference to the Laban frameworks, you can develop new levels of insight. You can more consciously absorb the subtlety and depth of nonverbal information, and more easily recognize the different sides and layers of someone's personality. Here are some explorations in observation.

40. Observing with your whole body

Observe someone you don't know, but who, for whatever reasons, has attracted your attention: someone on the street, in a café, at the gym … wherever!

- Sense them in your own body. Get a feel for what you imagine it's like being them. And, importantly, notice what they stir up in you as an observer.

- After observing for a time, subtly try on their movement patterns. Let this give rise to your own version of an inner monologue, or duologue between what you sense are two opposing aspects of the person you are observing.

- Write up the observation afterward, describing it so that someone else can get a feel for the person. Include language and ideas from the Laban vocabulary to describe the person: posture, gestures, kinesphere, body parts that stand out, as well as key Effort qualities, State(s), and/or Drives.

- What elements of Weight, Space, Time, and/or Flow stand out? What Effort Actions do they seem to use? Where do you feel their center is and the placement of weight on their feet?

- Don't feel restricted to using only "Laban language." Use your own words as well to describe them in relationship to the setting and to other people. Include your own thoughts and feelings observing them.

41. Embodying characters from observation

- If you are in a class, bring written observations of two people to class (as described in the previous exercise).

- Each person embodies one of their two characters, taking time to be precise and layered.

- Characters then mingle freely as a group. Discover what you feel about the others ... who you can relate to ... who you clash with ... Improvise in silence first, and then add speech.

- The leader tells the assembled group of characters they have been selected randomly and brought here to gauge their concerns about life in their local community. Seat them in a row, and select a leader to moderate a discussion.

- Characters may also present themselves one by one to the group. Again, you can set it up so that they are there to answer questions on an issue of the day, or simply to describe what's on their mind, and receive questions from others, who can be instructed to remain in character, or not.

42. Embody someone else's character

- Give one of your written observations to someone else in the group. Everyone embodies the character they've been given. Do not consult the observer. Then half the class watches the other half meet and improvise a scene.

- Or, each person introduces themselves to the audience and takes questions. Imagine your backstory and your wants and needs as this person. Describe something this person is passionate about.

- Share afterward with the person whose character you embodied.

43. Observation as a group

Organize an outing for a group of actors. Go to a busy street, where each actor has the task of finding someone to observe, and to embody when you return to class. (At RADA, we could simply go around the corner, onto London's ever-bustling Tottenham Court Road.)

- Try going out in three groups, each group with a different relationship to space, using the planes: Vertical—Door plane;

Horizontal—Table plane; Sagittal—Wheel plane. Prepare yourselves carefully in class beforehand. (RADA classes ranged from 12–16 people and this was a very manageable size, with four or five people in each group.)

- Feel the rhythms and imagine the thoughts of people you observe. Notice—and later, when you return to class, discuss—the different ways of perceiving from the three planes. What was noticed and experienced from each of the three perspectives?

44. Watch TV or a segment from a film with the sound off

- Watch news anchors, interviewers, political figures on TV with the sound off. Notice their nonverbal tics, what Laban referred to as *shadow movements*. Try to put names to the movement qualities, States, and dimensional orientation to the space; and describe their gestures and postures. Bring an observation to embody and discuss in class.

- Choose a segment of a film to watch together in class, without the sound. What can you say about the character(s) in Laban terms? I used *Taxi Driver* for this exercise. Watch with the sound only after you watch and discuss a small segment without.

Other Effort-inspired movement themes to explore

In the following exercises, you don't necessarily begin from LMA, but rather use it to assess what you have done, and/or to explore different interpretations and a fuller range of possibilities.

45. Objects

Much can be revealed about a character's inner life by how he chooses to handle objects. Use any objects, hard and soft, small and large, for this exercise—not too many at once though, so that you can focus in depth, and have plenty of room to move. Objects can be anything, from books, clothing or cooking utensils, to ropes, umbrellas, ladders—absolutely anything you want. This is a creative and effective exercise for a group, in which participants can play with placing, sorting, holding, choosing, giving, taking, offering, receiving, and handling.

- What qualities are engendered by an object? How does an object make you feel? How does it make you want to move? What do you want to do with it? What else can you do with it? Surprise yourself.

- You can create a character from your work with the object. Let a scene and situation arise from that.

- Work with objects that you will be using or could use in a scene you're working on. Bring objects and clothing to handle that evoke the setting for the play.

46. Activities

You can find out much about characters by exploring their activities, with and without objects, both inside and outside the confines of the play. Activities can be anything a character might do: sewing, putting on clothes, tidying up, looking in a mirror ... whatever fits with the world of the play. Try out a range of States and notice how the activity and your state of mind change. Also try out different Effort Actions and Transformation Drives. Is there an *inner* attitude that colors or conflicts with an *outer* execution of an activity? Let the subtext take shape. If speech comes, allow that, but work primarily in silence, taking account of your breathing and any sounds, or melodies, you emit.

47. Eating

A character's eating onstage reveals subtext. Practice by inviting one person at a time to eat in front of the group. You might bring fruit to class or whatever else you think is appropriate. The person can select a slip of paper before choosing a piece of fruit, with emotional qualities like aggressive, fearful, lusty, sneaky, preoccupied, messy, picky, careful, raging, starving, disgusted, guilty, mournful, joyful, seductive.

After each performance, the group can discuss what they saw in terms of Effort qualities, States, and Drives.

48. Costume

Everyone in a group puts an article of clothing into a pile in the middle. Extra bits and pieces can be added by the group leader. Everyone chooses an item. Develop a character from the clothing, and let the group decide a setting and/or relationships for small group improvisations. Let the costume influence the character's movement, voice, and thinking. This is a good exercise for exploring the boundaries of gender and roles. Afterward, discuss the improvisations in terms of Effort qualities, States, and Drives, as well as what stood out as valuable and/or surprising.

49. Portraits

Using my collection of postcards from museums, portraits of men, women, and children, historical and modern, I ask students to choose a picture and embody the character as fully as possible.

- Be exactly true to the pose. If there is only a face, discover the rest of the body.

- Begin to see through the character's eyes, and notice the character's thoughts as you move through the space.

- Recognize how you use the space, what you think of the others, who you gravitate toward, and who repels you.

- Hear the sound of your internal voice. If you are moved to speak to someone, notice how the character's voice differs from your own.

- Write a monologue as the character. Read it to the group in character, using the person's gestures, voice, and rhythms of speech. The group can watch you as well as your picture.

- Discuss the primary State of each character afterward.

This exercise can also be done using photographs from the newspaper, carefully selected for the impact of their physical life.

50. Making music and sound

Provide percussion instruments, so that half the group can be an orchestra, and improvise music to support the others in movement. There can be a wonderful unity of expression between movers and musicians, as everyone opens their eyes, ears, hearts, and minds to being a part of the whole ensemble.

- Begin formally, in silence and stillness, movers having chosen starting positions in the space, musicians having chosen instruments.

- This can be a great exercise for rehearsing a play, as it liberates the actors from the script and allows unusual, often insightful, ways of interacting with fellow players, as the subtext comes to the fore.

- This exercise can also be done using voice only to support the movers. In this case, each mover has a specific partner who watches and makes sound to support her. The vocalists can sit round the periphery of the space.

- The segments can be five minutes, or longer, if all is going well. Let the group know when to start to find an ending, so the conclusion can be organic.

Two culminating projects: Bringing it all together

51. Developing and presenting a scene

This project is an important vehicle through which actors take over responsibility for incorporating LMA into their working process.

- Actors prepare scenes outside of class, usually duologues, but they may also choose a trio or solo piece.

- In addition to preparing and presenting the scene, each actor prepares a *Laban-based preparation* for the scene.

- Actors will lead the class in their preparations before presenting the scene. It is important that although the performers are leading others in the preparation, they also participate in it themselves, as it is their preparation for presenting the scene.

Students who will be the audience enjoy preparing with the actors who will be performing. It allows them to strongly identify with the roles before they witness the scene. They also learn from each other about different ways of applying LMA to their working processes.

Here are two examples of preparations created by students at RADA.

Two actors presented a scene from Strindberg's *Miss Julie*. For the preparation, the women were asked to follow the actor playing Julie, who led them in producing a vocabulary of three Effort Actions the character portrays. The men followed the actor playing her servant, Jean, who led three different Effort Actions. The men were then asked to choose a partner for a waltz, to music the presenters provided. The complexities of power and class between the characters was embodied in the dance, and set the scene for the duologue. In fact, a dance between these two characters actually opens the play.

In a scene from *Waiting for Godot*, the actors playing Vladimir and Estragon divided the class in half. Those following Vladimir were led in the experience of the Effort Action of Float, and also a sense of timelessness, in Dream State in particular. Those following Estragon were led in the Effort Actions of Flick, Slash, and Punch, as well as the Awake State. They were asked to come together with a partner from the opposing group, and see how they related.

52. The Enchanted Forest

Creating characters in the Enchanted Forest is as vivid now as it ever was. I remember the characters and the passionate ways they would interact. It was so real.

(Student response, RADA, a year after the exercise)

This is an extended group exercise that spans several sessions, and requires someone to guide the improvisation, and have an outside eye. The Enchanted Forest differs from the other exercises presented in the Transformation section of this chapter. Here, LMA is used after a series of three extended improvisation sessions, as a tool for reflecting back on the characters created, and their psychophysical life.

I created this project for actors with whom I'd already been working for almost two years, at which point they had had much experience working together, and using LMA as a catalyst for exploring movement. In that sense, this is an "advanced" exercise. With minimal guidance, the actors were able to create unique characters in the Enchanted Forest, as they formed and inhabited this imaginary world.

As the Enchanted Forest takes shape, it becomes populated by an exotic mixture of beautiful, ugly, magical, terrifying, shape-shifting creatures the actors create. Their imaginations are informed, first and foremost, by their movement. Characters emerge, crystallize, and transform through actors' synchronizing their movement and imagination. They respond to the highly dramatic and emotional relationships and situations that arise from moment to moment.

The encounters—in improvised scenes, mostly nonverbal—can be both tender and daring. Passions run high, as the forces of good and evil are close to the surface, and good can change to evil at the drop of a hat. Nothing is necessarily as it seems—there can be deception, rivalry, hatred, and murder as well as compassion, tenderness, and love. All the elements of good drama are there.

I use background music to help create the atmosphere for this exploration. (If you google Enchanted Forest music, you will see many examples.) You can select pieces with differing emotional qualities from each other. I like to use soothing music at the beginning and the end, and wilder, more disturbing and rhythmic music in between. Equally, participants find their own sounds and voices in this exercise, so you may find that outside music is not essential.

To add to the imaginative world, I have collected a large assortment of fabric remnants of different sizes, shapes, textures, and colors. I describe below how I use them. The fabric, as well as whatever (hopefully limited) furniture is in the space, helps actors create the characters and the setting of this fantastical, surprising world.

You can devote at least three one-and-a-half-hour sessions to the development of this world. I describe three instalments below.

Session one

- Start by talking about the theme as a group, asking participants to free-associate a list of what images and characters are conjured up when they think about the Enchanted Forest. This engages everyone's imagination and creates a sense of excited anticipation. Ask someone to write down the list as people speak and read the whole list back to the group. Because the theme harks back to childhood, it is important to discuss the richness of this world for adults, so participants don't feel they are being infantilized—rather that they are invited to embody the openness of a child.

- Next, everyone finds a relaxed resting position in the space, lying down or leaning against a wall or other support, eyes closed, as if entering a dream.

- From there, guide participants to focus on their position, physical sensations, breath, and contact with the physical environment. Some peaceful Enchanted Forest music will help set the mood.

- Then, participants start to allow small movements, maybe just hands and feet at first. They continue, spreading attention throughout their bodies, following any desire to move, roll, stretch—changing shape in any way … allowing imagination to blossom as they start to embody creatures or characters in the forest.

- The person who is guiding this experience can scatter pieces of fabric throughout the space after participants' eyes are closed, so that as participants start to move, they encounter the fabric; and this informs their imagination. Encourage participants to let their imagination and movement synchronize so they begin to crystallize a character or creature from the impulses of movement.

- Keeping their awareness of physical sensations, participants open their eyes, and also take in the terrain and the others, fully entering the realms of Space, Time, Weight, and Flow.

- Characters can make use of the fabric in any way—as costume or set or to endow something with magical powers. In the Enchanted Forest, anything is possible—love, hatred, death, rebirth; spells are cast, battles are won and lost. The music underlying this more active section of the work can be more lively or disturbing, in order to support the dramatic encounters that ensue.

- This improvisation can go on for up to an hour. When the guide feels it's time to end a session, instruct characters to slowly settle back down, entering into a dream again. Guide them to review their journey, as if remembering a dream, before fully awakening to themselves.

- End this session with everyone sitting in a circle. One person begins telling a story: "Once upon a time ..." Each person adds to the narrative from their own experience of being a character in the forest.

Session two

- The next session can pick up exactly where the last one left off for each character, including any use of fabric to create a costume or an environment. Or it can begin again from scratch. Follow the same development, slowly immersing into the physical world, actively engaging, and returning to rest and review.

- End this session with participants drawing their characters, using gentle music to sustain the mood. Allow time for each actor to show and describe their drawing and character, and to give some information about the creature/character's traits to the group. It is wonderful if these can be hung on the wall, so they are visible for the next session in the Enchanted Forest. This helps everyone to visualize all the characters.

Session three

- Before the final session begins, let participants know this is the last instalment, and that the narrative will end.

- Give plenty of warning, so that each actor can bring things to a definite conclusion for their character.

- When actors come to rest at the end of the story, ask participants to stay in their characters, as if waking from a dream, and, as they come back to the "real world," to gradually transform to a contemporary human character, retaining the essence of the forest character.

- Immediately ask them to play a scene together—it's a family reunion! Have them introduce themselves, and improvise a scene. The improv will undoubtedly reflect the narrative and relationships that were established in the forest.

- After the improv, leave time to reflect on each of the characters in LMA terms. Ask participants to name the States, Drives and/ or Effort Actions that define their characters' essential qualities, and the key elements of their vocabulary of movement.

This series of sessions has never failed to engage a group of actors. I think it is because there is such intensity in the experience of being in an unknown world with their colleagues; and yet they have a flexible container, the Enchanted Forest, for all the action. The trust is near total—of the guide, each other, and the world they've created. This is possible, I feel, because of the previous building of LMA movement vocabulary as a group, over time, before this exercise is introduced, so that trust and safety are already embedded in the working process.

As not everyone will have the opportunity to work with a group of over such an extended time, and you may want to try this exercise, here are some notes that may be of help to guide the exercise.

- The extent of the guide's involvement in the Enchanted Forest will depend on the needs of the group. For example, the group may need encouragement to sense their bodies, and to move if they are stagnant for too long; or, if they leap into planning and action, they may need a reminder to slow down, and let their imaginations follow from sensing their bodies.

- You can let actors know that if you sense anyone is at risk of getting hurt, you will call out "freeze," and they will stop the action; they will go on when you give the cue, starting in slow motion.

- The guide will have to tolerate a certain amount of chaos, and not knowing what is going on, just as the actors do; but this is not usually a reason to stop the improvisation.

- I have used a deck of symbol cards with this exercise. Actors choose, discover, or are given card(s); the image on the card can inform the journeys and individuals' wants and needs.

Using the Laban vocabulary after this extended exercise, as a tool for reflecting on what has been discovered—for analyzing the States and Drives of the characters, rather than as an inspiration for creating characters—gives actors a chance to sharpen their intuitive impulses and then to reflect on them.

Summary

You can understand a play until the cows come home, but unless you physically and emotionally commit to it, you'll never be able to perform it.

(Tom Hiddleston, actor, and former student at RADA)[9]

Our bodies are barometers of the truth. Working with and from your body can liberate truthful responses, helping you to transform and, as Hiddleston says, to "physically and emotionally commit" to a play.

The movement explorations in this chapter help you tap into hidden depths via the unconscious pool of nonverbal experience, in order to more deeply *in-form* yourself and your characters. As with human development, our physical life comes first. We perceive and express physically, before we have words or understanding.

In his later years, Stanislavski emphasized the importance of creating a line of physical actions in order to organically fulfil a role. He said:

The "small truth" of physical actions stirs the "great truth" of thoughts, emotions, experiences, and a "small untruth" of physical actions gives birth to a "great untruth" in the region of emotions, thoughts and imagination.

(Richards 1995: 65)

LMA can help you plot a through line of physical actions from the beginning to the end of the character's journey. It can enable you to make specific choices, while also developing the flexibility to adapt to variations with your acting partners from moment to moment—to play, with utmost belief and commitment.

When actors are given the freedom to explore a piece of work via movement, they inevitably discover different kinds of choices and rhythms than the ones they would instinctively make if working from discussion and research alone. What one gains from movement explorations will always be fresh and surprising and, as with dreams, there can be layers of insight to be harvested. In short, LMA provides a language for shaping the subtext—the tone, rhythm, and atmosphere that underpin the words of any play.

Acknowledgments

My thanks to Juliet Chambers, Katie Laris, and series editors David and Rebecca Carey, all of whom read the chapter and offered extremely useful feedback and suggestions. Thanks also to all my students at RADA, from whom I learned so much, and to Suprapto Suryodarmo, whose Amerta Movement practice greatly deepened my experience of LMA.

Notes

1 Prapto Suryodarmo, a Javanese movement teacher, whose non-stylized practice, called Amerta Movement, has greatly influenced my teaching.
2 Adam Bradpiece is a movement teacher, and one of the first Western students to work with Prapto Suryodarmo.

3   Body-Mind Centering® is an approach to movement, the body, and consciousness.

4   Susanka Christman was one of the first Westerners to work with Prapto Suryodarmo.

5   Personal communication with Juliet Chambers.

6   This image was originally published in *The Embodied Self: Movement and Psychoanalysis*, by Katya Bloom (Karnac Books, 2006), and is reprinted with kind permission of Karnac Books.

7   The term *Flexible* is also known as *Indirect* use of Space.

8   Juliet Chambers is a Laban-based Teaching Fellow at the University of Surrey, UK.

9   Taken from www.rada.ac.uk (accessed 28 April 2017): "A word with …Tom Hiddleston," filmed September 2012, with kind permission of RADA.

Further reading/resources

Bloom, Katya (2003). "Moving Actors: Laban Movement Analysis as the Basis for a Psychophysical Movement Practice." *Contact Quarterly* 28: 11–17.

Bloom, Katya (2006). "The Language of Movement: Embodying Psychic Processes," in *The Embodied Self: Movement and Psychoanalysis*. London: Karnac, 17–29, 40–2.

Bloom, Katya (2009). "Laban and Breath: The Embodied Actor," in *Breath in Action: The Art of Breath in Vocal and Holistic Practice*, J. Boston and R. Cook (eds). London and Philadelphia: Jessica Kinglsey Publishers, 227–38.

Dick, Michael (2014). "Ever Speaking Being," in *Embodied Lives: Reflections on the Influence of Suprapto Suryodarmo and Amerta Movement*, K. Bloom, M. Galanter, M., and S. Reeve (eds). Axminster: Triarchy, 231–40.

Podcast with Juliet Chambers. Available online: www.Labanarium.com/featured contributor/dr-katya-bloom/ (accessed 28 April 2017).

Porter, Claire (2008). *Dynamics in a Bag*. Self-published cards.

3

MOVING YOUR VOICE: EXPANDING YOUR VOCAL CREATIVE POTENTIAL THROUGH LMA

Barbara Adrian

Introduction

The purpose of this chapter is to expand your vocal expressiveness. The explorations developed through Laban Movement Analysis (LMA) are to be applied towards integrating movement with voice, speech, and text. The explorations will guide you to physical and vocal choices that are rooted in the specifics of the text, ignite the imagination, promote character development and clear story telling. A Caliban speech from Shakespeare's *The Tempest* will serve as the model for the explorations and several videos will ensure that the reader understands the more complex explorations. I encourage you to extrapolate and adapt the exercises to a text of your own choosing. There is one codicil. Not every exploration will be immediately applicable to every text. Ultimately the individual will choose the tools best suited to the needs of the moment. As you play with this LMA-based approach to voice and text, I recommend that you keep a journal that will include discoveries, frustrations, and questions.

Voice, speech, and movement

The healthy well-tuned voice is capable of leaping, spinning, diving, whirling, and permeating space to a distance much greater than our corporeal body is capable of reaching even when stretched to the outermost boundary of its kinesphere. While the body is in active stillness[1] the voice can move around corners and through obstacles aurally touching the listener. The voice can reach heights that would be a taxing journey for the body to climb. Ideally, outstanding feats of voice and speech occur when the *need* to speak is united with healthy applications of the breath through the vocal folds, an expansive vocal range, and efficient muscular activity of the articulators to produce speech sounds. If all are in harmony, your voice will radiate your presence into the environment, leaving a "voice-print" or "sound-picture" of your unique essence.

In this chapter, I use the words "sound" and "voice" interchangeably to mean any sound that passes out of the throat and mouth. Furthermore, when I write, "add voice" or "add sound," I am referring to "unstructured sounds." The unstructured sounds are shaped moment to moment by how you are feeling and/or how your imagination is affected by the exercise. Unstructured sounds lack the precision that would identify the sounds as particular consonants, pure vowels,[2] or diphthongs.[3] They are primitive, giving the listener a sense of what you are feeling. The actual literal meaning is not articulated through words, which would require refinement of the articulatory actions. Think how excellent pre-verbal children are at letting their needs and feelings be known without actual words. They are using unstructured sound.

When I use the word "speech," I am referring to the precise movements of the articulators that shape the unstructured sound into recognizable speech sounds and ultimately words. During speech, the individual consonants and vowels are sequenced with enough precision that the literal sense of the thought is conveyed to the listener. Speaking a text requires both voice and speech. For instance, your character is grief-stricken and your voice reflects the grief in the form of a wail without specific articulatory structure. The hearer absolutely understands that you are sad, distraught, and mournful but until the articulators move with precision the hearer doesn't know why. The hearer cannot glean the specifics of your distress until you say: "My dog was hit by a truck." In a sense, speech rides the wave of unstructured sound. The words, "My dog was hit by a truck," ride the wail of grief.

Why integrate LMA, a movement practice, with voice and speech training?

LMA is practical and readily adaptable to a variety of needs, which may or may not lie in the realm of the arts. I discovered how flexible LMA is regarding actor training when I team taught with a movement coach who was using LMA as the lens for observing and creating movement. Everything the movement coach said and did with the actors was immediately applicable to their voices and to the text at hand.

Similarly to voice/speech, I observed that when the body was moving in ways which were not particularly structured or detailed, I could understand the general emotion that was being portrayed but little of the specifics. As the LMA vocabulary induced more and more physical specificity, the expressiveness of the actors' bodies also became enriched and the stories became clearer. Their bodies literally became more articulate. When you integrate the body, voice, and speech with specificity, then you have a performance.

Overview of the chapter and the explorations

This chapter begins with the actor's relationship to breath integrated with Laban's concept of Shape. You will explore how this integration supports nuancing the tone of voice and experiment with how your text may be spoken. To that end, you will be guided towards examining the actual articulation of the words as they relate to Shape, thus enhancing both the clarity of the articulation and the meaning of the text. Central to this chapter is the idea that an articulated thought must be treated as a gesture traveling on a specific trajectory through space to affect the listener in the same manner as our limbs do when gesturing to under-score our meaning. To flesh out the text even further, Laban's concept of Effort will be employed to guide you towards filling the words with psychological truth and specificity and to provide a tool for affecting your partner in ways perhaps previously unimagined. Detailed explora-tions are provided throughout the chapter for your investigation. It is important to empty your mind of judgment. Give over to the experience and bring your joy. This is play! You really can't do the explorations wrong. So please do not try to be "right." Let it be messy and take all the time you need with each exploration.

Shape

"He is in bad shape." "You look like you are in good shape today." "You looked so sad yesterday; what kind of shape are you in today?" We have all used or heard these statements regarding an individual's state of being. The word "shape" is used to describe the inner attitude of an individual as it radiates outward changing the visible shape of the body. Shape is one of the four main concepts housed in LMA, the others being Body, Effort, and Space. In regard to acting, Shape reveals the ever-changing relationship of the individual to the Given Circumstances. The term "Given Circumstances" refers to the conditions under which a character is living regarding both the environment and situation.

Given Circumstances and Shape

The shape of your body at any given moment potentially reveals your emotional response triggered by your relationship to self, the environment, others, and/or your situation. Your body literally changes shape, albeit sometimes very subtly, when you are happy, disappointed, or scared, to name just a few examples.

Exploration 1: Create a scenario

- Create a scenario that could induce deep disappointment, such as not getting the job you desperately need and thought you were perfect for. Observe how your body adapts to those feelings.

- Change the stimulus to a success, such as being nominated for a Tony Award. Note how your body changes shape.

You may have been sensitive enough to notice that the first change that takes place is in the flow of the breath and all else follows that shift. So that is where we will start—with the breath.

Shape Flow of the breath

Shape Flow of the breath refers to the shape changes that manifest in your torso as you breathe. The breath moves in and out of your lungs without an agenda—except to keep you alive. The flow is subtle, fluid, and unstoppable. The general movements inherent in the Shape Flow of the breath are identified as *growing* and *shrinking* and they occur in rhythm with the inhalation (*growing*) and exhalation (*shrinking*). We could also call Shape Flow of the breath the "infant's breath." You have been *growing* and *shrinking* with your breath since birth without giving it a thought. Additionally, soon after birth you began to lay down breathing patterns that eventually became your baseline for the movement of your breath. Therefore, Shape Flow manifested before you had any thought of sharing yourself with others or influencing your environment. Shape Flow of the breath is between you and YOU!

In addition to the sense of *growing* and *shrinking* with the inhalation and exhalation, there are other subtle movements within the torso. These are identified as *lengthening* and *shortening, widening* and *narrowing, hollowing* and *bulging*. At its most efficient, the breath radiates three-dimensionally. *Lengthening/shortening* the spine emphasizes the vertical dimension of the breath (up/down). *Widening/narrowing* the ribcage emphasizes the horizontal dimension of the breath (side/side). *Hollowing/bulging* the sternum towards and away from the spine emphasizes the sagittal dimension of the breath (backward/forward). When the dimensions are activated simultaneously, you are breathing three-dimensionally. It is this movement of the breath that eventually radiates out into the limbs allowing the whole body to become attuned with the breath.

In order to vocally and physically support a character, we need to start with the movement of the breath. It is always helpful to identify your own breath patterns to delineate the traits you and the imagined character have in common and traits that mark you as distinctly different from one another. Examining our selves first and then the character will be the pattern of presentation throughout this chapter.

See: 5 Explorations 2, 3, 4: Shape Flow→Shape Forms→Standing with Unstructured Sound
https://vimeo.com/channels/thelabanworkbook/199996417

Exploration 2: Shape Flow

- Lie on your back (supine). Without managing or forcing the breath, be aware of the ebb and flow of your breath and the subtle internal changes within your torso (*growing* and *shrinking*).

- Give over to the natural rhythm of your breath. You are discovering the impulsive breath rather than the planned overly conscious breath. If you are breathing on impulse,[4] you are likely to feel a slight pause or suspension of the breath just before the next impulse to inhale.

- As you give into the rhythm of the breath, allow your limbs (six limbs: head, tail, arms, legs) to expand away from the spine and contract towards the spine with each inhalation and exhalation. Allow the inhalation and exhalation to be the impulse for the external body's observable physical changes, which are fluid and free.

- Allow the energy of the breath to manifest in the dimensions discretely at first and then allow that energy to radiate even more fully into the limbs.

- Take a few moments to emphasize the *lengthening/shortening* of the spine with the breath.

- Emphasize the *widening/narrowing* of the ribcage.

- Emphasize the *hollowing/bulging* of sternum towards and away from the spine.

- Return to step one and allow the breath to manifest in all the dimensions simultaneously.

By the last step, were you well balanced in the three-dimensionality of the breath or were you aware of favoring one dimension over another? There are many possible permutations of our habitual breathing patterns. Perhaps you feel most comfortable privileging *lengthening* over *widening* or *hollowing* over *bulging*. The movement of the breath can be very subtle so it may take several passes before you can identify the dimension with which you are most affined. Observing the movement of your limbs during the previous exploration can help you with this identification. For instance, did you favor stretching your limbs lengthwise along the floor, enclosing your limbs towards your naval, or spreading your arms and legs forming a large X?

As you are exploring the breath, don't think in terms of right or wrong. Your impulsive breath is guiding you and is the sole arbiter of the flow of the breath. Keep in mind that all human beings begin life experiencing the Shape Flow of the breath. Even if your character is a fully mature adult, beginning your warm-up with the Shape Flow of the breath is an excellent starting place towards identifying where you have an affinity with your character and where you do not.

Still Shape Forms (Shape Forms): Pin, Ball, Wall, and Screw[5]

Figures 3.1–4 3.1 (Pin), 3.2 (Ball), 3.3 (Wall), 3.4 (Screw)

Shape Forms are born out of and supported by the Shape Flow of the breath. On the face of it, these four Shape Forms are an oversimplification of the complexities of the human condition. But the simplicity of the designations, as you will discover, is also their strength relative to discovering character.

Exploration 3: Shape Forms

- Remain on the floor on your back. Return to the Shape Flow of the breath and relax into the ebb and flow (*growing/shrinking*). Feel the rhythm of your breath.

- Allow the limbs to stretch farther and farther away from your naval along the floor until you are in the shape of a Wall. Then contract the limbs closer and closer to your navel until you are in the shape of a Ball. Keep in mind that there are six limbs (two arms, two legs, head, and tail). Consider all six limbs as you expand and contract. You will most likely find yourself evolving principally towards Wall and Ball Shapes in this activity.

- When the previous step feels organic, allow unstructured sounds to ride the trajectory of the breath. Is your voice reflecting how you are affected as you travel between the two Shape Forms? The value of the exploration is not necessarily in the Shape Form you arrive at but rather the physical and vocal journey *between* Shapes.

- Explore the relationship between body and voice as you evolve from Pin to Ball to Pin, etc. A Pin Shape is evident when you "narrow" the body by extending the arms and hands along the floor beyond the top of your head and stretching your legs out aligning your heels with your sit bones.

- Introduce Screw Shapes by allowing the spine to twist and untwist. A Screw Shape manifests when rotation is apparent in the spine.

- Explore all the Shape Forms allowing them to influence both your body and voice. Keep in mind it is the journey not the destination that helps us discover the influence of the Shape Forms on our body and voice.

The next exploration emphasizes moving from floor to standing while sounding. It is important to be aware of any moment during which you tense the muscles that support the sound. This means you need to find a balance among the muscles so they do not over-effort or under-effort either activity: rising or sounding. If the voice begins to become restricted, stop. Return to the floor and begin again. Remind yourself to balance the effort among the muscles that support moving and sounding. Do not rush. Be goal-less, and you may surprise yourself when you finally arrive at standing and sounding with ease.

Exploration 4: Coming to standing with unstructured sound

- As you explore the Shape Forms with more and more freedom, fluidly sequence from one Shape Form to another. This sequencing will lead to overlapping Shapes such as upper body Pin, lower body Wall. You may also move towards level changes such as sitting, kneeling and, eventually, standing.

- Are certain Shape Forms or combinations of them more effective as you make this journey towards standing?

- Continue to allow the unstructured sounds to be inspired by the flow of the Shape Forms and the weight shifts that support the journey to standing and back to the floor.

Shape Forms and character

Shape Forms reveal the inner state of the character to the audience. Shape Forms, like our breathing patterns, are influenced by our state of being and the environment in which we function. Through the Shape Forms, you discover how the character is affected by the specific circumstances of his life such as: age, environment, culture, health, work, or relationships. If the character is *enclosed*, i.e., round-shouldered and stooped towards a Ball Shape, the observer will immediately begin to draw some specific conclusions about this individual as opposed to an individual who *spreads* into a Wall Shape.

Regarding the addition of voice and speech: as the spine goes, so goes the voice. As you have discovered, this is partially due to how your imagination may be affected by the specific Shape Form. And on the practical anatomical side, the voice is affected by the physical changes within the torso. The torso *widens* and *narrows*, *lengthens* and *shortens*, *hollows* and *bulges* with the movement of the intercostal muscles (which lie between the ribs), the contraction and relaxation of the diaphragm (the "floor" of the ribcage), and the movement of the sternum towards or away from the spine. The diaphragm (the principal muscle for breathing) has attachments to the ribs, the spine, and the sternum. It is interesting to note that the movements of the muscles that help control the breath also initiate the Shape Form we embody and contribute to radiating our state of being or the character's state into the environment.

The next exploration refines the effect of the Shape Forms on your imagination. Keep in mind that there is no right or wrong as you explore. The result is totally dependent on your imagination and your body/voice interaction. Additionally, there is never one answer to the questions posed in the exploration. The answer today may not be true tomorrow or even an hour from now. But you will begin to discover some repeating qualities that surface depending on whether you emphasize a Pin, Ball, Wall, or Screw Shape Form.

Exploration 5: Shape Forms and imagination

- Play with each specific Shape Form one at a time.
- Investigate the effect each Shape has on your imagination, which means intuiting the answers to questions below without a lot of forethought or analysis.

For example:

- "Who am I when I am dedicated to a Pin Shape?"
- "What are the Given Circumstances that come to mind when I emphasize a Pin Shape?"
- "How is my breath affected?"
- "How is my voice affected?" For instance: "Does the quality of my voice change depending on which Shape Form I am privileging?"

- Observe individuals in real life for the Shape Form with which they seem most aligned.

  – How is your imagination affected? What do you glean about this person from their predominant Shape Form?

  – How are you affected by taking on this Shape Form yourself?

- Find pictures in a book or magazine or portraits in a museum in which the Shape Forms of the individuals are clear and dynamic.

  – How is your imagination affected?

  – How are you affected by taking on this Shape Form yourself?

  – Can you develop characters from the individual Shape Forms?

- Choose a few of the characters that were born of your explorations with Shape Forms. Allow the characters to further make themselves known through unstructured sound or speech. You can also use a monologue, improvised text, or even the alphabet. You are attempting to get a sense of how the character sounds and/or speaks, influenced by his predominant Shape Form.

Caliban's turn!

The Tempest by William Shakespeare
Caliban: Act 1 Scene 2

I must eat my dinner.
This island's mine, by Sycorax my mother,
Which thou tak'st from me. When thou cam'st first,
Thou strok'st me and mad'st much of me, wouldst give me
Water with berries in't, and teach me how
To name the bigger light, and how the less,
That burn by day and night: and then I loved thee
And show'd thee all the qualities o' the isle,
The fresh springs, brine-pits, barren place and fertile:

Cursed be I that did so! All the charms
Of Sycorax, toads, beetles, bats, light on you!
For I am all the subjects that you have,
Which first was mine own king: and here you sty me
In this hard rock, whiles you do keep from me
The rest o' the island.

Caliban and Shape Forms

How do Shape Flow and Shape Forms relate to Caliban? A character's relationship to the breath is critical to who he is and what he values. In Caliban's case, the evidence in the text is that he is stuck in the developmental stage of early childhood. Caliban has been abused and neglected most of his young life. Caliban uses the pronouns "me" and "I" and the possessive "mine" and "my" fourteen times in fifteen lines. At the heart of Caliban's words is a condemnation of Prospero, first for betraying him and then punishing him for being ignorant of how to behave in a civilized manner. Caliban's feelings of betrayal are compounded because Prospero initially treated him like a son and accepted Caliban's gifts "o' the isle." While exploring Caliban, it is informative to re-experience the most infant-like breathing patterns: Shape Flow. This isn't important just for Caliban but potentially for any character that you are investigating.

Exploration 6: Caliban's Shape Form preferences

- Begin with the breath. Allow your imagination to be affected by Caliban's circumstances and background. While you are exploring the breath of Caliban, your imagination is guiding you and is the sole arbiter of the flow of the breath.

- Influenced by your knowledge of Caliban, allow the inhalation and exhalation to be the impulse for the external body's observable physical changes.

- Allow unstructured sounds to grow out of the breath connection. Do not force yourself to make sounds. Allow your unstructured sounds to be the inevitable response to your explorations.

- As you work through the explorations, which Shape Forms (Pin, Ball, Wall, Screw) does Caliban privilege?

Now that you are warmed up physically, vocally, and imaginatively to the breath and the Shape Forms, let's look at Caliban's text more closely and attempt to be specific regarding his most frequent Shape Form. We are starting at the end of the speech when Caliban reveals the environmental limitations to which Prospero has relegated him:

> and here you sty me
> In this hard rock, whiles you do keep from me
> The rest o' the island.

There are those who will say Caliban was restricted to a cave-like dwelling but, in my imagination, I see him literally captured inside of a boulder, a rock. This prison would have a profound effect on both his body and voice. My supposition is that he cannot stand upright or even spread his limbs very far when encased in the "hard rock." He is trapped in a ball—literally. Perhaps Prospero has let him out of this prison, at least briefly, for this interaction. What are the repercussions on him physically and vocally to finally be able to *lengthen* and *widen*?

Exploration 7: A hard rock

- Explore being trapped in a "hard rock" and the manifestations on your body and voice. No need to worry about specific words yet. Live in the rock for several minutes. What happens to your breath? What happens if you make sound? Can you accomplish an everyday activity in this confinement, such as scratching your head?

- Explore being released from the rock. How does your body and voice respond?

- Imagine being sent back into the "hard rock," perhaps for all eternity. What is your visceral response?

- Identify and explore the Shape Form for a character from a play you already know. How is the character's voice and speech affected by this exploration?

Consider that most characters, regardless of the script, are trapped or encased in some sort of container and this container has deep ramifications on the character's Shape Form and resulting tone of voice. What is the container for Laura in *The Glass Menagerie*? For her brother Tom? How about Willy Loman in *Death of a Salesman*? His sons? His wife? The character of Electra in Sophocles' *Electra*? They are all confined to a container, i.e., a Shape Form from which they would like to be released.

Like a Japanese line drawing, these are broad strokes that can be detailed out by you in any number of ways, not the least of which is the expressive voice. Shape Form supported by the breath emanates from the core and influences the spine, which in turn creates the shape of the whole body. The Shape Form is a snapshot of the character's relationship to the Given Circumstances.

Articulation and Shape

Articulation relates to Shape. To demonstrate this relationship, we are leaping into the specifics of the articulation of Caliban's speech. Let's once again return to the words "I", "me", and "mine" that are so often repeated in this text. Inherent in the intellectual meaning of the words are the shapes that the articulators must make to produce the specific sounds and resonances.[6]

The phonemes[7] that comprise the diphthong "I" and the pure vowel "EE" are front vowels. Front vowels are created when the body of the tongue arches towards the hard palate while the tip of the tongue remains relaxed behind the lower front teeth.[8] The articulators shape the vibrating air as it bounces off the pharyngeal cavity, hard palate, nasal cavity, and teeth. This in turn produces resonances that emanate from the face or head (referring to front vowels) permeating space. This is important because if your articulator—the body of the tongue in this case—is accurate in arching towards the hard palate causing a Ball-like Shape while the tongue tip is relaxed behind the lower front teeth; then the face/head resonance will produce a sound that, when repeated again and again, will cause both you and the listener to hear and feel the plea and insistence in Caliban's words. You are no longer just giving information clearly but filling the container of the words with your character's point of view. Look in a mirror and watch the body of your tongue arch towards the hard palate as you speak "I" and "EE."

It is also possible to examine the movement of the tongue spatially. Again using a mirror, watch the movement of your tongue as you say "I" or "EE." You will observe the arch in the body of the tongue moving towards the hard palate along the vertical dimension. Perhaps the body of the tongue is reaching for something needed but out of reach since the tongue does not actually connect with the roof of the mouth. Is it possible that Caliban's tongue is mimicking his situation? He is trapped in a "hard rock" which implies a forced Ball Shape and his tongue, in order to produce the dominating "I" and "EE" sounds, is also compelled into a Ball Shape while simultaneously attempting to reach upward. Perhaps this articulation is a mirror of Caliban's attempts to overcome his obstacles. In spite of his determination, he never reaches his goal as everything conspires to pull him down into an abyss. Such a detailed examination won't reveal juicy secrets in every instance. But you might be surprised to learn that when your articulators are both precise and flexible, they can become a mini picture of the character's condition as well.

Speech is movement. How we produce individual sounds is a significant part of our voice print. I recommend that if you haven't yet, take a speech class that examines the movement of the articulators in detail. Do *not* do this for the purpose of correcting or standardizing your speech but for the purpose of challenging your articulators to move in unfamiliar ways and to identify your personal habitual speech patterns. We all get locked into ways of moving not just our gross body, but even the smaller (observed and unobserved) refined muscles that govern speech. As an actor, it always behooves you to identify habitual patterns and expand your expressivity by challenging yourself to move in unfamiliar ways.[9]

Repeating Shape = Repeating Sound = Emotional Reveal

The results of the following explorations will be very subtle as resonance itself is subtle. Proceed gently. If you over pressurize the words in an attempt to force the resonance you will actually dampen it.

Exploration 8: Articulatory Shape and Specific Resonance

- Repeat sounding "I" and "EE" at least five times each.

- Become aware of the specific shape the body of the tongue makes as it arches from the bottom of the mouth towards the hard palate. (A mirror can be a helpful tool.)

- As you repeat the sounds again and again with the knowledge of Caliban's Given Circumstances, how do these movements of the tongue and the preponderance of face resonance affect you?

- Repeat the words: *I, me, mine,* and *my* five times applying what you learned from the previous three steps.

- Put these words back into the text and say the lines.

- Repeat the previous exercises with this expanded list containing "I" and the pure vowel "EE": *eat, teach, light, by, night, thee, brine, beetles, sty, whiles, keep, island.*

- Restore all the words back into the text and speak the entire text with the benefit of the exploration.

"I" and "EE" are not the only Ball-like tongue shapes in this text. There are other front-loaded vowels/diphthongs that may contribute to the over all affect of Caliban's speech. In addition to "EE" and "I", the other front vowel sounds in this speech are: e (rest), i (which), a (bat), and AY (place). I have reproduced Caliban's speech with *all* the words that contain front vowels in **bold**.

I must **eat my dinner**.
This island's mine, by Sycorax my mother,
Which thou **tak'st** from **me. When** thou **cam'st** first,
Thou strok'st **me and mad'st** much of **me**, wouldst **give me**
Water **with berries in't, and teach me** how
To **name** the **bigger light, and** how the **less,**
That burn **by day and night: and then I** loved **thee**
And show'd **thee** all the **qualities** o' the **isle,**
The **fresh springs, brine-pits, barren place and** fertile:

> Cursed **be I that did** so! All the charms
> Of **Sycorax**, toads, **beetles, bats, light** on you!
> For **I am** all the subjects **that** you **have,**
> **Which** first was **mine** own **king: and here** you **sty me**
> **In this** hard rock, **whiles** you do **keep** from **me**
> The **rest** o' the **island**.

In 131 words, more than half of them require the tongue to assume some form of a Ball-like Shape. These words ignite the face and head resonators. This over abundance of face/head resonance, if allowed, will have a profound effect on the sound of the content in this speech.

See: 6 Exploration 9: Repeating Articulatory Shape = Repeating Sound = Emotional Reveal with Caliban's Text
https://vimeo.com/channels/thelabanworkbook/200001763

Exploration 9: Repeating Articulatory Shape = Repeating Sound = Emotional Reveal with Caliban's text

- Repeat Exploration 8 with the expanded list of front vowels. How are you affected by the repetition of the mouth shape and resonance?

- Speak only the bolded words as if these are the only words provided to tell this story.

- What is revealed about Caliban? Or rather, how does Caliban reveal himself?

- Restore all the words and speak the entire speech.

Consonant repetitions

The repeated sound may be a specific consonant sound or a type of consonant sound. The consonants are often described as carrying the specific meaning while the vowels carry the emotion. However, if you have an abundance of stop-plosives[10] in a short amount of text you will certainly be affected by it emotionally and you will discover something about what the character is doing and feeling that goes beyond the literal meaning of the words.

Here is an example from Shakespeare's *Richard III*. It is Lady Anne's speech to Richard who has just entreated her to love him and become his queen. Her reply is given over the body of the King, whom he has slain.

> Cursed be the hand that made these fatal holes!
> Cursed be the heart that had the heart to do it!
> Cursed the blood that let this blood from hence!
> More direful hap betide that hated wretch,
> That makes us wretched by the death of thee,
> Than I can wish to adders, spiders, toads,
> Or any creeping venom'd thing that lives!

There are a striking number of stop-plosives in these seven lines: forty-nine to be exact. If you articulate these lines you might actually feel your Lady Anne spitting on Richard as you curse him in revenge. It doesn't hurt a thing that the word "cursed" is repeated three times and "cursed" begins and ends with unvoiced stop-plosives,[11] the most explosive sounds of all. The value of articulation to the emotional condition or action of the character relies on the abundance of a particular type of sound in relation to the length of text.

Exploration 10: Consonants

- In the following lines, underline all the sounds that are stop-plosives (p, b, k, g, t, d). You are not looking to the spelling of the word, but rather the pronunciation. Consequently the "g" in "springs" would not be underlined because the sound in this instance is not a stop-plosive.

  > The fresh springs, brine-pits, barren place and fertile:
  > Cursed be I that did so! All the charms
  > Of Sycorax, toads, beetles, bats, light on you!

- Lean on the stop-plosives with particular vigor. Does the curse come alive?

In any text, when a particular sound or types of sounds are repeated frequently you may feel the profound effect of those articulations on the character's state of being, and gain deeper insight into their worldview and motives for their actions. Examples of what is meant by "types of sounds" are front vowels, mid-vowels, back vowels, stop plosives, fricatives,[12] and nasal consonants.[13] In my experience, the better the playwright, regardless of the century in which the play was written, the more likely you are to be gifted with new insights through this exercise.[14]

Exploring vocal and physical gestures through Modes of Shape Change[15]

At this juncture, we have a basic Ball-like Shape Form for Caliban. We have also discovered that the actual articulation of the words and the resulting resonant area that is ignited are aligned with Caliban's wants and needs. In this speech, it is the face and head resonators that are predominant.

Now, let's look at vocal gesture-life and the interplay between the possible gestural choices that influence voice and speech. To that end, we will be employing the Modes of Shape Change, which are designated as: Shape Flow, Spoke-like Directional, Arc-like Directional, and Carving. We will marry these to Pathways in Space, which are Central, Peripheral, and Transverse.[16] To understand Pathways it is important to pause for a moment and introduce the term kinesphere. Kinesphere is the space you claim as your own. Psychologically you can call it your "personal space." Technically, it is the space between yourself and the distance you can reach with a limb. Your kinesphere travels with you, like a surrounding bubble. We make this personal space known to others through the Pathways. Movement on a Central Pathway radiates out from and back to your center; movement on a Peripheral Pathway defines the edge of your kinesphere; and a Transverse Pathway literally transverses or sweeps between the center and the edge of one's kinesphere. Can you see the potential for affinity among the Modes of Shape Change and Pathways? For the purposes of this chapter, we will designate Spoke-like as affined with Central, Arc-like as affined with Peripheral, and Carving as affined with Transverse. But how do we establish the kinesphere of the voice? I propose that the kinesphere of the voice is the distance you can project your voice and speech with ease. Like physical gestures, vocal gestures can manifest in near-reach (close to your body), intermediate-reach (between your body and the edge of your kinesphere), and far-reach space (the far edge of your kinesphere).

The delicious complication of exploring vocal gestures is that the voice is not *seen*. It is heard and felt both by the speaker and the listener. Once you release your words into space it is not possible to change the words, the trajectory, or "Mode" with which the words are traveling. We have all thought with regret: "I wish I could take those words back"; "I knew as soon as I said it, I shouldn't have." However, if you launch a physical movement with the intention of punching someone there is always the option to retract your fist before it strikes its goal. Not so with speech. Like the pebble in a slingshot, once launched it will sail until it hits its target. It is easy to picture a physical gesture as an attempt to form a relationship or bridge between yourself and someone else, the environment, or even oneself. The voice, though invisible, does exactly the same. The *intention* of the vocal or physical gesture will determine its trajectory.

Shape Flow and gesture

We have already identified Shape Flow as being all about *you*! The breath pattern established in infancy stays with us throughout life and is at the core of Shape Flow. We will now expand the meaning of Shape Flow to include self-to-self gestures. Shape Flow gestures, also known as shadow movements, are usually in near-reach space and can provide self-comfort, relief, or an expression of introspection. Though often described as subconscious, observers might be acutely aware of the gesture, particularly if it is repeated frequently. Examples include a man who pulls at his beard, a woman who continually wraps her hair around her finger, a teen who keeps straightening his shirt, patting his thighs, or biting his fingernails. If a behavior is repeated again and again then the behavior can reveal something about an individual's state of being.

Exploration 11: Shape Flow gestures

- Can you identify your own habitual self-comforting gestures?

- Observe others throughout the day for self-comforting gestures. If the individual you are observing is speaking simultaneously with the gesture, how are the voice and speech affected?

- Create a self-comforting gesture that is not yours. Repeat the gesture several times as you improvise a short text. How is your imagination affected? Does a character come to mind? Can you imagine the Given Circumstance that prompts the gesture?

Spoke-like Directional

As a baby becomes more aware of the outside world, Spoke-like Directional gestures begin to manifest. These might include reaching for an object of desire (the bottle, the cookie), pushing away the spoon full of food held by an adult, or throwing the food or utensil at the caregiver or to the floor. The mantra at this point in development is: "Give me";

Figure 3.5 Spoke-like

"Take it away"; "I want"; "I don't want." A Spoke-like Directional gesture is goal-oriented and moves on a Central Pathway from the center of the body outward or from outward towards the center of the body.

**See: 7 Explorations: 12, 13, & 14: Modes of Shape Change and Pathways with Unstructured Sound and Words
https://vimeo.com/channels/thelabanworkbook/199997315**

Exploration 12: Spoke-like gestures

- Experiment with Spoke-like gestures. Keep the objects of your desire or rejection very concrete for now. Remember—any limb can gesture! You are either reaching to bring something close to self or releasing something from self into the environment on a Central Pathway.

- Say as you are gesturing: "Give me"; "Take that away"; "This is mine"; "This gift is for you"; "Let me help you."

- Observe your responses. How does it make you feel to have an abundance of Spoke-like gestures? What does it feel like you are doing? In your imagination, what kind of character primarily employs Spoke-like gestures?

Relationship to voice and speech
When you are speaking principally in a Spoke-like manner you may be perceived as being direct, to the point, or having a singular point of view. You may be giving the listener a picture of yourself as a no-nonsense individual, interested only in the facts, insistent, determined, unwavering, or even attacking. Keep in mind that the level of intensity within the Given Circumstances with which you are speaking will affect the outcome. For instance, is your voice offering to help a child or attacking a perpetrator? The level of intensity is critical in understanding the potential outcome of all the Modes of Shape Change.

Figure 3.6 Arc-like

Arc-like Directional

As the child matures and takes in more of his environment, he begins to discover the perimeters of the space in an Arc-like Directional manner. The focus in this section is on the relationship between voice and Arc-like gestures that indicate the circumference of the space and move on Peripheral Pathways. Additionally, the reach space emphasized in this chapter will be intermediate and far reach. The statements that might produce this particular Arc-like Directional vocal and physical gesture could be: "Look at all this land. It encompasses from here all the way around to there."

Exploration 13: Arc-like gestures

- Experiment with Arc-like gestures.
- Say as you gesture: "Look at all this land"; "All this acreage belongs to everybody here"; "I want to give you all of this."
- How does it make you feel to have an abundance of Arc-like gestures? What does it feel like you are doing? In your imagination, what kind of character principally employs Arc-like gestures?

Relationship to voice and speech

When one is speaking in an Arc-like manner one may be perceived as being all-encompassing, observant of the environment, vocally sharing or claiming an expanse of territory physically and/or ideologically, skirting around an idea, or sizing up the situation. You could say the speaker's voice is traveling on the periphery of the environment or idea in order to outline the big picture for the listener, or to avoid making a pointed comment.

Carving[17]

Carving is about molding and adapting to the environment and or the people. Carving gestures reveal your kinesphere by moving on Transverse Pathways between your center and the periphery. Carving is process oriented and emerges when the child matures sufficiently to rotate in the joints and spine. Carving requires that the individual take in her surroundings, digest what she sees or hears, reorganize the information and send it out in a new form. Does this sound like something you do every day, many times a day? Doesn't a mature

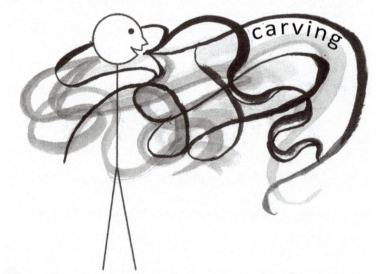

Figure 3.7 Carving

individual take in and "digest" other people's points of view while formulating her own position? Whether deciding where to go to dinner with friends or buying a house with a partner, decisions large and small are no longer just about you. You are adapting to another individual's point of view.

Examples of statements that might produce Carving include: "I heard what you said and have considered it"; "Can we negotiate a compromise?"; "I can understand this problem from several points of view"; "Let's consider other possibilities"; "I am sure we can carve out a mutual agreement."

Exploration 14: Carving gestures

- Carve with your hand and observe the rotations in the wrist.

- Carve with your arm and observe the rotations in the joints of the wrist and shoulder.

- Carve with your whole body and feel the rotation in the spine.

- Experiment with Carving gestures that are near, intermediate and far reach. How does changing the reach space affect you?

- Say as you gesture: "I want everyone to get along"; "Can we negotiate?"; "Well ... I am not sure what to think"; "Maybe ..."

- Observe your responses. How does it make you feel to have an abundance of Carving gestures? What does it feel like you are doing? In your imagination, what kind of character principally employs Carving gestures?

Relationship to voice and speech

When speaking in a Carving manner one could be perceived as digesting what others have to say, attempting to achieve a consensus, negotiating a point, winding around the truth, adapting to the points of view of others. Again the intensity will influence whether you are perceived as manipulating the ideas, being seductive, easily changeable, unsure of where you stand or what you think, or attempting to influence others to adapt to your point of view through negotiation. Carving could also be used to avoid confrontation.

In the following exploration, you will integrate all the Modes in one fun exercise. The goal of the exploration is to explore and develop vocal gestures.

Exploration 15: Conducting an orchestra!

- Imagine you are a conductor of an orchestra. You can even put on music!

- Observe yourself as you conduct the music. Sometimes you will be Carving as you negotiate the violins, violas and the bass. Sometimes you will be Arc-like as your arms swoop over the musicians in far reach to create the swell, and other times Spoke-like as you pinpoint to the tympani to strike.

- Hum along with the music as you conduct.

- Repeat with your jaw released so more tone escapes.

- In active stillness, lead the orchestra with only unstructured sounds. How specific can you make your vocal gestures?

Have you been struggling to connect your vocal-gestural expressions while in active stillness? Does the capacity to gesture vocally feel illusive? Let's build on the conductor exercise by simplifying the approach. The following explorations can be called "outside-in" exercises because you will be arbitrarily changing your choice of Mode. But you are also allowing the choices to ignite your imagination regarding the underlying intention of the sounds or words. Give yourself time and many repetitions with the following exercises to allow the voice to get used to the vocal stretch and your imagination to respond.

More fun discovering vocal gestures!

One of the easiest ways to embody vocal gestures is to imagine your sound as a color with which you can "draw" in the air, on the wall, on the ceiling, on the floor, or on someone else.

Exploration 16: Coloring with the Modes of Shape Change

- Imagine a color for Spoke-like Directional and with just your voice "draw" straight lines.

- Imagine a color for Arc-like Directional and with just your voice draw arcs.

- Imagine a color for Carving and with just your voice draw circuitous, winding routes.

The following exploration will make your vocal gestures even more concrete. You will need crayons!

Exploration 17: Keep coloring!

- Tape to the wall very large pieces of paper on which you will draw. Pick a colored crayon for each of the Modes of Shape Change. Draw straight, arcing, and winding lines with the chosen colors allowing the voice to match the movement of the arm. In this case, the body is leading the voice.

  - To see more of the Carving potential in your drawings, rather than using the point of the crayon use more of the surface of the crayon by peeling off the paper from the crayon and laying it on its side on the paper. Move the crayon on the paper in swirling, sweeping motions again allowing the voice to reflect the movement of the drawing arm. The picture drawn will be very distinct from Spoke-like or Arc-like.

- Reverse the above procedure. Let the voice lead the body. This tends to be more challenging because most of us are unaccustomed to moving the voice in unsubtle ways.

- After several go rounds of the first two steps, it may become difficult to distinguish whether the body is leading the voice or vice versa. Good!

- Compare the drawings made with the body leading the voice with the drawings made with the voice leading the body.

Partner work can be very helpful towards exploring vocal gestures; therefore the next explorations are done with a partner or partners. During Exploration 18, when you are the sounder, you are discovering the power of your voice to literally move people. When you are the mover you are sensitizing your body to respond in both subtle and not-so-subtle ways to the vibrations felt and sounds heard from another's voice. You are sensitizing yourself to respond on impulse to vocal gestures.

See: 8 Exploration 18 Partner Work: Vocal Gestures with Unstructured Sound
https://vimeo.com/channels/thelabanworkbook/200002743

Exploration 18: Partner work: Vocal gestures with unstructured sound

- Your partner takes a shape. Come into very close proximity with your partner. With your mouth a few inches from your partner's body (avoid the face and ears), sound into your partner's body causing the vocal vibrations to be felt. Based on the vibrations, your partner will reshape her body as you sound into it. Switch.

- Group exercise:[18] A group of actors starts in active stillness with their backs to you the sounder. As the group hears your unstructured sounds, the actors will move in any way that they are affected. The actors are showing you a moving picture of your voice through their bodies. Keep switching up who is the sounder and who are the movers. The beauty is that you get to see several different physical responses to your unstructured sounds simultaneously.

The instructions for **More fun discovering vocal gestures** are deceivingly simple and short. Depending on the speaker, it may take many repetitions before the voice begins to draw, to gesture, to affect and be affected by your partner. It is time to add words to the previous exercises. You can count, use the alphabet, or a text that you know well. Be patient. Have courage. Play!

Exploration 19: Vocal gestures and text

- Explore each of the Modes and Pathways in turn using words of your choosing. Keep in mind that it is important that you know to whom and/or where you are bridging the voice. (Quick review: Spoke-like travels on Central Pathways, Arc-like travels on Peripheral Pathways, Carving travels on Transverse Pathways.)

  – How does the Spoke-like vocal gesture influence the text? Arc-like? Carving?

  – Can your words travel to a specific object or person, real or imagined, forming an invisible but audible bridge while the body remains in active stillness?

  – Does the story alter if you change the dominant Mode and Pathway for each repetition of the text?

  – How is your imagination ignited by the above explorations? Does a character emerge? Given Circumstances? Action/ Object?

  – Can you identify a Mode that feels most like you?

  – Which Mode is distinctly more difficult for you to access?

How you are affected by these vocal gestures is contingent on the context, Given Circumstances, and the intention with which you are speaking. The Given Circumstances give rise to the objectives and the objectives will determine the action to be taken. When vocal gestures are applied to text from a play, you are in essence playing an action and discovering a variety of vocal tactics to achieve the objective. Listeners perceive vocal gestures in exactly the same way that they interpret physical gestures. An arm gesturing in an Arc-like manner may be showing off or sharing the goods, so might the voice do the same.

An actor strives to be able to access all the Modes of Shape Change in her physical and vocal gesture-life. However, most of us have valued one Mode over another for any number of reasons. We usually gesture in a way that supports what we are thinking/doing and will hopefully have the desired effect on the listener/observer. Most of us want to get our own way in all kinds of matters so the tactics we use, consciously or unconsciously, will have an impact on that outcome. Additionally, our upbringing, personal experiences, and culture greatly influence which Modes of Shape Change we will favor.

If you look at the Modes as a continuum with Shape Flow at one end and Carving at the other, you may discover that you utilize one of the four Modes more frequently than the others. Observing your gesture-life preferences (physical and vocal) is an interesting journey to self-discovery. These discoveries will enhance your observation skills and increase your choices when developing a character.

There is an on-going interplay between your outer (environmental influences) and your inner (internal emotional and physical influences) that inspires your personal wants and needs and those of the character you are portraying. In order to be comprehended by others, specific physical and vocal actions must radiate into the environment.

Caliban and the Modes

Now it is time to incorporate the Modes into Caliban's text. What follows is my interpretation of the text. I am using it as a template for how you can explore text with the Modes. You may have a different response and therefore wish to make different choices than I suggest here. Do it! Make other choices inspired by your imagination. Without choice there can be no artistry!

The objectives of the explorations that follow are to discover vocal and physical choices that support the internal logic of the character, the Given Circumstances, and encourage new discoveries. But it is also possible that much of what you discover may not be logically playable. Don't worry. Another benefit of these explorations, regardless of whether the discoveries are ultimately viable or not, is that the text will remain elastic as opposed to becoming fixed or rigid. Static line readings are less likely to take hold because the words have a better chance of being freshly discovered with each rendering of the text. The goal of Exploration 20 is to fill the spoken text with gesture life.

See: 9 Exploration 20: Unstructured Sound into Caliban's Text with Modes of Shape Change and Pathways
https://vimeo.com/channels/thelabanworkbook/199998212

Exploration 20: Unstructured sound into Caliban's text with Modes of Shape Change and Pathways

- Follow how the text has been divided up and utilize the designated Mode and Pathway for each segment of text.

- Say each segment in active stillness.

- Body moves with the designated Mode and Pathway with unstructured sound.

- Body moves with the designated Mode and Pathway with Caliban's words.

- Say each line again in active stillness.

- Observe the difference between the first time you spoke the lines and the second time.

- Spoke-like on a Central Pathway:

> I must eat my dinner.
> This island's mine, by Sycorax my mother,
> Which thou tak'st from me.

These first lines seem to emphasize Spoke-like gestures moving from the outer towards the inner. Grabbing food. Staking a claim on the land. Accusing Prospero of taking his land.

- Shape Flow:

> Thou strok'st me and mad'st much of me,

Like a babe in the crib being comforted, perhaps Caliban's hands move in self-comforting gestures as he remembers how it felt to be "stroked."

- Spoke-like on a Central Pathway:

>   wouldst give me
> Water with berries in't,

Is Caliban Spoke-like reaching with his hands for the berries thus acting out the memory? Or is he opening his mouth to receive the berries like a baby bird being fed by its mother? Perhaps his mouth is gesturing in a Spoke-like manner, lips and tongue reaching for the food that is dangling from Prospero's fingertips above his head. Note that the intensity is quite different from the first two lines that also suggest Spoke-like gestures.

- Spoke-like on a Central Pathway:

> and teach me how
> To name the bigger light, and how the less,
> That burn by day and night:

These lines imply a Spoke-like reaching towards the sky. Specifying "the bigger light" makes Caliban pinpoint his reach to a specific object, in this case the sun. Again, the intensity of the Spoke-like gesture has evolved once more from the previous two manifestations.

- Arc-like on a Peripheral Pathway:

> and then I loved thee
> And show'd thee all the qualities o' the isle,
> The fresh springs, brine-pits, barren place and fertile:

- Arc-like changing to Spoke-like on the last line:

> and then I loved thee
> And show'd thee all the qualities o' the isle,
> The fresh springs, brine-pits, barren place and fertile:

Perhaps, Caliban is gesturing for the first time in an Arc-like Directional manner. He is showing the island to Prospero and not just claiming it as his own. He is sharing with Prospero what the island contains, putting it on display. Therefore, it is possible that his gestures are Arc-like as they describe all the "qualities" of the island. However, in regard to the last line, one could argue that Caliban is Spoke-like

Directional, as he pinpoints the specific qualities to Prospero. Do you have a preference?

- Spoke-like on a Central Pathway:

    Cursed be I that did so! All the charms
    Of Sycorax, toads, beetles, bats, light on you!

The first thought implies a beating-up of self. Caliban, with a Spoke-like gesture, grabs all the sharing he did with Prospero and brings it back to himself with a high degree of intensity. The second thought is a curse on Prospero. Caliban's curse flies directly from himself to Prospero with the intensity at its maximum.

- Arc-like on a Peripheral Pathway:

    For I am all the subjects that you have,
    Which first was mine own king:

- Spoke-like on a Central Pathway:

    For I am all the subjects that you have,
    Which first was mine own king:

It is possible that Caliban indicates himself with an Arc-like gesture implied by the word "all" or even the word "I." Perhaps the Arc-like gesture makes Caliban's predicament even more poignant than if Caliban adheres to Spoke-like gestures. Or maybe he *is* Spoke-like drawing Prospero's essence into his center, claiming Prospero to be his "own king" first and foremost. Do you have a preference?

- Shape Flow into Carving:

                              and here you sty me
    In this hard rock,

In the lines above, Prospero is once again acting on Caliban's body, but this time for an entirely different effect. Assuming that Prospero's stroking, recalled early on in the speech, made Caliban *lengthen* and *widen* in his Shape Flow, then Prospero "stying" him "in a hard rock" causes Caliban to *shorten* and *condense* into a Ball-like Shape. Caliban is once again reactive to Prospero's handling of his body. The words bring up images of being forced into a Ball-like Shape, dictated by the container of a hard rock. Caliban is once again pre-gesture, he is an infant for the moment. Another tactic is to recognize that Caliban has been forced to adapt, to mold himself (Carving) into his confinement. His body and voice accommodating his environment by twisting into the enclosure.

- First line Spoke-like on a Central Pathway
- Second line Arc-like on a Peripheral Pathway:

> whiles you do keep from me
> The rest o' the island.

Finally, with the last thought, two more gestures. The first one is Spoke-like to himself, "keep from me ..." And the second one grows from Spoke-like to an Arc-like gesture, indicating all that he has lost, namely "... the rest o' the island."

Clearly, in my interpretation, Carving is at a minimum—at least on the surface. This could be because Caliban can only honor one point of view—mainly his own. He does not easily mold or adapt to new circumstances. To him the world is black and white, without nuance. However, this is not the whole story regarding Caliban and his potential for Carving. I have been focusing specifically on Caliban's relationship with Prospero, but what about prior to that? Caliban's relationship to the physical and spirit world in which he lived was primarily a feral one. In my imagination, his feral nature reveals his Carving inclinations. So as you can see, there is much more exploratory fun to be had here. So let's mess it all up!

Exploration 21: Change up the Modes!

- Reconfigure Caliban's speech with alternate Modes of Shape Change. It will help to write out the phrases and identify your specific choice for each phrase. Use your choice as a leaping-off-point and not an end in itself. In other words: play and let your imagination go free!

- Allow just the body to reflect your choice in silence.

- Allow the body and text to reflect your choice.

- Speak the text reflecting your choice but remain in active stillness.

• How does changing up the Modes of Shape Change affect the story being told?

• How does the character of Caliban shift as you privilege the new choice?

• Repeat this exploration with a text of your own choosing.

• As you explored, did you discover organic shifts in pitch (high↔low), volume (loud↔soft), and rate (fast↔slow)?

Pitch, volume, and rate are the usual suspects when we talk about dynamic changes in voice and speech. They are what we typically attempt to vary when we are searching for vocal variety. But as you have discovered, the inclusion of Modes and Pathways helps to flesh out the vocal dynamics possible and supports forming vocal relationships with the environment and others. Though invisible, voice and speech fills space! And when the expressive choices made by you are specific, the listener can capture the aspect that is most salient at any given time bringing the story and character into sharp focus. Now we need to color in the lines with even more dynamic and nuanced choices.

Effort

Effort is the aspect of LMA that gives us a color palate with which to work. With the inclusion of Effort, we are nuancing the portrait and simultaneously complicating (in a good way) the qualities that define us as human.

Effort is the concept typically taught in many acting and movement classes. It is the easiest of the concepts for actors to access and understand on a practical level because Effort relates to "playing an action" so handily. Effort can be defined as the psychological inner attitude an individual holds at any given moment towards the **Effort Factors: Time, Weight, Space**, and **Flow**, which are defined in the next paragraph. This inner attitude manifests in behavior that helps define a character and the character's attempt to fulfill the wants and needs within the Given Circumstances. Effort offers you an endless range of tactics from which to choose. I think we can agree that there are many ways "to grieve," "to seduce," "to defend." However, we tend to get stuck in what it means to us personally and play only those qualities. Effort helps you avoid clichés and generalities.

The voice and body must form an active relationship with the four Effort Factors in order for the choices to become available to you. Depending on the objective prompted by the Given Circumstances, one or more of the Factors may be salient at a time. For instance, if "to be urgent" (*quick/sudden*) or "to luxuriate" (*sustainment*) are primary then **Time Effort** will be relevant. To overcome an obstacle, it may take great force (*strong*) or gentleness (*light*) to achieve the goal; therefore **Weight Effort** will become most relevant. If the action that is most important is discovering where things or people are, then **Space Effort** will become most salient either by pinpointing the location (*direct*) or scanning the environment (*indirect/flexible*). **Flow Effort** underlies and supports all that we do. Flow can take the lead from Time, Weight, and Space but relative to acting it tends to be the underlying support for the other three Factors. Flow addresses the question: Is my character careful (*bound*) or easy going (*free*)?

On both a vocal and physical level, Effort provides rich, varied, and often, unpredictable choices. Effort life throws the doors wide open to possibilities that, heretofore, may have eluded you. And all those possibilities can fill your voice, even when (particularly when) your body is in active stillness.

Similarly to the Modes and Pathways, Effort also organically encourages changes in pitch, rate, and volume, and even varies how we use the muscles required for articulation. Effort life helps us bend the words and phrases in a variety of ways to achieve the objective. Effort life easily activates the text while keeping you out of your head. Exploring Effort through your text will produce rich and varied possibilities from which, in collaboration with your director, the most effective choices can be made.

Effort life and voice/text

Let's begin with a self-exploration. The elements are the component parts of each Effort Factor and the component parts lie at the extreme ends of each Factor's spectrum. For instance, the Weight Factor's elements (*strong⇔light*) are positioned at either end of the continuum for Weight. Everything between the two extremes is a gradation of the Weight Effort.

See: 10 Exploration 22: Effort Elements with Unstructured Sound and Body
https://vimeo.com/channels/thelabanworkbook/199999450

Exploration 22: Effort elements with unstructured sound and body

- Move your body and voice (unstructured sound) influenced by each of the eight elements one at a time. Decide the order of the Factors (Weight, Time, Space, Flow) ahead of time. I find it useful to set a timer of one minute per element. Keep in mind that you want to challenge yourself to move and sound at the extreme ends of each Factor's spectrum, as well as the gradations in between.

- Repeat the exercise adding random words or phrases as you explore. You can even use numbers or the alphabet. What is important is to allow the numbers, alphabet, or random words to reflect each element fully. Let the body's exploration bend the words, distort them, reshape them.

The Tossing Up Game

The "Tossing Up Game" makes a mess, but the element of surprise it provides as you speak your text is worth it. This game prevents you from gravitating to the same elements over and over (we all have our preferences!) or thinking about which element you want to explore next. Another interesting challenge in the Tossing Up Game happens when you pick up the same element three or four times in a row. How do you keep varying the effect? Keep in mind it is possible that the manifestation of the element in your body and voice can vary quite a bit and still be recognized as *bound* or *free*.

Exploration 23: Make a mess!

- Write down the eight elements on bits of paper a number of times. For example, you might have the word *strong* on five different bits of paper. You will have forty bits of paper covering all the elements five times. Toss them up and watch them land willy-nilly. Pick up one of the papers and move the element written on the paper in your body and voice. Don't bother with the timer this time, let your impulses guide you when it is time to pick up another bit of paper and move/sound the new element.

At the conclusion of your exploration, note the elements with which you are most affined and dis-affined.[19] Not recognizing our own inclinations or resistances are part of what limits our choices when developing a character or telling a story.

Activating language with Effort

The language of Effort invites you to tease out and refine the expressivity of voice/speech. For instance, a high pitch may live in either *strong* or *light* Weight Effort depending on the intention and the particular obstacle to be overcome. Your high pitch can also live in Space Effort (*direct⇔indirect*), or Time Effort (*quick⇔sustained*), or Flow Effort (*bound⇔free*). In other words, your high pitch can be nuanced many ways. The voice has a story to tell and that story is dependent on the specific choices you make.

Exploration 24 is an example of how you can explore the relationship between Effort and pitch, volume, and rate. For this exploration, I chose the word "go" because, all by itself, it is a complete thought.

Exploration 24: Say "go!"

- Say "go" on a pitch that is high in your range of speech.
  - On the same pitch, say it again with *strong weight*.
  - Again, with *light weight*.
  - Again, *sustained*.
  - Again, *quick*.
- How many stories were you able to tell by varying the Effort element?
- How was your imagination affected?
- Did you get the sense that you were playing an action and that action changed with the element?
- Experiment with the remaining elements.

Effort elements and text

You are ready to apply Effort to text of your own choosing or Caliban's speech. Please know that you are not codifying how each element affects you or the text, but rather exploring each element moment to moment as if for the first time. The effect will change depending on all sorts of factors such as the context, your state of being at the time, and even the weather.

Exploration 25: Tossing Up Game with text

Body and Voice:

- Choose a line or lines of text from Caliban or a text with which you are comfortable. Repeat the Tossing Up Game. How does the story change depending on the element explored?

Active Stillness:

- Gather up some of the paper bits and turn them upside down in your hand so you cannot know ahead of time what you are selecting. Turn the papers over one at a time and in active stillness let the voice be filled with that element.

- Are the vocal shifts more difficult to achieve in active stillness?

- If your voice moves fluidly from element to element, consider how the story is affected. What is the action? For instance, what might be the action if you spoke the line(s) with *strong weight* as opposed to *light weight?*

To keep things simple, we started with considering a single Effort element at a time. However, we are too complicated and variable in our humanness to truly stay on task with one element. More typically, we operate in two or more Effort Factors simultaneously or consecutively. What you accomplished was making the element of choice the *most salient* one revealed, but other elements were certainly present in secondary or tertiary roles. For instance, *quick* may have been the most salient Effort element you were exploring but no doubt there were fluctuations in Weight, Space, and/or Flow happening simultaneously or consecutively. When two Effort elements manifest simultaneously and are predominate, the combination is called a State. There are six States: Dream, Awake, Near/Rhythm, Remote, Mobile, and Stable. When three elements manifest simultaneously and are predominate, it is called a Drive. There are four Drives: Action, Passion, Spell, and Vision. The last three are referred to as Transformation Drives.

The Action Drives are often the centerpiece of actor training that includes LMA. However, adapting the exercises described in this section and by consulting Chapter 2 you may also explore the States and the Transformation Drives. Chapter 2 gives a detailed explanation of Effort Theory and describes many exercises for physically exploring all the permutations of Effort.

Action Drives

For our purposes, we are going to focus on the vocal potential of the three predominant Effort Factors that comprise an Action Drive. An Action Drive manifests when one element from each of the Factors, Weight, Time, and Space, arise simultaneously. An element from the Flow Factor is an underlying support during an Action Drive.

Configurations of Action Drives
Float: *light, sustained, indirect*
Punch: *strong, quick, direct*
Glide: *light, sustained, direct*
Slash: *strong, quick, indirect*
Dab: *light, quick, direct*
Wring: *strong, sustained, indirect*
Flick: *light, quick, indirect*
Press: *strong, sustained, direct*

It is interesting to note that the Action Drives are the only set of Drives to which Laban assigned names for each configuration.

Exploration 26: Exploring Action Drives

- Move your body and voice (unstructured sound) influenced by each of the eight Action Drives one at a time. Decide the order of the Drives ahead of time to make sure you move each of the Drives. Set a timer for two minutes per Drive.

- Identify the Action Drives with which you are affined and dis-affined.

- Repeat the exercise adding random words or phrases or a text that you are very familiar with. What is important is to allow the words to reflect each Drive fully. Let the body's exploration bend the words, distort them, and reshape them.

As you conclude your Effort explorations, perhaps you noticed how your voice and text became more varied. There were, no doubt, spontaneous changes in pitch, rate, and volume. You didn't have to think about vocal variety. Likewise, the particular words that became emphasized may also have given you new, heretofore, not considered choices. Because you were connected to "action," these changes were not just technical explorations but fully embodied vocal explorations from which you discovered a cornucopia of possible choices. An exploration of Effort is multi-layered and in constant flux. In fact, the whole of LMA is like a kaleidoscope in that even a slight shift causes a dynamic re-arrangement of the component parts revealing a new picture and a new story.

Caliban and Action Drives

Rather than prescribe a specific Action Drive to each section of Caliban's speech, it is more effective for you to make the choices. Take the following blocks of text and explore each section with at least three different Action Drives. I am recommending Action Drives because typically a Drive is employed when the stakes for the character are very high or climactic. Caliban is certainly in a heightened condition throughout this speech fighting for his land and his freedom. However, it is also a worthy experiment to manifest a single element at a time or two elements (States) per block of text.

During the following explorations, begin with body and voice working together and then come to active stillness and discover how your voice and speech can manifest the Effort choices while your body remains in active stillness. I will make an example of Section 1, but then the rest is up to you!

Example

See: 11 Exploration 27: Caliban and Action Drives: Punch, Dab, and Wring
https://vimeo.com/channels/thelabanworkbook/200000784

- Section 1: Punch, Dab, Wring

Allow each Drive to manifest in body and voice. Then come to active stillness and speak the text with each Action Drive.

> I must eat my dinner.
> This island's mine, by Sycorax my mother,
> Which thou takest from me.

Now it is your turn!

Exploration 27: Caliban and Action Drives

- Assign three different Action Drives to each section. Allow each Drive to manifest in body and voice. Then come to active stillness and speak the text with each chosen Action Drive.

– Section 2:

> When thou cam'st first,
> Thou strok'st me and mad'st much of me, wouldst give me
> Water with berries in't,

– Section 3:

> and teach me how
> To name the bigger light, and how the less,
> That burn by day and night:

– Section 4:

> and then I loved thee
> And show'd thee all the qualities o' the isle,

– Section 5:

> The fresh springs, brine-pits, barren place and fertile:

– Section 6:

> Cursed be I that did so! All the charms
> Of Sycorax, toads, beetles, bats, light on you!

– Section 7:

> For I am all the subjects that you have,
> Which first was mine own king:

– Section 8:

> and here you sty me
> In this hard rock, whiles you do keep from me
> The rest o' the island.

- Repeat with a text of your own choosing.

Now let's add the surprise!

Exploration 28: Tossing Up Game with Action Drives

- Using Caliban's speech or a text of your own choosing, repeat the previous exercise using the Tossing Up Game with the Action Drives written on the slips of paper. Again, the element of surprise is key to making new discoveries.

- How difficult or easy is it to allow the voice and speech to carry the Effort qualities?

Detailed choices: Operative words and Action Drives

Operative words are those words you must stress and that the audience must hear in order to understand the sense of the line. Changing up the operative word can subtly and sometimes not so subtly alter the meaning of the text or even our perception of the character. Therefore, our choices must be both logical and surprising to the listener. Not only can we fill the whole word to make it operative, we can also look at the actual articulation of the word and load a particular phoneme within the word with Effort. The Effort life with which we infuse the operative words helps to flesh out the details of both character and intention leading to surprising inevitabilities. "Surprising inevitability" is my moniker for where the operative words lead us.

It is important to note that the rhythm of Shakespeare does most of the work for us. The iamb and any rhythmic variations to the iamb that emerge in Shakespeare tell us upfront which words are operative. Therefore, identifying the operatives is often much easier in poetry than in prose. However, how the operative is "pointed" is up for grabs regardless of whether the text is poetry or prose, classical or contemporary.

To facilitate the next exploration, I have bolded the operatives that may be pointed. Ultimately, however, one must be very selective as to which words are going to get the kind of detailing I am describing or you run the risk of making too many words important and thus losing the sense. The ear of the listener needs to be directed where to "land" and in that way the sense is made clear. Upon completing Exploration 29, apply what you learned about pointing the operatives to a text of your own choosing.

Exploration 29: Operative words and Action Drives

- Press: I **must** eat my dinner.
  - Press on the word "m**u**st" lengthening the short vowel "uh" until it becomes a long vowel. By lengthening the short

vowel we have almost turned the word inside out, we have distorted the word. Likewise, Caliban is "distorting" himself as he makes known the depth of his desperation about eating.

- Wring, Dab: This **island's mine**, by **Sycorax** my mother,

  – Lean into the diphthong "I" and the consonant /n/ in the word "m**in**e". Attempt to Wring all the truth that you can out of that word "mine."

  – Follow that with Dabbing the /k/ sound in the consonant combination /ks/ at the end of the name Sycorax – in this way you may make very clear who your mother is and her importance to your claim.

- Glide, Float, Dab:

  Thou **strok'st me** and **mad'st much** of **me**, wouldst give me
  Water with berries in't, and **teach** me **how**
  To **name** the **bigger light**, and **how** the **less**,
  That **burn** by **day** and **night**: and **then** I **loved thee**
  And **show'd** thee **all** the **qualities** o' the **isle**,
  The **fresh springs, brine-pits, barren place** and **fertile**:

  – In these six lines, Caliban is activating his memories of when things were good, safe, and comforting. Glide and Float the long vowels and diphthongs in words like: *strok'st, mad'st, teach, how, name, light, burn, day, night, thee, show'd, all, isle.* Of course, to honor all of them in this way would be too much, so choices must be made.

  – The last line of this section begins with short vowels *fresh, springs, -pits, barren.* Touch these sounds with a Dab Action Drive keeping the tone of the text *light, direct,* and *quick.*

  – Also note, in the first line the nasal consonant /m/ is alliterated in the words "mad'st much". And the word "me" is repeated three times! Lean into the /m/ with *lightness* and feel the affect. But be careful not to overdo this. Alliteration is often sufficient to catch the listener's ear.

- Punch: **Cursed** be I that **did** so! All the charms
  Of **Sycorax, toads, beetles, bats, light** on **you**!

- As discovered in Exploration No. 10, the bolded words highlight the stop-plosives, which in this context lend themselves handily to Punch. This Action Drive will bring Caliban (you!) and the listener back to reality and your resolve to get revenge.

- As an experiment, try touching the operatives with the Dab Action Drive (*quick, light, direct*). Note how changing just one of the Effort elements affects the sound of the desire for revenge.

One could say that we are now doing more and more with less and less. Yes, this is a lot of detailed exploration and too much of a good thing can simply be … too much! But unpacking some of the possibilities in this way can have a big payoff for both you and the listener.

Review

Let's take a moment to review what you have accomplished:

- You discovered Caliban's breath while exploring Shape Flow.

- Shape Forms helped you discover Caliban's Ball-like Form, a form that highlighted his feelings of abandonment, betrayal, and outrage. Shape Forms explored and illuminated Caliban's state of being and his feelings about himself.

- Through utilizing the Modes of Shape Change you discovered how Caliban forms a bridge between himself, others, and the environment. His relationship to his personal space (kinesphere) was revealed by his use of Pathways in space.

- By exploring Caliban's preferred Modes of Shape Change, you discovered he is arrested in an early developmental stage that influences how he is able or unable to understand or adapt to the outside world. However, though arrested at the Directional (Spoke-like, Arc-like) stage of development, he does indeed selectively employ Carving, the seeds of adaptability.

- Exploring Modes of Shape Change and Pathways began to reveal Caliban's wants, needs, and objectives.

- Breath, Shape Forms, Modes of Shape Change, and Pathways provided the scaffolding on which you built his Effort life.

- Effort life fills the text with action. Filling the text with Effort develops the story and character supplying the surprising inevitability for all the character's choices. In regard to Caliban, you experimented with many possibilities regarding the application of Effort and have by now culled the most relevant, logical, and playable choices.

- The explorations have provided you with an alternative process for expanding your vocal dynamics, which includes shifts in pitch, volume, and rate.

- You learned how to gesture with your voice and speech!

- You experienced voice and speech as movement!

- You applied the explorations to a text of your own choosing.

- You explored your personal preferences and inclinations regarding voice/speech and movement and, while embracing your personal preferences, you experimented with expanding your expressiveness to develop a character and tell a story.

Now put it all together!

What is there left to do with Caliban's speech or the text of your own choosing? Put it all together! Act the text! Let go of any conscious consideration of the explorations that have come before and now trust the discoveries and let the words fly, bend, ripple, twist, and soar into the environment. Let your conscious choices become "unconscious." You know in a very visceral way who your character is, what he wants, what he needs, and the obstacles to be faced. You know which actions to play in order to achieve the objectives. Then allow what began as a conscious foraging for dynamic choices that support the character and story to evolve into *conscious-unconsciousness*. It is at this juncture that your choices, if fully embodied, will appear to come from the impulse of the moment.

Conclusion: It all comes back to YOU!

How each actor synthesizes the material in this chapter will be highly individualized and dependent on the text at hand. The order in which you explore text through LMA is not sacrosanct in any way. You must assess each character and the text to determine which explorations are going to be the most beneficial to you and your work. Beneficial doesn't necessarily mean the easiest. Some of the most beneficial explorations may also be the most challenging. While each text you pick up can lend itself to the explorations put forth in this chapter, not every exploration will yield a well of discoveries. One must be patient and allow the text to unpack its mysteries as you explore.

When you pick up a text, let curiosity be your guide. LMA and its many component parts make up a kaleidoscope of possibilities. Eventually, your explorations will become the scaffolding that supports an integrated physical and vocal wholeness. Every time you make even a subtle shift all the component parts will shift and shift and shift again, creating an abundance of choices that will lead to a dynamic portrayal of your character. Therefore, it is critical that you unleash from your body and voice as many options as possible from which to choose. To arrive at that point takes time, discipline, dedication, and a huge amount of curiosity. You can't be in a hurry. Trust. Let go. And don't forget to bring your joy!

Acknowledgments

Thank you to Katya Bloom for inviting me to be part of the team that wrote this book. Thank you to our fabulous group of co-authors— the team! Your collective and individual support throughout the process was priceless. I wish to acknowledge Ilsse Garcia for her fun illustrations and Tom White, whose connections in the film world made the videos possible. To Joseph Quartararo, Producer; Donavon de Cesare, Cinematographer; and Jose Ramirez, Audio: thank you for your expertise and care for this film project. A special debt of gratitude to Joe, whose expertise in the editing room made it possible to craft the videos. To Adam Bachir, Lindsey Liberatore, and Lita Lofton: thank you for lending your beautiful talents to the videos.

Notes

1 Active stillness is the state of apparent stillness that is achieved when there is no perceivable movement of the limbs or torso. It is called "active" because there are uninterrupted internal movements that include blood flow, digestion, and breath. Each contributes to the body being fully present in the space even when in apparent stillness. The opposite of active stillness is rigidity, which is usually the result of a greatly diminished connection to the flow of the breath and results in a locking down of the muscles and joints.

2 Pure vowel is a vowel sound during which the articulators assume only one position. Example: /OO/ as in "soon."

3 Diphthong is a sound that is comprised of two pure vowels so closely blended together they seem like one sound. The articulators glide from one position to another during phonation of a diphthong. Example: /OH/ as in soul.

4 I am using "impulse" to mean "an instinctual urge that compels action."

5 Shape Forms or Still Shape Forms: Some LMA programs and practitioners are including the Pyramid. For the purpose of this chapter, the original Shape Forms (Pin, Wall, Ball, Screw) are sufficient.

6 Resonance occurs when the outgoing air passes through the vocal folds causing them to oscillate, resulting in vibrations that are amplified as they strike the pharynx, mouth, and nose. Some experts include the bony structure of upper chest and head as resonators.

7 Phoneme: Any individual speech sound. Examples: /t/ as in "hot" /OO/ as in "soon".

8 There are also "back vowels" and "mid-vowels". Back vowels describe the relationship between the arch in the back of the tongue and the soft palate. Back vowels tend to ignite the chest resonators. Mid-vowels describe the relationship between the arch in the body of the tongue and the place where the hard and soft palate meet. Mid-vowels tend to ignite the mouth resonators.

9 It is important to consider that there are a variety of spoken English dialects. Therefore, the mouth postures for individual phonemes will vary to some degree. For instance, in Standard American dialect the vowel sound in the word "ch**a**nce" is the same as the front vowel sound in the word "b**a**t." However, in Received Pronunciation the vowel sound in "ch**a**nce" is the same as the back vowel sound in "f**a**ther." Consequently, the various national and regional dialects and cultural influences will have an impact on how a frequently repeated sound in consecutive lines of text affect the speaker and the listener.

10 Stop-plosive: A consonant sound that is formed when the breath stream is completely stopped by the articulators and explodes upon release. Stop-plosives are: p, b, k, g, t, d.

11 Curse**d**: When speaking this word as one syllable, the pronunciation of the final consonant of this word is /t/ and not /d/ in spite of the spelling. If speaking this word as two syllables ('curs-**ed**) then the final consonant is a voiced stop-plosive.

12 Fricative: A consonant sound that is formed when the articulators impede but do not stop the flow of breath causing an audible friction of sound. Examples: f, v, sh, z. There are eleven fricatives in spoken English.

13 Nasal consonants: A consonant sound that is formed when the breath stream is directed into and out of the nose. There are three nasal consonants: n, m, and ng (as in si**ng**).

14 Translations are trickier. Peter Brook wrote: "the arrangement of vowels in Greek produced sounds that vibrate more intensely than in modern English— and it is sufficient for an actor to speak these syllables to be lifted out of the emotional constriction of the twentieth-century city life into a fullness of passion which he never knew he possessed" (Brook 1987: 130).

15 Modes of Shape Change are sometimes called Moving Shape Forms as a contrast to Still Shape Forms or Shape Forms.

16 Transverse movement cuts through three-dimensional space (vertical, horizontal, sagittal) in gradations. Example: portions of a spiral.

17 Carving: Carving and Shaping terms are often interchangeable. Also sometimes referred to as Shape Carving or Carving/Shaping.

18 With kind permission from Allworth Press, this exercise has been revised and adapted for an exploration of vocal gestures from Barbara Adrian (2008). *Actor Training the Laban Way: An Integrated Approach to Voice, Speech, and Movement*. New York: Allworth Press, 120.

19 "Dis-affined" is a term coined by LMA practitioners to mean "lacking relationship" or "lacking connection," as opposed to "affined" which means "related" or "connected."

Further reading

Adrian, Barbara (2008). *Actor Training the Laban Way: An Integrated Approach to Voice, Speech, and Movement.* New York: Allworth Press.

Boston, Jane and R. Cook (2009). *Breath in Action: The Art of Breath in Vocal and Holistic Practice.* London: Jessica Kingsley Publishers.

Carey, David and R. Clark Carey (2010). *The Verbal Arts Workbook.* London: Methuen Drama.

Carey, David and R. Clark Carey (2015). *The Shakespeare Workbook and Video.* London: Bloombury Methuen Drama.

Devore, Kate and S. Cookman (2009). *The Voice Book.* Chicago: Chicago Review Press.

Knight, Dudley (2012). *Speaking with Skill: An Introduction to Knight-Thompson Speechwork.* London: Bloomsbury.

Melton, Joan and K. Tom (2003). *One Voice: Integrating Singing Technique and Theatre* Voice Training. New Hampshire: Heinemann.

Skinner, Edith (1990). *Speak with Distinction.* New York: Applause Theatre Book Publishers.

4

LINKS BETWEEN LMA AND KEY ACTING TECHNIQUES

Jennifer Mizenko

Modern acting techniques

During the early twentieth century, great developments were taking place in the worlds of theater and dance. Constantin Stanislavski was developing his system of acting technique, and his pupil Michael Chekhov simultaneously performed in Stanislavski's company while developing his own methods that expanded those of Stanislavski. Sanford Meisner's technique from the mid-twentieth century is also an evolution of the work of Constantin Stanislavski. At the same time, Rudolf Laban was observing and analyzing movement throughout the early and mid-twentieth century and developing this wonderful system that links movement and meaning. Laban's ideas and theories have so much to offer the world of acting. In fact, they greatly enhance and deepen the methods of Stanislavski, Chekhov, and Meisner. This chapter will help you use various aspects of Laban Movement Analysis (LMA) to bring alive the psychophysical connection explored in these acting techniques.

In my experience, Stanislavski's technique can be boiled down to three main concepts: the Given Circumstances, the Magic-If, and Emotion Memory. Stanislavski revolutionized the approach the actor took to portraying the text from representing the character to experiencing the character's circumstances. Using this technique, the actor understands and knows the key events, situations, and actions in the character's life, as related to the plot. The actor must imagine himself into those events, situations, and actions, and use his memories of events in his own life that bring up the same emotions as the character.

The work of Michael Chekhov builds on the work of Stanislavski by including a more physical approach to acting. One of the central components of the Chekhov acting technique is the Psychological Gesture. A Psychological Gesture (PG) is a physical action that is an investigative tool for the actor. A PG can be created for each line of the text, a particular scene in the play, or from a single thought the character might have. Commonly, a PG is created based on the character's main drive or desire; this is called the Will-Impulse. A physical or bodily movement is created that represents the character's desire. The way this bodily movement is performed stirs up the character's desire and as a result stimulates the actor's muscle memory throughout the play.

Finally, Meisner's technique emphasizes *the reality of doing*. Meisner does not ask the actor to investigate memories, internal thoughts, or emotions, but teaches that good acting is not acting at all; rather, it is believing the Given Circumstances of the character and then reacting instinctively in the present moment. The actor must listen and respond in the present moment, *as if* everything happening on stage were happening in reality.[1]

Laban themes and LMA

Throughout Rudolf Laban's writings some general themes emerge. These themes are *Inner and Outer, Function and Expression, Exertion and Recuperation, Stability and Mobility.* Each theme reveals a different layer of expression and physical coordination for all movement, and examines movement psychophysically. Exploring the themes physically is very helpful for the actor and is supportive of various aspects of Stanislavski, Chekhov, and Meisner, really bringing alive the psychophysical connection.

The themes will be the main lens through which we examine the links between LMA and the acting techniques. For each theme I will first offer explorations focusing on the concept of the theme; how it relates to physicality and how it is useful for the actor. Then I will dive into application of a theme to a particular acting technique. Next, LMA concepts will be introduced that will deepen the physical experience and understanding for the actor. Along the way you will find video examples of some of the explorations. These videos range from 2–5 minutes, and I hope you find them helpful.

It is recommended that the explorations are done in a group setting with a facilitator. Some of the explorations are individual work, and some require a partner. I offer time suggestions, but they are merely a guide. When going through the explorations, take the time that you need (more or less) to complete and thoroughly experience each step of the exploration and the concepts presented. The explorations are offered in a specific order, designed to build one upon the other, layering concepts and deepening the experience. The order is designed to give a logical and thorough experience of the LMA themes, the various acting techniques, and LMA concepts.

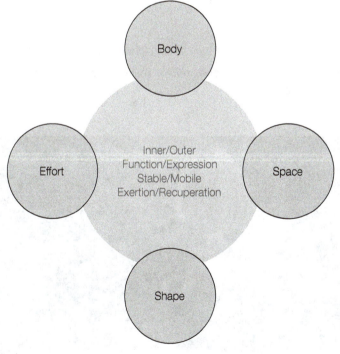

Enjoy!

The theme of Inner and Outer

Movement is meaningful. Movement that happens on the outside is reflected by movement that happens on the inside. For every inner thought there is an outer movement and for every outer movement there is an inner thought. There is a cyclical relationship between inner thoughts and feelings and outward action. One affects the other, creating a constant dynamic between what we are experiencing on the inside and how we are moving on the outside.

Inner/Outer Exploration 1: Movement Conversation and Inner/Outer (20–30 minutes)

Objective: To explore the theme through listening and responding. Allowing the exterior stimulus of a partner's movements to affect the inner life, resulting in an outer response.

Partner work:

- Beginning with a partner, decide who will be the first mover.
- Stand across from one another, making easy and gentle eye contact.

Figure 4.1 Karen Anne and Stephen in a Movement Conversation

- Breathe together, inhale and exhale, creating a connection across the space.

- If you are the mover, close your eyes for a brief moment. When you open them, respond in movement to the very first thing you notice about your partner.

The movement used in the Movement Conversation is not a simple gesture, nor is it a dance movement. It is a full-bodied movement that physicalizes inner impulse, using the spine and the limbs. The movement can change levels, facings, be fast or slow. There are no limits, except that the movement is purely connected to impulse, whatever you are observing and experiencing at that present moment. The movement is short and to the point, but has a beginning, middle, and end, 10–15 seconds long at the most.

- When you are receiving the movement, *listen* with the whole body. Using your eyes and your breath, empathize with the movement, breathing it in, allowing your partner's movement to impact your inner state. At the completion of his movement, respond in kind, by moving your inner state, allowing the outer stimulus of your partner's movement to affect and change your inner being. Then *move this inner change*, responding to your partner.

- Listen and respond with your partner, allowing the conversation to continue for 1–2 minutes.

- In the beginning make sure each of you completes your movement before the other begins. As the exercise continues, the responses may overlap, just as we often overlap our sentences in regular conversation.

- At the end of the exercise, "FREEZE," and notice your spatial relationship and ending shapes. Often these shapes are representative of the nature of the Movement Conversation.

- Discuss your experience with your partner.

Repeat the Movement Conversation, except this time about 1 minute into the exercise begin to add sound with the movement. No words, just sound that reflects the inner impulse and is also connected to the outer movement.

During the third round of the exercise, allow the sound to turn into a *word*. Allow the vocalization of the text to be as exaggerated as the movement. The vocalizing of the *word* once again reflects the inner impulse and is connected to the quality of the outer movement.

In a fourth round of the exercise, go through the whole process, Listening and Responding with movement, movement and sound, movement and a word, and then speak a line of improvised text. Be sure to let the vocalization of the text be just as exaggerated as the movement.

Using the theme of Inner/Outer, the text reflects the inner impulse and is connected to the outer movement.

See: 12 Inner/Outer Exploration 1
https://vimeo.com/channels/thelabanworkbook/200008928

Inner/Outer Exploration 2: Application of the Given Circumstances to the Movement Conversation (15 minutes)

Objective: To explore the physicality of the Inner/Outer connection within a scene, with awareness of the Given Circumstances.

In Stanislavski's approach to acting it all begins with the Given Circumstances, "the plot, the facts, the incidents, the period, the time and the place of the action, the way of life, how we as actors and directors understand the play" (2008: 52–3).

The next round of the Movement Conversation exercise is to use a scene, while applying Stanislavski's concept of the Given Circumstances. Choose and analyze a specific scene. Before beginning the Movement Conversation, focus on the Given Circumstances of your character.

What are your physical attributes: age, height, weight, eye and hair color, etc?
Where are you?
What does it smell like?

Are you outside or inside?
What time of day is it?
What is the light like?
What is the temperature like?
Who are you speaking to?
And why are you about to speak?

Add any other questions you can think of that will bring the Given Circumstances to life.

After answering these questions, go into the Movement Conversation with text from the scene. It is important that the text is committed to memory so you are not searching for lines. This can be done for an entire scene or only a portion of scene.

"FREEZE" at the end of the scene. Notice your spatial relationship and ending shapes. Consider these questions:

Is the ending tableau or relationship indicative of the scene?
What did you learn about your character from moving in this way?
What did you learn about your relationship with the other character from this movement interaction? Did the subtext come alive?
What do you know now that you didn't know previously about your character or this relationship?

Inner/Outer Exploration 3: Movement Conversation, Inner and Outer with Meisner's Mechanical Repetition exercise (40–50 minutes)

Objective: To apply the understanding of the Movement Conversation, along with the Inner/Outer connection of inner impulse and outer physical expression, to Meisner's Mechanical Mechanical Repetition exercise.

The heart of the Meisner work is Mechanical Repetition. Mechanical Repetition exercises are an attempt by Meisner to strip acting down to the bare essentials of listening and responding. The emphasis in Meisner technique is the moment, the now, and what is actually happening in the present moment, as opposed to recalling or remembering past emotions.

ACTING IS NOT EMOTING. Acting is doing something. Of course acting does demand of us the ability to access our own rich emotional life and the way in, the organic way, is through meaningful doing. (Silverberg, Foote, and Stern 1994: 4)

Partner work:

- In traditional Meisner training, this exploration is done sitting in two chairs opposite of each other. Decide who will begin the exploration.

- To establish a connection with your partner, begin in the same manner as the Movement Conversation in the first exploration, making easy and gentle eye contact and breathing together.

- Once a connection has been established, the partner beginning the exploration briefly closes his or her eyes and reopens them.

- Upon reopening the eyes, speak the very first thing you notice about your partner. Examples:

  - blue

  - bandana

  - stain

- The receiving partner responds by speaking the same text.

- As the text is continuously exchanged between the two of you, be sure there are no pauses while at the same time you are not cutting each other off.

- Additionally, stay connected observing you partner and receiving the text anew each time.

- Try this exploration several times, giving each partner a chance to be the initiator. Vary the duration of the exploration from 10 minutes to 10 seconds.

Now remove the chairs and try the exploration on your feet, applying the Movement Conversation. Begin again by making a connection through breath and gentle eye contact.

- The partner initiating the exploration closes his eyes, reopens them and makes a *movement* based off the first thing he notices about his partner, while speaking one word describing this observation as he is moving.

- The receiving partner *listens* to the movement with her eyes, while simultaneously taking the movement into her body with an inhale.

- The receiving partner responds on the exhale, saying the same word and performing the same movement as her initiating partner.

- Continue this moving Mechanical Repetition exploration for 1–2 minutes. The same rules apply, no cutting off your partner and no pauses.

- Be sure the *listening* (seeing) happens on the inhale, and the *responding* (moving) happens on an exhale.

See: 13 Inner/Outer Exploration 3
https://vimeo.com/channels/thelabanworkbook/200009017

Inner/Outer Exploration 4: Connecting the theme of Inner and Outer using the LMA concept of Shape in support of Chekhov's concept of Psychological Gesture (PG) (80–90 minutes)

Objective: To connect the theme of Inner/Outer and the concept of Still Shape to the creation of a Psychological Gesture.

Actors can create a Psychological Gesture to explore many different aspects of a character and a scene. For this exploration we will approach the PG from the character's Will-Impulse. Simply stated, the Will-Impulse is the character's overall desire or need. How to determine the Will-Impulse is included in the following steps. Once the actor determines the character's Will-Impulse, the actor creates a full-bodied movement that physicalizes the Will-Impulse. When the actor discovers a movement that hits home or creates sensations and feelings in the body that represent the character, he has found a PG that brings to life the character's Will-Impulse.

The *strength* of the movement stirs our will power in general; the *kind* of movement awakens in us a definite corresponding *desire*, and the quality of the same movement conjures up our feelings. (Chekhov and Callow 2002: 64)

The PG is then used as a way to warm up the actor into the character's body and psyche, bringing his understanding of the character into his own body and psychology. Instead of relying on an outside written analysis, the PG comes from the actor's own psychophysical experience. The PG is never used on stage. The actor carries the movement inside his body as a personal secret. Chekhov states: "through the gesture, you penetrate and stimulate the depths of your own psychology" (Chekhov and Callow 2002: 64).

- Begin by creating full-bodied, over-exaggerated LMA Still Shapes. The Still Shapes recognized in LMA are Wall, Ball, Pin, Screw, and Pyramid[2] (20–30 minutes).
- Create a game out of this by moving or walking through the space with a facilitator shouting out either Wall, Ball, Pin, Screw, or Pyramid.
- When the facilitator shouts out the type of shape, freeze in a full-bodied physicalization of the shape.

As the game proceeds, try not to recreate the same physicalized shape each time. How many different ways can you physicalize a

Figure 4.2 Karen Anne in a Screw Still Shape

ball? Use different levels, body parts, spatial orientations (i.e., upside down), etc. Or play the game in two different groups so that everyone can see how many ways there are to be a Wall, Ball, Pin, Screw, or Pyramid.

- Play the game a second time, and as you assume your shape, shout out a word reflecting how you are feeling.
- Record the feelings associated with the shape. For example, for every Screw Shape, what words literally just fall out of your mouth? Write these words down. Your record may look something like this:
  - Wall: *open, broad, strong, powerful*
  - Ball: *closed, small, scared, protected*
  - Pin: *narrow, straight, tight, skinny*
  - Screw: *twisted, conflicted, anguish, doubt*
  - Pyramid: *stable, grounded, balanced, full*

Next review your embodied Still Shapes, and turn these shapes into a realistic posture. Take your posture for each shape, and use the word you discovered for the shape in a sentence. Standing in your Wall posture state:

- I am open.
- I am broad.
- I am strong.
- I am powerful.

Notice how the statements go with the posture. In relation to the theme of Inner/Outer, how are your inside feelings and outside posture/form connecting? What is the relationship between the two?

The next step is to create full-bodied, over-exaggerated shapes for the following verbs recognized by Chekhov as being universal or archetypal movements: *push/pull, lift/smash, open/close, drag/throw, reach/embrace* (20–30 minutes).

- The same game can be applied. Walk through the space and

have a facilitator randomly instruct the group to *push*, or *open*, or *embrace*, etc.

- Again, as the game proceeds, avoid doing the exact same movement. Play with different levels, different timings, and different qualities of movement as you *smash, drag,* or *reach*.

As you are physicalizing these actions, notice if the movement is supported by any of the LMA Still Shapes. Which Still Shapes are utilized to achieve the action of *lift,* or *pull,* or *close,* or *drag?* Use the Still Shapes to add specificity to your movements.

- Play the game again, and as you move through your action, once again shout out a word or phrase reflecting how you are feeling.

  - What comes to your mind when you move *smash*?

    - Anger, despair, frustration, pissed off.

Record these words and also record what Still Shapes are being utilized to achieve the actions.

See: 14 Inner/Outer Exploration 4
https://vimeo.com/channels/thelabanworkbook/200009069

When creating a PG, choose a character and a piece of text from a play, not a monologue book. A full play is necessary to provide the actor with all of the details required for this exploration (20–30 minutes).

- Explore the character's Will-Impulse by reading the entire play noting the character's:

  - Thoughts (images, fantasies).

  - Feelings.

  - Wishes, desires.

- From these observations in the text, determine the main desire and psychological state of the character, the Will-Impulse.

- Create a one-sentence statement that succinctly states the character's Will-Impulse. Examples:

  - I want revenge.

- I surrender.

- I am giving my heart.

- Memorize 30–60 seconds of the text by heart.

Using the Will-Impulse statement, move the character's desire.

- Begin by speaking the statement out loud and creating gesture. Start small, perhaps only moving a hand or the arm.

- Repeat the statement over and over again, allowing the movement to grow. With each repetition of the statement, allow more of the body to get involved.

  - Shift your weight.

  - Let the spine move.

  - Where does the head want to go?

  - How do the legs respond?

  - What is the pelvis doing?

  - Are the limbs moving as a unit? Or is the movement more sequential, moving one joint after another?

  - What is the texture of the movement? Try different textures.

  - What is the timing? Try different timings.

As you repeat the line, become more and more physically engaged, using the entire body to physicalize the line. Allow the voice to reflect the movement, becoming one in timing, pitch, power and quality.

Bring all of these concepts together by performing the movement and text until it stirs YOUR will, YOUR desire, YOUR feelings. The resulting movement is your PG, connecting the Inner psychological state or Will-Impulse of the character to the Outer physical form.

- Notice what LMA Still Shapes are being utilized. How are Wall, Ball, Pin, Screw, and Pyramid supporting your movement choices? How do the words you chose for the Still Shapes give emotional subtext to your PG?

For the final step in the process, perform the PG for the group, immediately followed by the chosen memorized text. Do not actually physicalize the PG while speaking the memorized text, remembering that a PG is never to be used on stage. It is like the scaffolding of a building, ever present, but never seen. It is the actor's "technical secret" and serves as an internal director or guide and provides inspiration. The PG is an excellent physical warm-up for the specific character the actor is portraying on stage. Allow the PG to sit in your bones and sinews and inform the text.

See: 15 Inner/Outer Exploration 4 – PG into Memorized Text
https://vimeo.com/channels/thelabanworkbook/200009176

Discussion questions for the theme of Inner/Outer

1 How does the Movement Conversation reveal the concept of the theme? Impulse? Listening and Responding?

2 How does Stanislavski's concept of Given Circumstances enrich the Movement Conversation?

3 How does the physical connection of the Movement Conversation enhance Meisner's Mechanical Repetition? What is it like to breathe in your partner's movement, and exhale your movement response?

4 How does the Laban concept of Still Shape support the creation of a PG? Does the use of Still Shape enhance your Inner/Outer connection when creating a PG reflecting the Will-Impulse of the character?

The theme of Function and Expression

Function and Expression integrate to create meaning in movement. Every movement or action has a function and an expression. An expressive movement such as a hug may serve the function of deepening a relationship. A functional movement such as washing the dishes may serve the expression of anger or frustration. Functional movements are filled with meaning, and expressive movements function as communication within a type of situation or relationship.

Function/Expression Exploration 1: Noticing Function and Expression in gestures and movement (15–20 minutes)

Objective: To notice that all movement is both functional and expressive.

Pick a movement that you think is *functional*, i.e., it serves or accomplishes a function or task. Examples: Comb your hair into a new style, take a shoe off and on, move furniture, pick up a backpack.

- Perform this movement 3–5 times to secure the phrase or beginning, middle, and end of the movement.
- Perform this functional movement thinking of the following circumstances:
  - Your lover just rejected you.
  - You're late for an important job interview.
  - Your sweetest and dearest pet just died.
  - You're getting ready for your wedding to the love of your life.
  - You just got a huge job promotion.

Figure 4.3 Cory playing with a Functional Gesture

- Observe the different ways the same movement is performed.

- Perform these different ways of doing the *functional* movement for a partner. Have an outside observer guess what your circumstances are.

See: 16 Function/Expression Exploration 1
https://vimeo.com/channels/thelabanworkbook/200009209

Partner work:

With a partner, pick and perform a movement that is considered *expressive*, i.e., a movement that expresses feelings. Do the movement in relationship with your partner. Examples: hugging, a handshake, a wave, a push or shove, holding hands.

- Perform the movement 3–5 times to secure the phrase or beginning, middle, and end of the movement.

- As the two of you repeat the movement, notice how this *expressive* movement is inherently *functional*.

  – A hug serves the function of bringing two people together in close physical contact.

  – A handshake serves the function of a greeting between two people.

  – A wave serves the function of a greeting of hello or goodbye, depending on the context.

  – A push or shove serves the function of setting a boundary with the other person. It creates a sense of safety for the person doing the pushing or shoving.

  – Holding hands serves the function of creating a physical union between two people.

- What is the *function* of the movement you and your partner chose?

All movement is expressive and all movement is functional!

Function/Expression Exploration 2: Apply the Meisner concept of Imaginary Circumstances to Function and Expression

Objective: To enhance the idea of Expression by adding Imaginary Circumstances to gesture and movement.

A basic tenet of Meisner's work is: "Acting is living truthfully under imaginary circumstances" (Silverberg, Foote, and Stern 1994: 9). Meisner requires the actor to believe and accept the Imaginary Circumstances. This is the "Actor's Faith."

> Everything in acting is a kind of heightened, intensified reality—but it's based on justified reality. (Meisner and Longwell 1987: 45)

Accepting this intensified reality as real is the Imaginary Circumstances.

Partner work:
Add Imaginary Circumstances to the *expressive* movement chosen by you and your partner in the previous exploration. Each partner picks their own Imaginary Circumstances. Use the following list or create your own list of Imaginary Circumstances. (Be sure to define who is playing what role in the Imaginary Circumstances.)

- Your lover just rejected you.
- You're late for an important job interview.
- Your sweetest and dearest pet just died.
- You're getting ready for your wedding to the love of your life.
- You just got a huge job promotion.

Discuss with your partner how layering the Imaginary Circumstances on top of the already *expressive* movement increases both the *function* and *expression* of the movement. It adds layers and nuance to the movement.

For fun, try adding Imaginary Circumstances to an improvised Movement Conversation (Inner/Outer theme Exploration 1) and notice if the functional and expressive elements of the movement deepen. This is clearly something that happens in everyday life, all of the time. Notice as you go through your day and interact with others how your movements and gestures are both *functional* and *expressive*.

Function/Expression Exploration 3: Investigating the theme of Function and Expression as related to Chekhov's concept of Qualities, and supported by Laban's concept of Effort (100–120 minutes)

Objective: To explore how movement has function and expression in relation to "how" the movement is articulated. The "how" of movement is referred to as Quality by Chekhov and Effort by Laban.

Michael Chekhov believed that the inner driving force or the Will-Impulse of a character results in physical action, behavior, and decisions. From the driving force, the body responds with a particular energy. This resulting energy is the character's Quality of movement. Chekhov defines the possible Qualities as Molding, Flowing, Flying, and Radiating. These Qualities are often associated with the elements of the universe: earth, water, air, and fire. Creating these qualities in the body requires the actor to engage the imagination.

To explore the concepts of Effort and Qualities, we'll begin by reviewing Chekhov's Psychological Gesture (PG). This concept was explored previously in the Inner/Outer theme Exploration 4 (15–20 minutes).

- Begin by moving the following verbs: *push/pull, lift/smash, open/close, drag/throw, reach/embrace*:
  - Walk about the room and have the facilitator shout out one of the words above.
  - When you hear the word, move it in the most exaggerated manner possible. Over-emphasize the physical action of the verb. Experiment with different physical choices for each word. Once you have done this for each verb, choose verbs of your own:
  - To kick, to digest, to destroy, to scatter, to chase, to break, to caress, etc.

- Based on this improvisation, choose your favorite movement and allow it to be a new PG.

- Find a partner and share your PG. Answer the following questions:

  - What body parts are moving?
  - Where are the body parts moving in space?
  - What does it make you feel like on the inside? What emotions (if any) does the movement bring up?

The PG you just created will serve as your baseline PG for the rest of this exploration.

Playing with the "how" of the movement, consider the following scenarios and move your PG as if you were ...

- Molasses in a jar that transitions into moonshine being poured out of a bottle.

- A fairy transforming into a giant scary monster.

- A bee buzzing around every which way, becoming a laser-guided rocket headed straight for its target.

- A fish swimming downstream, then turning around and swimming upstream to spawn!

Title each of these movement variations of your baseline PG, with a short descriptive sentence. How did the Function/Expression of the PG change by moving it in these scenarios?

Now let's specifically explore the LMA concept of Effort. In LMA, Effort defines the "how" of movement. The term Effort does not refer to the difficulty or ease of a movement, but to the quality or texture of a movement. Just as there are three primary colors, there are four fundamental Efforts that are combined in pairs and trios to create a cornucopia of movement textures. For this exploration, we will stick to the four fundamental Efforts of Weight, Space, Time, and Flow.

Using your baseline PG, apply each of the four Efforts as explained below and see how the feeling or meaning of the PG changes. Keep the exaggerated style of movement, as well as exaggerated style of vocalization when adding words or text. Applying Effort to the PG may require the body to adjust a little bit to accomplish the instructions. Allow this adjustment to happen. Apply Effort to both the movement and the voice (20–30 minutes).

Weight Effort has two polarities, Light and Strong. Using Weight Effort in movement engages the muscles and bones of the body, and is connected psychologically to Intention.

- Light Weight

  - Allow your body to become very light. Feel as if you can linger in the air like a feather.

  - Perform your PG and notice the effect Light Weight Effort has on the meaning of your gesture.

  - Is there a Light Intention in your gesture?

  - Record your observations, and choose a one-word title for the PG performed with Light Weight.

  - Perform your PG with Light Weight Effort while speaking your new title.

- Strong Weight

  - Allow your body to become very strong. Feel as if you can move mountains.

  - Get up against the wall, and attempt to move the wall. Or pair up with a partner of similar size and work to move your partner across the room, as if they were a car stuck in snow.

  - Using this same kind of physicality, perform your PG and notice the effect Strong Weight Effort has on the meaning of your gesture.

  - Is there a Strong Intention in your gesture?

  - What is the title of your PG performed in this manner? Perform the PG while speaking your new title.

The two polarities of Space Effort are Indirect and Direct. Space Effort engages the senses of hearing and sight, and relates psychologically to your attention.

- Indirect Space
  - Allow your awareness of the room to become very broad. Notice everything at once. What's in front of you, behind you, above you, below you, to the side of you?
  - Even while noticing what's in front of you, simultaneously be aware or sense what's behind you.
  - This movement energy is Indirect in LMA, and requires a multi-focused attention of your body.
  - Move your PG with Indirect Space Effort.
  - Is your attention Indirect?
  - What is the title of your PG performed in this manner?
  - Move the PG with Indirect Space Effort while speaking the title.
- Direct Space
  - Allow your awareness to narrow in on a specific target.
  - Bring your whole body into relationship with this chosen target. Not just your face and vision, but also your chest, your belly button, your pelvis, your knees, your forehead.
  - Direct Space Effort requires you to zoom in on your target, with your whole being.
  - Choose a target for your PG and move it with Direct Space Effort.
  - Is your attention Direct?
  - Give the PG a new title for this performance, and move the PG while speaking this title.

The opposite ends of Time Effort are Quick and Sustained. Applying Time Effort to movement engages the nervous system of the body and psychologically is connected to thinking and decision making.

- Sustained Time
  - It is morning and you have nowhere to go, nothing to do, and you get to linger in your process of getting up, getting out of bed, and getting ready for the day ahead.

- Every movement is luxurious and indulgent.

- One tiny little movement can take as much time as you decide.

- With this indulgent and luxurious feeling in your body, perform your PG.

- This is Sustained Time Effort, when a movement or gesture lingers and continues on forever.

- Is your thinking or decision-making process Sustained?

- What is the title of your Sustained Time PG? Speak the title of your PG while moving with Sustained Time.

- Quick Time

    - Now all of a sudden, you realize it's actually a work day and you're late for your job. Holy cow!

    - You've got to get up, get dressed, and get out of the house lickety split.

    - Movement with this type of energy is Quick Time Effort. It has a sense of urgency, and immediacy.

    - Apply Quick Time Effort to your PG.

    - Is your thinking or decision-making process Quick?

    - What is the new title for your PG? Speak the title and move the PG in Quick Time.

The opposite ends of Flow Effort are Free and Bound. Flow Effort engages and is connected to the circulatory system in the body. Psychologically it connects to the flow of emotions.

- Free Flow

    - In your mind's eye imagine you are in a fast-moving stream. Or perhaps one of those lazy river rides you find at the water park.

    - Imagine yourself just floating along, literally going with the flow. The current is moving you and you simply cannot stop.

    - Imagine yourself actually swimming with the current. What

does that feel like? How does the current affect your swimming stroke?

- Moving in this manner (on dry land) is called Free Flow Effort.

- In Free Flow, movement has momentum, and is difficult to stop.

- Moving with Free Flow, try out your PG.

- Are your emotions Free?

- What's the new title? Speak the new title and move the PG simultaneously.

• Bound Flow

- Staying in your stream or lazy river, imagine yourself resisting the current.

- Walking or swimming, how does it feel to move against the current?

- Resisting the current is moving in Bound Flow. In Bound Flow all movement is restricted, and can be stopped at any moment.

- Try your PG with Bound Flow.

- Are your emotions Bound?

- What is the new title of your PG?

- Move your PG while speaking the new title.

Thinking back to the theme of Function and Expression, review your baseline PG. How you *originally* moved it. Notice the original Function and Expression of your baseline PG:

• What was the *function* of the movement, and what was the *expression*?

• How did the *expression* of your baseline PG change when applying the different Efforts?

• Did changing the Effort affect the *function*? If it didn't change the actual *function* of the PG, did it change the context in some manner?

Moving on to Chekhov's Qualities, we will use the four fundamental Laban Efforts to support the movement of the Qualities. Much like Laban's Effort Factors, Chekhov's Qualities are used to create a movement dynamic that reflects the inner driving force of the character, and create expression in the PG (20–30 minutes).

Chekhov recognizes four Qualities, and connects these qualities to the elements of the earth.

- Flying/Air
- Flowing/Water
- Molding/Earth
- Radiating/Fire

Like we applied Laban's Efforts to your baseline PG, in this step apply each of Chekhov's four Qualities, using Laban's Efforts to support the energy of the Quality.

- To explore Flying, literally think of flying through the air.
    - Use the Efforts of Light Weight and Direct Space simultaneously, adding Free Flow.
    - Move through the room as if you are about to take flight.
    - Keeping the energy of the flight in your body, complete your flight with your PG.
    - Notice what expression comes from using Fly as a supportive Quality for your PG.
    - As we did previously, title this Flying PG and perform this PG while speaking this title.
- To explore Flowing, literally think of going with the flow of a stream or river.
    - Use the Efforts of Free Flow and Direct Space.
    - Add a little bit of Light Weight.
    - As we did earlier while exploring Flow Effort, go with the Flow. See how this makes Chekhov's quality of Flowing more specific.

- As you are Flowing, try out your PG. What is the new expression that is created? How does it feel to Flow your PG?

- What is the new title? Move and speak the title of the Flowing PG together.

- To explore Molding, ground your body into the earth while simultaneously pushing the space in your kinesphere.

  - Use Strong Weight and Bound Flow to engage your body into the ground. Then simultaneously add in Space Effort, varying between Direct and Indirect.

  - Think of yourself standing inside of the earth. See the earth. Mold all that is around you. Use your back, your arms and legs to mold the dirt of the earth. Imagine your movements moving the earth around you.

  - As you are Molding, move your PG. Make your PG Mold.

  - What's the new expression of your PG when you Mold it? What's the new title?

  - Mold and speak the new title of your PG while you are Molding.

- To explore Radiating, think of yourself as a fire.

  - Allow Quick Time and Indirect Space to help you move your body as fire.

  - Think of all the different stages of fire: sparks, flames, burning embers, pops, etc.

  - Think of the Flow of the fire. Vary Bound and Free Flow in your fire movement.

  - With your body as fire, Radiate your PG. Give it sparks, and pops, and flames, and glowing embers.

  - How does this feel? What new expression is created?

Reflect back on all of the applications to your baseline PG in this exploration: Laban's four Efforts of Weight, Space, Time, and Flow (and their polarities) and Chekhov's Qualities of Flying, Floating, Molding, and Radiating.

THE LABAN WORKBOOK FOR ACTORS

Fill in Table 4.1, naming the expression of each PG variation.

Table 4.1: Baseline PG, Laban Effort compared to Chekhov Qualities

Baseline PG...	Laban Effort	Chekhov Quality
Expressing?	Light Weight:	Flying:
Expressing?	Strong Weight:	Flowing:
Expressing?	Indirect Space:	Molding:
Expressing?	Direct Space:	Radiating:
Expressing?	Sustain Time:	
Expressing?	Quick Time:	
Expressing?	Free Flow:	
Expressing?	Bound Flow:	

Which of the Laban Efforts or Chekhov Qualities was the most fun to perform and perhaps even surprised you? (20–30 minutes)

- Journal on this PG and create a character and a monologue based on the PG.
- Who are you? And what do you want to say?
- Choose a set of Given Circumstances for the character you are creating, and let your imagination go.
- Once you have determined who the character is, give the character words and write a brief monologue.
- Title the monologue.
- Perform the PG in the most exaggerated manner as possible, with the chosen title word.
- Then perform the created text, keeping the PG and the intention of the inner driving force in your body.

Even though your character was created through movement first, were you able to create a complete and full character?

Discussion questions for the theme of Function/ Expression

- How does applying Imaginary Circumstances to a gesture or movement enhance the Function/Expression?
- How can actors benefit from being aware of Function/ Expression in a scene?
- How does the creation of the PG relate to the theme of Function and Expression?
- How do Laban's Efforts support Chekhov's Qualities?
- How do Chekhov's Qualities and Laban's Efforts affect the Expression of the PG or the inner driving force of the character?

The theme of Exertion and Recuperation

All movements or actions occur within a phrase, or natural cycle, with a beginning, middle, and end, which replenishes movement vitality. Within the phrase there is an exertion of movement and a recuperation. The theme of Exertion and Recuperation puts the focus on the rise and fall of a sequence or phrase of movement and/or text. A phrase begins with an initiation movement. This movement may feel like it is rising up out of the body or falling out of the body. The initiation of movement is the beginning of a phrase, the follow-through is the middle of the phrase, and the completion of the movement is the end. Once a phrase completes itself, a new wave of movement is created and the process begins anew.

Exertion/Recuperation Exploration 1: To explore the theme of Exertion and Recuperation

Objective: To use the understanding of Exertion and Recuperation and bring awareness to the fact that there is a beginning, middle, and end to every sentence, activity or thought process, called a phrase or the Arc-of-Life.

Create a gesture, any gesture. Perform the gesture thoroughly, completely. Pay attention to exactly how the gesture begins and ends. Notice the initiation or beginning of the movement, how it travels through space, and how the movement resolves or ends.

- Bring into your awareness the complete physical journey of the gesture.
- Repeat the movement over and over again (at least five times), and notice how the movement is like a sentence or a phrase with a specific beginning, middle, and end. This is the Arc-of-Life of the movement.

Partner work:

- Get a partner and perform your gestures for each other.
- Observe the Arc-of-Life (beginning, middle, end) or phrase of your partner's gesture (at least three times).
- Using any type of sound (non-sense syllables or vowel sounds), sing along while your partner does his or her gesture.
- Move the gesture together and sing the gesture together.
- Share your understanding of the gesture and answer the questions:
  - What is a phrase?
  - What signals or suggests an ending?
- Now switch and watch your partner's gesture.

The pattern developed from Arc-of-Life of the phrase is often referred to in LMA as the Phrasing. Phrasing is created by Exertion and Recuperation. There are four basic Phrasing possibilities:

- Impulsive: emphasis on the beginning of the phrase.
- Emphatic: emphasis on the end of the phrase.
- Middle: emphasis on the middle of the phrase
- Swing: emphasis on the beginning and end of the phrase.

Notice what type of Phrasing each of you is using and how that affects the meaning and intention of the phrase. Try out different Phrasing and see if the meaning and intention of the movement changes.

See: 17 Exertion/Recuperation Exploration 1
https://vimeo.com/channels/thelabanworkbook/200009254

Exertion/Recuperation Exploration 2: Movement Monologue, utilizing the theme of Exertion and Recuperation and Phrasing, to explore Stanislavski's concept of Units and Objectives (40–50 minutes)

Objective: To create a Movement Monologue, utilizing the theme of Exertion and Recuperation to discover the Phrasing of the monologue. Phrasing the Units of the text to discover Objective.

For the actor to thoroughly understand the character's Given Circumstances, Stanislavski suggests breaking a play down into Units. A good analogy is the carving of a turkey. Start by separating the big parts that are different from each other. Then narrow down these big parts into smaller component parts. And then divide smaller parts even further. In the context of a play, find the main events. Examples may be the start of a war, a big party, two characters meeting for the first time, the death of a character. Break down these events into smaller parts, and even smaller parts still, arriving at each separate and individual want of the character. Finding these individual and distinct *wants* leads to the discovery of the Objective. "At the heart of every unit lies a *creative objective*" (Stanislavski 1936: 116).

The ultimate goal of this exploration is to connect the theme of Exertion and Recuperation to the character's ideas and thoughts (Objectives) to movement.

Begin by choosing a 1-minute monologue. For this exploration, commit the text to memory. Analyze the text of the monologue on paper as follows.

- Note the beginning, middle, and end of each *idea*. Each idea may include several sentences or as little as one sentence. To do this, notice when the character introduces and concludes a new thought or idea. Divide the monologue into sections.

- Apply the theme of Exertion and Recuperation to the text by noticing an Exertion of a group of new thoughts, and the Recuperation from those thoughts.

These sections are what Stanislavski would refer to as Units.

Let's explore the Phrasing of the Units in the monologue through movement. To do this we will examine the Phrasing of each sentence in the Unit. Depending on the monologue it might take 10–20 minutes to apply the following instructions.

- Begin by reviewing the Given Circumstances prep as discussed in Inner/Outer Exploration 2, and apply it to the monologue.

- Once you have determined the Units on paper, begin moving the monologue paying attention to the Phrasing of each sentence in the Unit.

- When you move the monologue, physically connect to what the character wants and how the character is going to get it. While moving the Objective notice where the Exertion is in each sentence. How do the sentences Recuperate or resolve, physically?

- Move and speak each sentence simultaneously. It is sometimes helpful to keep your eyes closed at first. Move and speak this sentence over and over. Play. Allow the text to propel you into movement by feeling the Exertion of the sounds and the meaning of the text and its resolution or Recuperation. Experiment with the Phrasing of the text: Impulsive, Emphatic, Middle, or Swing. See which emphasis suits the Objective. Or, discover if changing the Phrasing changes the Objective.

Your movement can stay on the floor or change levels; move any and all body parts. It is recommended that the movement is exaggerated and not realistic in any way. Let the movement ride on the sound of the text and the chosen Phrasing. Allow the vocalization of the text to be exaggerated as well. Pitch and volume may rise and fall, vowels may be extended, and consonants may be overly pronounced.

- Repeat the sentence over and over again, letting the movement, sound, and phrasing evolve into a loosely set or "choreographed" movement sentence.

Keep in mind that the focus here is to connect the theme of Exertion and Recuperation to the character's ideas and thoughts to movement. Your resulting movement sentence needs to have a beginning, middle, and end that reflect the Exertion and Recuperation of the sentence.

- Once you have thoroughly examined the first sentence through movement, move onto the next sentence. Go through the same process.

- Once you find the sound, movement and Phrasing for the next sentence, put the two sentences together.

  – When the two sentences are linked, notice the transition between the two.

  – How does the first sentence move into the second sentence, physically and also in thought? What thoughts propel the character into the next sentence?

- Repeat this process for each sentence in the Unit you are working on.

- Once you have completed a Unit, move through the whole thing and notice the emotional journey the character is taking.

- Take note of the Phrasing of the Unit *as a whole* (Impulsive, Emphatic, Middle, Swing).

- How does the character phrase her thoughts and how is the character propelled forward in her thinking process?

  – Recall this idea from the theme of Exertion and Recuperation. Once a phrase completes itself, a new thought or wave of movement is created and the process begins anew, with a new exertion of thought and movement, followed by recuperation.

  – Notice how the character phrases the Exertions and Recuperations of her thoughts.

Figure 4.4 Stephen's Puck Movement Monologue

Upon moving through each Unit, put them together and perform the entire monologue. You have created a Movement Monologue. Now that the Movement Monologue is complete, discover the union of the physical and vocal Exertion and Recuperation of the text. What is the Objective for the character in each Unit? How do these Objectives come together to move the character toward what she wants? How does the physicality of connecting the Exertion and Recuperation of the character's ideas and thoughts assist you as an actor?

See: 18 Exertion/Recuperation Exploration 3
https://vimeo.com/channels/thelabanworkbook/200009315

Exertion/Recuperation Exploration 3: The theme of Exertion and Recuperation applied to Stanislavski's Magic-If and the LMA concept of Shape (40–50 minutes)

Objective: To discover the character's reality while applying the concept of Moving Shape, using the Phrasing of the text discovered in Exploration 2.

Stanislavski discusses the Magic-If in his seminal text *The Actor Prepares*. The Magic-If requires the actor to literally put herself in the character's predicament. Using the Given Circumstances, the Magic-If stimulates the actor's imagination. The actor asks herself, what would I do if I were in this situation? Applying the LMA concept of Shape helps the actor understand the character's relationship to the environment, thus giving the actor more insight into the character's predicament, situation, and state of mind. The various Modes of Shape Change or Moving Shape include Shape-Flow, Directional, and Carving.

Using the same monologue from Exploration 2, review the Given Circumstances of the character. From this review, determine how the character is relating to the environment in each Unit of the text. Use the following definitions of Modes of Shape Change or Moving Shape to help you with this examination. These definitions look at how the body is changing shape in relationship to the environment. As you examine the character's Moving Shapes, ask yourself *why* this relationship choice being made for this moment or Unit of the text?

Shape Flow: Is the character only relating to herself? Perhaps she's speaking to someone else, but not really relating externally to that person. Perhaps the character is making a self-discovery as she's speaking to another character.

- Within the concept of Shape, this definition of relationship is called Shape Flow, or self to self relationship.

- The movement of Shape Flow tends to be very breath-motivated and is usually very subtle.

- Often a movement like touching your hair, or neck, or heart is an example of a Shape Flow movement. In LMA this is referred to as self-touch.

Directional Shape: Is the character specifically, and purposefully directing her statements to another character or even a specific object on stage? Is the character narrowing in on a specific relationship? Making a very specific point?

- Within the concept of Shape, this definition of relationship to the environment is called Directional Shape, or self to other or external object relationship.

- Directional Shape change may result in a curved or straightway pathway of a limb or any body part (Directional Arc-like or

Spoke-like). The movement is connected or linked to another person or object.

- Pointing is an obvious example of a Directional Shape Movement.

Carving: Is the character trying to be inclusive of her entire environment? Such a relationship would require the character to be aware of every-thing around her, even perhaps inclusive of the universe. In such a case the character may be addressing universal human problems or needs, or may be wanting to bring love and happiness to the world.

- Within the concept of Shape, this kind of relationship is called Carving, or self to the entire world relationship.
- Carving Shape change usually results in rounded movement, gestures that gather or contain the space or people.
- A hug is an example of Carving Shape, as well as a gesture of opening and rounding the arms as if to include an entire group.

Note your discoveries of how the character is relating to the environment on paper. From these observations make Shape choices for each Unit of your text, and note why you made these choices.

Now we'll apply the physical and vocal Phrasing of the text discovered in Exertion and Recuperation Exploration 2, adding in Moving Shape choices.

- Move the monologue again and rediscover the Exertion and Recuperation of each phrase/sentence and Unit.
  - Over-emphasize the Phrasing. Let the movement ride on the text and physically experience the Exertions and Recuperations.
- Review the Given Circumstances and perform the Movement Monologue again.
- Notice if the relationship and Shape choices you made on paper are showing up as you are now physically moving the monologue.
  - Are you physicalizing what you theorized? Or are different

choices being made? Allow the choices to now come from physical impulse.

- – Allow the rises and falls of the Exertion and Recuperation help you discover the type of relationships the character needs.

- Let the physicalization of the monologue put you in the character's shoes—the Magic-If, moving the appropriate Moving Shape choices.

- What does it feel like when you physically specify these environment relationships? What is it like to physically be in this situation? To live in this predicament? Do the Moving Shape Modes deepen your experience of the Magic-If?

Compare the discoveries you are making about relationship from both the text to the movement and the movement to the text. Neither has to be right or wrong. Just note where there is agreement and where there is disparity between your paper work and your actual physical choices. Use Table 4.2 to help you make this comparison (add or remove cells as needed).

Table 4.2: Shape Choices – Paper Work vs Physical Choices

Unit of Text (Write text in the box)	Moving Shape Choice	
	Paper Work	**Physical**
Unit 1		
Unit 2		
Unit 3		
Unit 4		
Unit 5		
Unit 6		

In those places where there is a disparity, try to move the text with both choices. Move it in context with what occurs before and after. Make a choice by allowing your physicality to help you determine what feels right for the Given Circumstances.

Now you are ready to put it all together. Perform the Movement Monologue with exaggerated movement and text.

- Make choices and integrate what you discovered. How did applying Exertion and Recuperation lead to Phrasing? Did your understanding of Modes of Shape Change or Moving Shape bring alive the Magic-If?

Use Table 4.3 to help you clarify your choices (add or remove cells as needed).

Table 4.3: Clarifying Phrasing and Moving Shape Choices

Unit of Text	Phrasing Choice	Moving Shape Choice

Use the table to help you physicalize your Phrasing and Moving Shape Choices. Achieve this integration by repeating the Movement Monologue with full energy at least three times, using your final Phrasing and Shape choices.

Repeat the movement until you are physically experiencing the situation of the character, creating the Magic-If within your body.

Conclude the exercise by performing the Movement Monologue first, immediately followed by a "realistic" performance, and notice the transference from one to the next. Be aware of how your body feels when performing the text realistically. What stays with you from the Movement Monologue? How does the Phrasing propel the character forward? What is your awareness of the reality of the character? How have the two different approaches—Text to Movement and Movement to Text—supported each other? Or were they in complete conflict? Which way do you prefer to work? Why?

Discussion questions for the theme Exertion/ Recuperation

1 What is a phrase and what is Phrasing?

2 How did the theme assist you in discovering Units?

3 Did discovering and isolating the Units of the text help you discover the Objectives and help you determine your Shape choices?

4 How does the theme of Exertion/Recuperation influence change or transitions from one thought to the next?

5 Did exploring Exertion/Recuperation help you recognize when change in the monologue, relationship, or scene is evident and/ or necessary?

The theme of Stability and Mobility

Stabilizing and mobilizing elements interact continuously to produce effective movement. For any movement or action to occur, one part of the body must be stable to allow mobility. Stabilizing the left leg to the ground allows the right leg to move freely. Stability and Mobility interact to allow all movement.

Stability/Mobility Exploration 1: Exploring Stability and Mobility in your own body (20–30 minutes)

Objective: To feel the interplay between Stability and Mobility in your body, to notice how physical stability creates freedom of movement.

Begin lying on the floor and stabilizing one part of your body. Ground that part of your body to the floor.

- Examples: stabilize the following body parts and find the freedom of movement in the rest of the body.
  - Left scapula
  - Whole right side of the body
  - Pelvis
  - Rib cage
- Explore the movement potential in the parts of your body that are not grounded to the floor. What can you do with the mobile parts of your body?
- Let the different sides of the body play off one another, creating a kind of dialogue within the body.
- Explore this theme with different levels:
  - What happens if you try the same process sitting on the floor?
  - On your hands and knees?
  - Kneeling?
- Now, do this same exercise standing. Stabilize the following:
  - Left scapula
  - One whole side of the body

Figure 4.5 Stephen playing with Stability and Mobility

- Pelvis
- Notice how the stable part of the body assists the mobile parts.

See: 19 Stability/Mobility Exploration 1
https://vimeo.com/channels/thelabanworkbook/200009370

- Now create a short sequence of movement. Examples:
  - Lift your backpack up and carry it to a different part of the room.
  - Take a walk, then bend down to tie your shoe.
  - Walk over to a friend and give her a hug.
- Chose a sequence above or create your own. Perform the sequence and notice how you have to stabilize parts of your body to initiate the movement.

Stability/Mobility Exploration 2: Exploring Stability/Mobility within a scene (20–30 minutes)

Objective: To notice the effect of Stability and Mobility on the relationship between characters in a scene.

Apply the theme of Stability/Mobility to a scene.

- Scene 1: What happens if two people are both extremely mobile while trying to have a conversation?
  - Each partner picks a physical task, and repeats this task over and over again. Use any of the examples provided previously, or come up with a new one.
  - Now choose a topic to discuss: current events, politics, a movie you just saw.
  - Begin your physical task and also the conversation. Don't stop moving and don't stop the conversation with your partner. It is okay to speak while your partner is speaking. Continue until the facilitator tells you to stop!
- What was the conversation like? Did you hear what your partner had to say? Do you think your partner heard you?

- Scene 2: What happens if two people are both extremely stable during a conversation?

  - Both partners find a place in the room and ground their bodies. Neither of you move. You both need to feel anchored to your spot.

  - Now choose a topic to discuss: current events, politics, a movie you just saw.

  - Begin your conversation. Don't stop the conversation or grounding until the facilitator tells you to stop.

  - What was that conversation like?

Stability/Mobility Exploration 3: Applying the theme of Stability and Mobility to Meisner's exercise of Doing Fully the activity (40–50 minutes)

Objective: To prepare the actors to fully engage in activity, while playing off of one another—one actor as Stable, the other as Mobile.

In the world of Meisner:

> Acting is Doing. It is not talking about; it is doing something and when we are not really doing on stage we have stopped acting.
> (Silverberg, Foote, and Stern 1994: 56)

This next exploration requires the actor to be completely engaged in a particular physical activity. Being involved in this activity forces the actor to respond truthfully to what is actually happening in the present moment.

Partner work:
Use the basic concept of the Movement Conversation exercise, except this time as the exploration develops, only one partner will move while the other partner remains stable in one spot.

- Begin the Movement Conversation with both partners moving in exaggerated style—one person, then the other (refer to Inner/Outer Exploration 1).

- After 30 seconds, allow the actors to begin to make sound.

- Once the actors are comfortable with sound, cue them to speak simple improvised text with their movements.

- Let the actors move and speak text simultaneously for about 15 seconds. Then instruct one partner to continue to move, while the other partner stays stable, standing in his place.

  – The moving partner moves on her text *and* the text of her partner.

- Keeping eye contact with the partner is not essential, and in fact may hinder the choices of the moving partner.

  – However, the stable partner stays in relationship with the moving partner, watching her, relating to her and allowing his responses to be affected by the moving partner. The stable partner may turn in his place to keep the moving partner in his view.

  – Each partner allows their voice and posture to be influenced by the movement or non-movement of their partner.

As the exercise continues, notice the effect the stable partner has on the mobile partner and vice versa. How can the mobile partner "play" off the stable partner? And how can the stable partner play off the mobile partner, even though the stable partner can only turn on his spot? Is there any *movement* happening inside the stable partner?

- Switch roles and repeat the exercise.

Now transition into Meisner's exercise The Activity. Choose a physical activity. The initial activity in this exercise must be extreme and require full commitment. It must be all-encompassing and require your complete and full attention, physically and mentally. It needs to be something that is possible, but very difficult and not easy to accomplish. Physical activities may include putting back together a shattered model airplane, juggling while continuously adding balls or different items to juggle, playing a song on an instrument you've never played before, using all fifty-two cards to create a house of cards, etc. The activity must also have a clearly identified completion or end.

- Begin your activity and go into Meisner's Mechanical Repetition exercise as described in Exploration 3 of the Inner and Outer theme Explorations, except this time the text can be a short sentence.

- Choose which partner will be doing the activity first. This partner is mobile. The other partner is stable: sitting, or standing, not doing an activity.

- Complete the Mechanical Repetition exercise with this Stable/Mobile relationship, with one partner actually performing the physical activity while doing the Mechanical Repetition exercise. The moving partner is multi-tasking, focusing on the activity at hand, as well as responding in the moment to his partner. The other partner is stabilized, focusing only on her partner.

- Continue the Repetition exercise for 10–15 minutes.

Repeat the process, changing roles. It is suggested that each partner do a different activity.

Stability/Mobility Exploration 4: Applying the theme of Stability and Mobility to the creation of Chekhov's Imaginary Body, supported by the Laban concept of Body Organizations (40–50 minutes)

Objective: To apply the practical knowledge of stabilizing part(s) of the body and mobilizing other parts of the body to the idea of Imaginary Body, as supported by Body Organizations.

Chekhov's idea of the Imaginary Body is a rather simple one. Create a "body" that belongs to the character. The actor goes about this by visualizing what the character looks like. Obviously the actor cannot actually change her physical features, but can use her imagination to think of herself as taller, wider, thinner, or rounder. Imagining herself this way, the actor creates a new center in the body and her body occupies space in the same manner as the character.

Through analyzing personality traits from the text answer the following questions: Is the character aggressive? Shy? Sneaky? Sexy?

Vengeful? Other questions? With this process the actor imagines the character's posture and gestures. Chekhov believes:

> the imaginary body stirs the actor's will and feelings; it harmonizes them with the characteristic speech and movements, it transforms the actor into another person!
>
> (Chekhov and Callow 2002: 79)

Creating an Imaginary Body for a character deepens and enlivens the understanding of the character's Will Impulse and is also complimentary to the development of a PG.

Body Organizations are a part of the Body category within Laban Movement Analysis. Body Organizations are connected to the physical and psychological development a child goes through from birth to walking. There are six stages of development and awareness: Breath, Core/Distal, Spinal, Upper/Lower, Body Half, and Cross Lateral. Application of the Body Organizations provides excellent physical support and psychological insight for all physical postures, including those created through Chekhov's Imaginary Body.

- Choose one of your favorite characters from a play. Read the play and examine the physical attributes and personality of your favorite character.
  - Notice physical descriptive words that pertain to your character, words that describe mood, intention, or atmosphere.
- From these words begin to form a mental picture of your character.
  - Embody this shape.
- Notice what part of your body has become "the center," i.e., has your own physical center shifted higher, or lower?
  - Do you feel taller, shorter, wider, thinner?
  - How are your limbs relating to and extending from this new center?
  - What kind of shapes do your limbs make in space? Do they stay at your sides, or do they reach out into space in a unique way?

- How is your head resting on your spine? Is it tilted or turned?
  If so, in what way?

- Notice what part of your body feels grounded or stable.

- Allow this body part to connect with the floor, to allow
  freedom in the other body parts.

- In the Imaginary Body of your character, try out some text from
  the play while doing everyday actions.

  - How does the Imaginary Body affect your walk, how you sit,
    how you stand, how you gesture, your state of mind, how
    you relate to the environment?

  - How is this outward physical posture affecting your inner
    mood and general feelings?

**See: 20 Stability/Mobility Exploration 4 – Embodying the
Imaginary Body
https://vimeo.com/channels/thelabanworkbook/200009480**

The next step is to explore each of the Body Organizations identified in
LMA. Begin each of these exercises lying on the floor, and move slowly
to standing, and from standing to walking. Try various gestures and
movements within each Body Organization. What is it like to sit, stand
up, wave to another person, threaten or dismiss someone in each

Figure 4.6 Stephen's Imaginary Body for Puck – Sitting

Body Organization? Notice how each Body Organization affects your outward physical posture, as well as your inner state of mind.

- Breath: begin lying on the floor, feeling your in-breath and out-breath. Emphasize the breath in your body. Feel your body growing with each inhalation and condensing with each exhalation. Allow your actual breath to breathe life into each part of your body. Move from the floor to standing, each movement you make is motivated by either an inhalation or an exhalation. When you arrive to standing, feel your whole body breathing and moving and responding to your breath. Move through the space with Breath as your Body Organization. Come up with movements and gestures that relate to your character chosen for this exploration. Does this Body Organization relate well to your imagined physicality of the character?

  – Breath Body Organization is associated with the psychological component of trust and yielding. The character Blanche from *A Streetcar Named Desire* is a good example of a character that uses Breath Body Organization.

  See: 21 Stability/Mobility Exploration 4 – Body Organization – Breath
  https://vimeo.com/channels/thelabanworkbook/200009524

- Core/Distal: begin lying on the floor and allow yourself to move like a starfish. Radiate out from the center with your limbs and then allow your limbs to come back in towards the center at the completion of a gesture, creating a relationship from the center of your body to the tips of the fingers, toes, head, and tail. Move in this way from the floor to standing. When you arrive to standing, feel your posture radiating out from your core to your distal ends (head, tail, fingers and toes). Move through the space with Core/Distal as your Body Organization. Try out your character's movements and gestures. Does this organization fit what you imagined for the character?

  – Core/Distal Body Organization is associated with the psychological component of reaching out to the world and bringing information back into yourself for internal understanding and examination. Gollum from *The Hobbit* is a character that might be served well by Core/Distal.

See: 22 Stability/Mobility Exploration 4 – Body Organization – Core/Distal
https://vimeo.com/channels/thelabanworkbook/200013244

- Spinal: begin lying on the floor and allow your spine to move you. Move from the top of your head, your tail, rotate your spine and roll on the floor, inchworm, swish around. Move your spine in any way you can think of and let the rest of the body go along for the ride. Allow your spine to become fluid and articulated. Allow this movement to take you to standing. Once you come to standing, move your head and/or tail in over-exaggerated ways. Feel the entire spine, from head to tail, as an expressive limb. Move through the space with Spinal as your Body Organization. Try your character's movements and gestures. Does this Body Organization match your imagination of the character?

  – Spinal Body Organization is associated with the psychological component of individuation or independence. Becoming one's own self, literally and figuratively getting a backbone. Voldemort and even Harry Potter are two characters that might be physically supported by Spinal Body Organization.

  See: 23 Stability/Mobility Exploration 4 – Body Organization – Spinal
  https://vimeo.com/channels/thelabanworkbook/200009648

- Upper/Lower: begin lying on your belly with your hands right underneath your shoulder joints and the tops of your feet to the floor. Engage your hands and feet into the ground and then press the hands into the floor, forcing your body to fold at the hip joints, moving into child's pose. Once you have folded at the hips, move forward and backward into child's pose, keeping the hands and feet engaged into the floor. Rock back and forth and feel the separation and connection between the upper and lower body. While lying on the floor, move the upper body while grounding the lower body. Or move the lower body while grounding the upper body. Keep this relationship with your upper and lower body as you move slowly to standing. Once you come to standing, ground yourself firmly to the floor from the pelvis to the feet and allow the upper body to move and reach out into space. Then let the lower body move (either stationary or traveling) and keep the upper body grounded and firm. Move around the space with Upper/Lower Body Organization. How much movement is possible? Is it easy to travel through the space? How does this organization make you move? Is it a match with the imagined physicality of your character?

– Upper/Lower Body Organization is associated with the psychological component of setting boundaries, of deciding when to allow something or someone to come close or when to push something or someone away. Muhammad Ali is a great example of someone who utilized the power of Upper/ Lower Body Organization.

See: 24 Stability/Mobility Exploration 4 – Body Organization – Upper/Lower
https://vimeo.com/channels/thelabanworkbook/200012626

- Body Half: begin lying on your back on the floor and feel as if your body is split in two from the pubic bone, up through the torso to the top of your head. Notice your distinct right and left side, splitting your torso in half, right down the middle of your body, with vertical right and left halves. Move in this manner lying on your belly. Keep this right and left half relationship as you work your way to standing. While staying grounded on the right side of your body, move the left. Then ground the left side of your body and move the right. Try this on your back. Work your way to standing and walk with an exaggerated sense of the right and left sides of the body. Take yourself on a walk through the space in Body Half Organization. Do you feel confused by the split down the middle of the body, torn between two desires or goals? Does this Body Organization fulfill your imagined physicality of your character?

– Body Half Body Organization is associated with the psychological component of making a decision, or weighing two different alternatives. Classic example of a character embodying Body Half is Hamlet: "To be, or not to be …?"

**See: 25 Stability/Mobility Exploration 4 – Body Organization
– Body Half
https://vimeo.com/channels/thelabanworkbook/200009574**

- Cross Lateral: lying on the floor, notice the quadrants of your body: upper right (navel, right chest, right arm, and right side of your head), lower left (navel, left pelvis, left leg down to your toes), upper left (navel, left chest, left arm, and left side of your head), lower right (navel, right pelvis, right leg down to your toes). Feel the diagonal that is created from the upper right to the lower left, and also the diagonal from the upper left to the lower right. Allow your body to twist and rotate, or spiral. Notice how the quadrants interact with each other. Use this twisting, spiraling movement between the quadrants to bring you to standing. While standing play with the quadrants of the body, moving one against another. Make gestures that require twisting. Walk around the room with an exaggerated twist and swing of the arms. Perform movements your character might do with an over-emphasis of twisting and spiraling. Does Cross Lateral Organization support or enhance your character's imagined physicality?

  – Cross Lateral Body Organization is associated with the psychological component of complex thinking and decision making. My favorite character example for Cross Lateral is Tevye in *Fiddler on the Roof*. Throughout the play he is weighing tradition vs modern ideas (classic Body Half); when he finally comes to a decision he takes a step forward, moving into Cross Lateral, and declares: "There is no other hand!" He's there, he's made a decision, and it's a definitive moment in the play!

**See: 26 Stability/Mobility Exploration 4 – Body Organization
– Cross Lateral
https://vimeo.com/channels/thelabanworkbook/200009699**

Using the Imaginary Body you created for your favorite character at the beginning of this exploration, get it back into your bones and breath, and notice which Body Organization seems to apply the most: Breath, Core/Distal, Spinal, Upper/Lower, Body Half, or Cross Lateral. All six Body Organizations are required for a human being to stand up and move functionally through the world, so you may notice that more than one Body Organization is happening in your posture. Yet, most of us have one Body Organization that stands out and is also a part of our psychophysical personality—how we physically interact with others and the world.

- Notice if one Body Organization is more predominant in your Imaginary Body and also how the psychological component of the Body Organization connects to your character's personality and objective.
- Move the character around with this Imaginary Body; try out the text while walking, standing, sitting, waving, etc.
- Give extra support to your Imaginary Body with the chosen Body Organization(s) and also notice how applying the Body Organization(s) deepens the psychophysical connection for you, the actor, to the character.

Now apply the theme of Stability and Mobility. From the chosen Body Organization, choose the body part that feels more grounded. Move the Imaginary Body of the Character with this choice.

- For example, if Upper/Lower is the discovered Body Organization, notice the part of the body—Upper or Lower— that is most stable or grounded and move the rest of the body around this body part.
  - This may mean stabilizing the chest and the shoulders, and letting the lower body move freely underneath.
  - Or this may mean grounding and stabilizing the hip joints, and allowing the upper body to move freely and explore.
- Use the simple movements offered earlier to explore the movement of your Character's Imaginary Body (walking, sitting, standing, waving, etc.).
- Perform the monologue with the Imaginary Body using Body Organizations as support.
  - Concentrate on using the stable part of the body to support the mobile part. This will help you maintain ease and freedom in your Imaginary Body.

Discussion questions for the theme of Stability/Mobility

1 How does Stability/Mobility help the actor's physicality?

2 How does Stability/Mobility affect relationships and communication?

3 How does Stability/Mobility, within a chosen Body Organization, support the creation and use of an Imaginary Body?

Concluding thoughts

The main intention of this chapter has been to explore the acting techniques of Stanislavski, Chekhov, and Meisner through the window of Laban's themes. I encourage you to try any of the exercises applying any of the themes. Take an exploration from Function/Expression and apply the theme of Inner/Outer. Or an exploration from Stable/Mobile and apply the theme of Exertion/Recuperation. It's interesting to see how changing the theme changes the psychophysical perspective and gleans new information for the actor.

I wonder if you noticed as you were working that, of all the themes, Inner/Outer seems to relate to each exploration? I believe this to be true. I believe that Inner/Outer is in essence "*the mother*" of all themes. That everything is related to this idea of what's happening on the inside gets expressed on the outside, and then what happens on the outside changes the inside. Therefore, all the movement ideas and explorations presented in this chapter always affect what's happening on the inside, which changes what's happening on the outside, and then comes back again and changes what's happening on the inside. This is the circular nature of all of the themes, and especially the theme Inner/Outer. This circular approach is also at the heart of the idea of approaching a character psychophysically.

Each one of the acting techniques presented—Stanislavski, Chekhov, and Meisner—connect the mind and the body, the inner with the outer. How do you define an inner vs outer approach to acting? Is the text considered outer because it's outside of the body, or is it inner because it requires an intellectual inner process? Is movement of the body considered outer because the movement is on the surface and is seen on the outside, or is it inner because it requires movement from all of the tissues including the muscles and the sinews and the viscera? Regardless of how you answer these questions, the point is the two are connected; one cannot exist without the other and the circle of Inner/ Outer and its relationship to the creation of a character psychophysically is at the heart of believable, honest, exciting acting!

Applying the themes to the acting techniques of Stanislavski, Chekhov, and Meisner, is a unique approach. And adding the various LMA concepts from Body, Effort, and Shape embellishes and deepens the work. Now that you have an understanding of LMA, feel free to take a concept from any of the acting techniques and apply any of the chosen LMA concepts used in *this* chapter (Body, Effort, or Shape).

When we sum it all up, bringing awareness of the psychophysical connection for the actor can be done from a multitude of approaches applying the themes and LMA. I hope you have expanded your actor toolbox and will use these new tools as you continue to explore the art and craft of acting.

Acknowledgments

I am honored to be a part of *The Laban Workbook for Actors*. A special thanks to Katya Bloom for inviting me to contribute to the book. I also thank my readers Liz Shipman, Dawn Arnold, and Matthew Wilson, as well as my colleagues Barbara Adrian, Katya Bloom, Tom Casciero, and Claire Porter. Your insights and wisdom have been invaluable. It has been an honor to work with all of you.

Notes

1 All the Meisner exercises have been paraphrased and adapted from the text *The Sanford Meisner Approach* (1994) by Larry Silverberg, Horton Foote, and Stewart Stern.

2 Still Shapes classically include Wall, Ball, Pin, and Screw. In recent years

the Laban Movement Analyst community has begun to include Pyramid in this category.

Further Reading

The following list includes sources from the bibliography as well as additional sources. Use these sources to enhance your practice of applying Laban Movement Analysis to Stanislavski, Chekhov, and Meisner.

Bartenieff, Irmgard with D. Lewis (1980). *Body Movement: Coping with the Environment*. London: Routledge.
Bradley, Karen K. (2009). *Rudolf Laban*. New York: Routledge.
Cerullo, Jessica and Sloan (2009). *MICHA Workbook*. Hudson, NY: The Michael Chekhov Association Inc:
Chekhov, Michael and D. H. Du Prey (1985). *Lessons for the Professional Actor*. New York: Performing Arts Journal Publications.
Chekhov, Michael, M. Gordon, and M. Powers (1991). *On the Technique of Acting*. New York: Harper Collins Publishers, Inc.
Chekhov, Michael and S. Callow (2002). *To the Actor, On the Technique of Acting*. New York and London: Routledge.
Daventry French, Stephanie and P. Bennett (2016). *Experiencing Stanislavsky Today, Training and Rehearsal for the Psychophysical Actor*. New York: Routledge.
Hackney, Peggy (2002). *Making Connections, Total Body Integration Through Bartenieff Fundamentals*. London: Routledge.
Hagen, Uta (1973). *Respect for Acting*. New York: Macmillan.
Laban, Rudolf von and L. Ullmann (1975). *Mastery of Movement* (rev 3rd edn). London: Dance Books.
McCaw, Dick (2011). *The Laban Sourcebook*. New York: Routledge.
Meisner, Sanford and D. Longwell (1987). *On Acting*. New York: Random House.
O'Brien, Nick (2011). *Stanislavski in Practice, Exercises for Students* New York: Routledge.
Potter, Nicole (2002). *Movement for Actors*. New York: Allworth Press.
Silverberg, Larry, H. Foote, and S. Stern (1994). *The Sanford Meisner Approach, An Actor's Workbook*. Lyme, NH: Smith & Kraus.
Stanislavski, Konstantin (1989). *The Actor Prepares*. London and New York: Routledge/Theatre Arts Books.
Stanislavski, Konstantin and J. Benedetti (trans.) (2008). *An Actor's Work, A Student's Diary*. London and New York. Routledge.

5

GENERATING AND STRUCTURING A MOVEMENT AND TEXT PERFORMANCE

Claire Porter

There is no end to how to begin.
This is one way.

(Claire Porter)

The goal of this chapter is to take you through the steps of creating a movement theater piece. After first zeroing in on an idea, we will use Laban Movement Analysis (LMA) to manipulate and play with that idea in order to generate movement and generate text. We will then merge the movement and text in different ways. And finally, organize what we have.

Introduction

LMA provides a rich toolbox for creating work. It makes many distinctions in movement that give the artist a variety of ways to embody an idea physically.

I have chosen the five-pointed **Star Model** for this chapter. I find it to be a clear and useful tool for movement invention. I learned the

Star Model from Marion North and Valerie Preston-Dunlop, students of Rudolf Laban, who taught, along with Choreography Professor Bonnie Bird, a seminar on Laban Theory at the Laban Centenary Conference in 1979 held at Goldsmiths College, London, UK.

I have extended the Star Model, taking liberty with the exact nature of LMA. When studying LMA in depth, which I highly recommend, it is important to embody the distinctions and learn the specific and exact language of the theory. However in devising for theater I find that a looser Star Model provides those unfamiliar with LMA, as well as LMA practitioners, a simple structure for generating movement material in response to an idea.

Notes on use

- All practices and exercises are given for a workshop/class setting with a leader/teacher and group of participants. If working alone, please adapt.

- This chapter is not about interpreting what a movement *means* but a practice in generating movement responses to given prompts. It is about creating. Meaning can be interpreted much later in the process.

- This chapter is not about doing anything correctly. It is about using LMA to evoke ideas for performance, freeing you to *play* with your material and generate something new. Expect to not have answers and to move into unknown territory. There is no right way to create!

- The sharing of what you are creating with a partner or a group is important for anchoring that material in your body. The shared material, as a result, becomes a "something," a something that can be named and referred to. For those reasons there are many prompts for sharing and discussing your work.

- Take your time. This chapter can be a college semester or a one or two week workshop and it can be returned to over and over. Adapt for your own time frame.

- This chapter focuses on creating your own individual responses to prompts. The responses you generate can be organized into a solo performance and/or modified for group work. Please adapt as needed.

Theme, Content, Structure

It is helpful to view what is created as a combination of Theme, Content, and Structure.

The Theme (the idea, the subject, the source) is what the piece is investigating, its possible meanings and its possible hidden meanings.

The Content (the movement, text, music and staging) is the word to describe what we see and hear when viewing something. It is in Content where LMA excels. LMA makes generating and clarifying material easier to see and understand. It makes it easier to talk about, and it provides support for the Theme and for addressing Structure. This is where the Star Model lives.

The Structure (the organization of the performance) is the way the material is put together, how it flows from start to finish. For example, it might begin simply and become more complex. Or begin in complexity and resolve to simplicity. Or it might have quiet moments amid many peaks and climaxes. Or it might be a combination of these.

When Theme, Content, and Structure connect and interweave, a performance piece appears cohesive and true to itself.

The Star Model

What is in each category?

The LMA model taught in many training programs is the BESS model, which stands for Body, Effort, Shape, and Space. Shape is a rich study in itself, combining all five points of the Star Model, and can greatly inform your work, particularly in how your body and breath adapt to space and carve out lines and volumes in space. In this chapter on

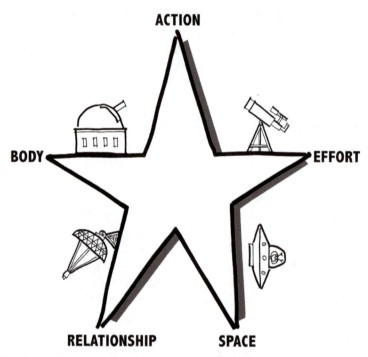

Figure 5.1 Star

generating and structuring, however, Shape is subsumed in one or more of the five points.

Body (who) refers to *who/what part* is doing something. Examples: arms, legs, whole body, torso, elbow, right half of the body, left half of the body, upper body, lower body. It also refers to initiation point, posture, gesture, alignment, grounded-ness, symmetry (right side of the body same as left side), asymmetry (right side different from left side), and sequencing (top of head to the tail, right foot through the torso to left hand).

Action (usually the verbs) refers to *what* is happening. Examples: jump, roll, speak, maintain stillness, arrive, balance, wait, consider, bark, fall, laugh, blink, run, retreat, march, lift.

Effort (usually the adverbs and metaphors) refers to *how/when* something is happening, including qualities, feelings, colors. Examples: hot, stormy, feathery, like a monster, powerfully, like a bird, quickly, loosely, like the wind, like an angry lion, red, carefully, blue, immediately, wildly. Effort also includes *Rhythm*, the patterns of quick and slow, and *Phrasing*, the preparation, emphasis, and follow-through of movements, words, or sounds.

Space refers to *where* something happens, including facings, levels, directions, size, place. Examples: up, low, big, small, in a figure 8, facing front, facing a wall, diagonally, centrally (a movement through the center of the body), peripherally (a movement on the edges of your reach space), dimensions, planes, volumes, roundness, flatness, width, length.

Relationship (often prepositions) refers to *connection* to something or to someone. Examples: behind him, through me, around the body, next to you, here, on top of the piano, far away from the wall, looking at the book, caressing the wall. Some words in Relationship also fit in other categories. For example, the word *"focus"* can refer to eyes (Body), direction (Space). And the word *"caress"* suggests a connection to someone or something, and can refer to what is happening (Action) and how it's happening, probably gently (Effort).

Practice observing using the Star Model

The following practices are designed for those in a group setting to become familiar with the Star Model.

Star Practice 1

Participants: Demonstrator(s), notator, observers
Props: Chair, book

Demonstrators: (With instruction in hand, take a moment to decide as a group how you will interpret and perform this.) Begin slouching in chairs close together, reading one big book. Gradually become aware of ghosts all around. Very slowly gather yourselves together, holding onto the book. Carefully and slowly, rise. Then zigzag and beeline across the room escaping out the door. Slowly slide the book back into the room.

Notator: On a big board or paper, write down what is said for each aspect of the Star, one aspect at a time, listing what the observers saw. Note that some words may fit more than one category.

Observers: Without knowing the instructions given to the demonstrators, what did you see? What was important? The language you use, of course, will depend on how the sequence was performed. No two performances are the same. The following *might* be what one group of observers saw:

Body: Three actors, heads, eyes, arms.
Action: Slouch, read, look, condense, gather, stand, embrace, run, exit, slide.
Space: Down, up, all around, out, straight lines, zigzag lines.
Effort: Slowly, determinedly, quickly, sneakily, fearfully, furtively.
Relationship: Close together, toward a book, in chairs, across the room, out the door.

Deepening

- Discuss what might have been going on with the characters and why you drew that conclusion.

- Address **Structure/Organization**. How was the study organized? Was it mysterious at the start and did it resolve itself at the end? Did it start with surprise and stay surprising? Was there a story structure of some kind? If so, what was it? And if so, how was it revealed and resolved?

- Repeat the exercise with different demonstrators, recording what is seen each time. Note the differences.

Star Practice 2

Participants: Demonstrator(s), notator, observers
Props: Bench

Demonstrators: (With instruction in hand, take a moment to decide as a group how you will perform this.) Begin spread out on a bench, draped like sloths. Several times, change your position in attempts to get comfortable. Gradually increase your determination to get very, very comfortable. Pause. Then "hear" something under the bench. Leading with your head, very slowly follow your head, snake-like, until your whole body is under the bench. Pause. Now try to get comfortable there. Pause. Then "hear" something from the top of the bench. Draw just your head up to the top of the bench. Very slowly twist your head to look at one person and ask (or express): "Well?"

Notator: Collect what the observers saw. On a big board or paper write down what is said for each aspect of the Star, one aspect at a time. Remember that some words may fit more than one category.

Observers: Category by category, what did you see? Depending on how it was performed, the language might be analyzed in the following way:

Body: Three people, heads, sequencing through the spine.
Action: Sleep, draped, repositioning, molding, snore, point.
Space: Around, flat, horizontal.
Effort: Like a bag of potatoes, sloppy, slithery, slowly, snake-like.
Relationship: On the bench, under the bench, around the bench, toward one person.

Deepening

- Discuss what might have been going on with the characters and why you drew that conclusion from what you saw?

- Address **Structure**. How was this event organized? Did all the participants move at once? One at a time? What caused them to move?

- Repeat the exercise with different demonstrators, and record what is seen each time. Note the differences.

Star Practice 3

Participants: Demonstrators, notator, observers

Demonstrators: (Confer as a group how you will perform this. Need three points of view. Keep the vocals fairly quiet so that viewers can focus on the movement.) Several friends discuss where to go for dinner. One wants the nearest place (right here) to save time, while the other wants a faraway fine French restaurant for the best entrees, best wine, and best service. Gradually intensify the discussion to a fight. End in a frenzy of head to head, nose to nose, gesticulation and yelling, pushing each other across the room. Have a third participant resolve the dispute in some way.

Notator: Collect what the observers saw. On a big board or paper, write down what is said for each aspect of the Star, one aspect at a time. Remember that some words may fit more than one category.

Observers: Category by category, what did you see (not hear)? Dependent on how it was performed, the language might be analyzed in the following way:

Body: Five people, arms, nose.
Action: Talk, point, gesticulate, yell, push.
Space: Over there, over here, far, backward, forward.
Effort: Friendly, in a frenzy, intensely, angry.
Relationship: Next to, face to face, nose to nose, through.

Deepening

- Discuss what might have been going on with the characters and why you drew that conclusion? How did the movement reveal the characters' desires?

- Address **Structure**. How did the performers structure this event? Was there a story? How did it progress? Did one event cause another?

- Repeat the exercise with different demonstrators, and record what is seen each time. Note the differences.

Star Practice 4

Participants: Demonstrators, notator, observers
Props: Chairs, stools, or bench

Demonstrators: (Confer as a group how you will perform this.) Begin seated on a moving subway/bus/car, backs to the audience. In sync, have the bus/subway/car stop and start several times (freeze then resume together). Then imagine you hear music in the distance that gradually gets louder. Keep time to the music. Then begin dancing together. Stand up and dance up a storm. As the music you "hear" fades and finally stops, slow down, return to sitting as though alone, responding to only the movement of the vehicle.

Notator: Collect what the Observers saw. On a big board or paper, write down what is said for each aspect of the Star, one aspect at a time. (Some words may fit more than one category.)

Observers: Category by category, what did you see? Dependent on how it was performed, the language you use to describe what you saw might be analyzed in the following ways:

Body: Five people, one very tall, backs and spines.
Action: Sitting, shifting, sequencing, jiggling, gesticulating, boogie-ing.
Space: Cramped, side to side, up and around.
Effort: Carefully, rhythmically, freely, wildly.
Relationship: Side by side, close together, intertwined, individually.

Deepening

- Discuss what might have been going on with the characters and why you drew that conclusion?

- Address **Structure**. How was this organized? Was there a story? A pattern? How did it progress?

- Repeat the exercise with different demonstrators, and record what is seen each time. Note the differences.

Star Practice 5

Create your own movement sequence.

- Form into small groups. Create your own sequence (with or without text).

- Perform for observers.

- Observers: Analyze what you saw as you did in the previous practices.

- Discuss what might have been going on with the characters, how the movement influenced your conclusion, and how it was organized.

PART 1: A WAY IN

Find a topic
Create movement for that topic

Figure 5.2 Zeroing in

There are infinite ways to start building a performance. And there are no rules for how or where to start. (Suggestion: If you have only a short amount of time, start with **Exploration 3**.) Let's begin.

Exploration 1: Find initial idea

Ask yourself, what is it I wish to explore/investigate? Have it be something that interests you, something you want to spend time exploring. This could be a particular character in a play, for example. Or it could be a simple movement idea, such as opening and closing. It could be the weather, grammar, or the stock market, or it could be manners, gossip, an historical character, a haiku, a newspaper article, a Greek play, a story, poem, or kind of food. It could be rain, the oceans, or garbage. It could be conflict in personal friendships, politics, equal rights. Any subject! Choose one that interests you. Suggestion: if you choose a metaphysical subject such as peace, love, hope, spirit, angel, find a real-life specific instance of it. For example, if your choice is *hope*, a specific example of *hope* could be listening and waiting by a door, *hoping* the person outside will knock and enter. If it's *peace*, a specific example might be finding agreement on what to serve for Thanksgiving in a warring family.

Exploration 2: Name it

Begin the research of your selected **Idea** by immersing in it. Collect and write down your thoughts about it. Collect photos, trinkets, articles of clothing related to it. Read, read, read about it. Create a notebook of your writings. Set aside an **Idea Box** for related things, photographs and trinkets. Let the idea play in your mind. What is the dictionary definition of the subject? Are there other words for it? Recall stories you heard about it. Discuss it with others. Interview people about it. Look it up in the encyclopedia, Wikipedia, quotation books, atlas. Find poems that refer to it. Listen to music that suggests it. If, for example, your subject is *The Deep Sea*, you might collect seaweed, shells, a starfish. See what these articles provoke. Write it all down. And finally, give this idea, this subject, a name. For example, names might be: *Irises, Intersections, Food to Go, Tossing and Turning, Hackensack River, Mirrors, Bones, Tsunami, Hoover Dam, Oats, Camping with Babies,*

Cooking Apple Pie, Niagara Falls in a Barrel, Heat Wave, Entering Doors Escaping Through Windows. Call this your **Initial Idea**.

Exploration 3: Postcard

- Start with a large collection of assorted postcards. Or start with your Idea Box.

- Having honed in on an Initial Idea, choose a postcard or something from your Idea Box that reminds you of that idea. If you have a script you are working with, find a related postcard. If you have *no* idea where to start, choose a postcard that you like.

- Freely write about the image on your postcard. Take your time. Fill the page. Generate. Don't censor. Some questions you might ask:

  - If you were to insert yourself in the postcard, where would you be, what would you be doing, what might you want?

  - What are the Efforts, the colors, qualities, feelings, images, memories, emotions, dynamics, in the postcard?

  - What are the Actions of the postcard?

  - If there is a Body in the image, how would you describe it?

  - Do you see any Relationship between things, people, colors?

  - Does the image have any Relationship to an event in history, to an environment?

  - Can you describe the Space, the shapes, lines, floor patterns, directions, levels?

- Give a title to all your thinking/writing, for example, **First Writings**.

Exploration 4: Movement from action

- **Find actions**

  - Read what you've written and circle all the **Actions** in your writing. Think verbs or words that suggest action. If you are not sure it's an action, go ahead and consider it an action. Then choose your favorite *three* Actions. Write them down below your writing. Suppose you find the actions "help," "supported," "tumble-dry."

- Of those three Actions, choose one favorite Action. For example, "help."

- **Move**

  - Get up and physically do that one Action. Do it several times. Do it some more. Become familiar with it. For example, "help" another sit on a chair, "help" an imaginary bird fly away, "help" shape one's mouth into a word, "help" one of your legs cross the other, or "help" yourself or another down to the floor. What is it to physically express, "to help"?

  - Save your favorites. Call them **Actions**.

- **Do the Action with different parts of your body**

  - Explore your Actions with different body parts. Instead of your hands and arms helping, for example, "help" with your legs. Continue "helping" with other parts of your body, your pelvis, chest, face, scapula, spine, whole body. You might find your forehead "helping" another sit on a chair, your knees might "help" your elbows touch each other, your back "help" a partner across the room, your nose "help" an imaginary bird fly away, your feet might "help" a partner by supporting his weight. Discover/invent what it means, to "help" with all parts of your body.

  - Choose what you like from these explorations and organize them by stringing them together. Practice and remember what you have. Call this your **Action Phrase**.

- **Show and discuss**

  - Show your Action Phrase to a partner.

  - Discuss. What did you enjoy that you saw? Become interested in how it was realized. Instead of like/dislike, good/bad, right/wrong, be curious and describe what you saw and felt.

  – Share your postcards. Notice how the movement related to
    the postcard, to the Initial Idea.

Exploration 5: Movement from space

- **Draw what you see, interpreting the postcard with lines
  and shapes**
  – Draw the lines you see in the postcard, real or suggested.
  – Draw the shapes and figures you see.
- **Move the space with different parts of your body**
  – Draw these lines with your hands in the space around you.
  – Make the line and shapes with your whole body.
  – Create the lines and shapes with parts of your body, your
    head, legs, your arms, your pelvis.
  – Choose what you like from this exploration, organize what
    you've chosen and remember it. Call it your **Space Phrase**.
- **Show your Space Phrase to a partner**
  – Share your postcards.
  – Discuss how **Space** transferred from one medium (printed
    postcard) to another (movement).

Exploration 6: Movement from Effort

- **Move**
  – Recreate the **Effort**, the qualities, colors, feelings, in the
    postcard through movement. For example, the postcard
    might suggest hot, energetic, wild, calm, airy, foggy, murky,
    wild, foggy. Or it might elicit sadness, anger, disgust, or fear.
    How might your body express the feelings elicited from the
    postcard?
  – Collect some of the movements you have generated, string
    them together and practice what you have until you are able
    to reproduce it. Name this material, your **Effort Phrase**.

- **Show your Effort Phrase to a partner**
  - Share your postcards.
  - Discuss. How did the qualities in the image transfer from that medium (printed postcard) to another (movement)?

Exploration 7: Structure/organize what you have

- **Choose**
  - Choose some or all of your material from the previous exercises. They are the following:
    - Actions
    - Action Phrase
    - Space Phrase
    - Effort Phrase
- **Organize**
  - **Organize** what you have in any way you like. You might do this by simply stringing it all together. Or you might choose only your favorite parts.
  - **Attend to Effort**: Look at where the peaks of energy/ excitement land and where they subside, where there is evenness, where there is stillness.
  - **Attend to Effort Phrasing**: Vocalize your movement as you do it noticing the rhythms that appear. Become aware of these rhythms and exaggerate them. Emphasize the pulse and intensities and quiet moments.
- **Practice, Show, Discuss**
  - Practice what you have chosen. Call this your **Trial Run**.
  - Show your **Trial Run** to a partner.
  - Discuss. For the viewer: What seemed important to the creator? What were the key moments? What intrigued you? How was it organized? What would you like to see developed? For the performer: Take note, and write down,

how your Trial Run was received. Avoid defending your choices but focus on collecting the responses you hear.

Exploration 8: Reflection

Having explored some ideas in movement, and having received feedback from viewers, notice, and write down, what you have discovered, uncovered, realized, about what you made and about your Initial Idea. Can these discoveries take you deeper? Questions you might ask: What have I realized so far? Has the subject changed? If so, how? What more would I like to know? Where might this be leading?

Exploration 9: Breather

In this break, converse with others about their projects, look at what they are making. Comment about what you see. Share ideas.

PART 2: FROM MOVEMENT TO TEXT

Figure 5.3 Writing

Exploration 10: Feedback in the form of Titles

- Observe your partner's Trial Run.

- Respond to what you see by creating a **Title** for it. Work to respond to what you *see* is *there*. The Title might be prosaic, poetic, and any number of words. All fine.

- Your partner then writes down the Title you have created for him/her.

- Switch roles, and collect a Title from your partner.

- Repeat with a second partner. (You now have been given two Titles.)

- Repeat with a third partner. (You now have been given three Titles.)

Exploration 11: Working with Limitation

The Titles you collect can be viewed as feedback on what you created and showed.

The following is an exercise in **Limitation** and the start of a text. Limitation—and in this case, limiting your language to the Titles given— can be surprisingly freeing.

- Using only the words of the three Titles you were given, create ten new Titles. Feel free to repeat words. Feel free to change verbs to nouns, adjectives to adverbs, plurals to singular, etc. Call this list **Title Play**. For example, suppose you were given the titles "Over the River," "Deep and Dark," "Blue Moon." The first few titles of Title Play might be "Over the Deep," "Over the Dark Moon," "River Blue Moon," "Over Dark Over," "Blue," "Darkly Deep Deepening Blue."

- Read your titles aloud to the group. Sometimes this list becomes part of the script itself. Sometimes not. Sometimes this list is poetic, sometimes not.

- Listen for how Limitation opens up possibility.

- What have you learned? Does your list, Title Play, inform your Initial Idea (from Exploration 1)? If so, how?

- Address the value of Limitation with each other, in partners or with whole group.

Exploration 12: Reflection

- Add to your writing. What does the movement that you created in response to your Initial Idea, suggest? What does Title Play suggest? Anything new? What have you learned about your explorations so far? Might a character be emerging? A situation?

Exploration 13: Making word choices

- Review all your writings, the description of the postcard, the titles you received, Title Play (created in Exploration 11) and what you just added in Exploration 12.

- Highlight words and phrases that intrigue you.

- Group your highlighted words and phrases in a way that makes sense to you. There is no correct way to do this! A favorite way is to just list these choices on a separate page. Call it **Favorites**.

- Anything you'd like to add? Anything missing? Add it to your writing.

- Anything you'd like to eliminate? What's not needed? Create a **Discards** pile for these and save for later. You can always return to Discards for ideas.

- Examine the verb tenses. Are you in past tense? (He went.) Present? (He goes.) Present continuous? (He is going.) Future? (He will go.) Past perfect? (He had already gone.) Future perfect? (He will have gone.) Check any list of verb tenses for more tenses.

- Examine verb modes. Are you in declarative mode? (He goes.) Subjunctive mode? (What if he goes?) Interrogatory mode? (Is he going?) Imperative mode: (Go! You must go!)

- Notice how a change of tense or mode affects the impact of your writing. Choose what you like.

- Read Favorites to a partner. What intrigues you here? What is being revealed? Are themes emerging? Discuss. Listen to your partner's Favorites. Discuss.

Exploration 14: Keeping track

Take note and review what you have.

What you now have:

Movement:
Actions
Action Phrase
Space Phrase
Effort Phrase
Trial Run

Text:
Initial Idea
Writing
Title Play
Favorites

PART 3: STRUCTURING: WORKING WITH INTERNAL STRUCTURES

Exploration 15: Practice structuring

- **Structuring Practice 1** (with five things)
  With all participating, have each person gather five articles found in the room and have each create a sculpture with those five articles. Once complete, tour the room and notice all the sculptures. Address how each one is organized. For example, you might find one weighted, with large articles on the bottom, small ones on top (structured around Effort and Relationship). Or you might find one composed only of red things in a row side by side (structured around Effort, Space, Relationship) or find one with all articles at angles within a circle (structured around Space and Relationship). Or you might find one organized like socks overflowing a drawer (structured around Action and Relationship)

- **Structuring Practice 2** (adding a person)
  In two groups, repeat Practice 1 but replacing one article with a person. What effect did adding in a real person have on the structure, if any? How was it organized?

- **Structuring Practice 3** (adding movement)
  Repeat Practice 2 but with the one person moving slowly in some simple way (perhaps rising or sinking). What effect did this have? How was it organized?

- **Structuring Practice 4** (more bodies, one article)
  Repeat Practice 2 with three people and one article. Have the article be moved simply and slowly (Effort). What effect did this have? How was it organized?

- **Structuring Practice 5** (with five people)
  Repeat Practice 2 with five people. Beginning and ending in stillness (Action), perform one simple movement very, very slowly (Effort). This movement could be the same for all or each person could have a different movement. Address what you see. How was this organized?

Exploration 16: Structure of Repetition and introducing Movement Motif

Repetition is performing something in the same way several times.

- Choose *one* movement from your Action Phrase that you consider its essence. Call it your **Motif** (which means, main idea). This might be: turning away while condensing your chest. It might be: flinging yourself out onto the floor. It might be: a startled jump off the floor. It might be: waving goodbye to a loved one.

- Perform this Motif for a partner, repeating it 10x (ten times).

- Notice and address what happens through the structure of Repetition. You have more material. What else? Is it interesting to you? If so, why?

Exploration 17: Structuring Movement Developments

Development is repeating something while growing it in some way. Here are some ideas.

- **Space**: Repeat your Motif 10x by beginning extremely small and on each repetition get larger and larger in size until the movement is as large as it can be. Make it huge. Call it **Motif Size Development**.

- **Effort**: Repeat this Motif 10x by beginning very slowly and on each repetition get faster and faster. Call it **Motif Speed Development**.

- **Effort**: Repeat this Motif 10x by beginning neutrally and on each repetition get stronger and more forceful. Call it **Motif Strength Development**.

- **Effort**: Repeat this Motif 10x by beginning neutrally and on each repetition get lighter and gentler. Call it **Motif Lightness Development**.

- **Body**: Repeat this Motif 10x by beginning with one body part and on each repetition add more body parts, getting fuller and fuller. Call it **Motif Body Development**.

- **Action**: Repeat this Motif 10x by beginning neutrally and on each repetition add an action. For example, adding to your Motif, a jump, then jump while stretching out, then jump, stretch out and sing, and then jump and stretch out and sing and shake. Call it **Motif Action Development**.

- Review these Developments and choose your favorites. Call this your **Movement Developments**. In small groups, perform them for each other. Discuss what intrigued you.

Exploration 18: Structure of Repetition and introducing Text Motif

Just as you used Repetition to expand your movement material in Exploration 16, use **Repetition** to expand your text.

- Choose your favorite short phrase, two or three words, from First Writings. Call it your **Text Motif**.

- Suggesting to yourself a reason for repeating, say and repeat your Text Motif to a partner 10x. A reason might be: you're trying to remember something. Or you're not sure your listener understands you.

Exploration 19: Structuring Text Developments

Just as you used Development to expand your movement material in Exploration 17, use **Development** to expand your text. Feel free to choose the same or different short phrases. Here are some ideas:

- **Effort**: Say your Text Motif 10x gradually getting louder, stronger, and more determined, as though working to convince your listener.

- **Effort**: Say your Text Motif 10x gradually getting faster and wilder, as though building a storm.

- **Effort**: Say your Text Motif 10x gradually getting slower and quieter, as though calming a child to sleep.

- **Space**: Say your Text Motif 10x gradually taking up more space,as though your listener moves farther and farther into the atmosphere.

- **Space**: Say your **Text Motif** 10x gradually taking up less and less space, as though your listener comes closer and closer until directly across from you.

- Review these Developments and choose your favorites. Call this your **Text Developments**. In small groups, perform them for each other. Discuss what intrigued you.

Exploration 20: Structuring with Movement Theme and Variations

Theme and Variation is a structural device to expand material but, unlike Development, expands material by varying a longer sequence

of material, called a *Theme*. There is no end to possibilities here. Here
are some ideas.

Begin by choosing a short segment of your movement from First
Movement Response (about five to eight movements). Call it **Phrase
One**.

- Create **Space Variations** by performing Phrase One in the
  following ways: Perform it while changing facings several
  times. Perform it while having every movement travel. Perform
  it all to the space behind you. Perform it changing levels.
  Perform it upside down (often a favorite). Perform it "inside-out"
  (another favorite, because no one knows what "inside-out"
  means which can be quite freeing). Perform getting extremely
  tiny or immensely huge. Choose your favorites. Call it **Space
  Variations**.

  – Show it to a partner. Notice and discuss how Space affects
    the movement and your experience of it.

- Create **Effort Variations** by performing one of your Space
  Variations with changes of Effort. Try the following: Perform
  your Space Variation with the qualities of your postcard.
  Perform it with the rhythm of your postcard (Exploration 3).
  Perform it exaggerating the speed (only extremely fast or
  extremely slow.) Perform it with one Effort quality, end with
  its opposite (from Strong as an Ox to Light as a Feather, or
  from Direct as a Cat to Indirect as a Moth, or from Quick as
  a Chipmunk to Slow as a Melting Ice Cube, or from Free as a
  Child in a Playground to Bound as if in a Tight Bag). Save what
  you found that you like. Name it **Effort Variations**.

  – Show it to a partner. Notice and discuss how Effort affects
    the movement and your experience of it.

- Create **Body Part Variations** by changing the emphasis in
  your Body. Begin by choosing either an Effort Variation or
  Space Variation. Then try one or all of the following: Have your
  head do what your feet were doing. Have your pelvis do what
  your head was doing. Have your arms do what your legs were
  doing. Have your legs do what your arms were doing. Have

just your hands do the whole variation, then just your face, then just your chest. Save what you found that you like. Name it **Body Part Variation**.

- – Show it to a partner. Notice and discuss how a change of emphasis in the Body affects the movement and your experience of it.

- Create an **Action Variation** by adding **Action**. Begin by choosing one of your Variations. Then try the following: Perform it while jumping, running, or falling. Perform it while doing one of your Actions (Exploration 4) or one suggested by the postcard. Save what you like. Name it **Action Variation**.

  - – Show it to a partner. Notice and discuss how adding Action affects the movement and your experience of it.

- Create a **Relationship Variation** by changing your connection to a thing. Begin by choosing one of your Variations. Then try the following: Perform it while connected to a chair, on, under, through the chair. Perform it with a book, water bottle, eyeglasses, or another prop. Save what you like. Name it **Relationship Variation 1**.

  - – Show it to a partner. Notice and discuss how adding a Relationship to something affects the movement and your experience of it.

- Create another **Relationship Variation** by adding connection to a partner. Both begin by each choosing one of your **Variations**. Try the following: Perform these variations circling each other. Perform them back to back. Perform then while always in connection to each other, while interweaving, on, under, through each other. Save what you like. Name it, **Relationship Variation 2**.

  - – Show it to a small group. Notice and discuss how adding a **Relationship** to another affects the movement and your experience of it.

Exploration 21: Structuring with Text Theme and Variations

Just as you used Theme and Variation to expand your movement material in Exploration 20, use **Theme and Variation** to expand your text.

Begin by choosing a short segment of the text, about five to eight words. Call it **Text Phrase**.

- **Space**: Create a **Text Space Variation** by changing your attention to Space. Try the following: Send your voice to different places, sometimes near, sometimes far. Change the size of the voice. Have it be tiny. Then huge. Speak inwardly to yourself, then outwardly to others. Speak the lines as though they are riding a Figure 8. Save what you found that you like. Name it **Text Space Variation**.

  – Show it to a partner. Notice and discuss how Space affects the text and your experience of it.

- **Effort:** Create a **Text Effort Variation** by changing attention to the quality of the delivery. Try the following: Say your lines with the qualities of your postcard (Exploration 3). Say it with the rhythm of your postcard. Exaggerate the speed by, for example, speaking it rapidly or extremely slowly. Begin the text with one Effort quality and end with its opposite. Whisper it, mumble it, sneer it, laugh it. Deliver it smoothly, jerkily, singsong-y. Deliver it like a snake, a hummingbird, a vulture. Save what you found that you like. Name it **Text Effort Variation**.

  – Show it to a partner. Notice and discuss how Effort affects the text and your experience of it.

- **Body**: Create a **Text Body Part Variation** by emphasizing where in your body the language originates. Try the following: Deliver the text exaggerating the movement from your tongue, then lips, breath, lower lip, back of your mouth. Have your pelvis speak, your spine, the top of your head, your chest. Save what you found that you like. Name it **Text Body Part Variation**.

  – Show it to a partner. Notice and discuss how Body affects the text and your experience of it.

- **Action**: Create a **Text in Action Variation** by adding Action to the delivery. Try the following: Jump your voice. Slither your voice. Fall your voice all over yourself and down the stairs. Toss, catch, blow, chew, your text. Watch it as it leaves your mouth. Let your voice by affected by one of your Actions (Exploration 4) or one suggested by the postcard. Save what you like. Name it **Text in Action Variation**.

  – Show it to a partner. Notice and discuss how Action affects the text and your experience of it.

- **Relationship**: Create a **Text Relationship Variation 1** by adding a connection to a thing. Try the following: Speak to a chair, on a chair, under a chair. Perform it while addressing the wall, a telephone, a rock, a piece of chalk. Perform it while savoring the aroma of fine meal or while sensing the length of a knife, or the length of a leg (yours or someone else's). Keep the object stationary or move the object while you move as well. Save what you like. Name it **Text Relationship Variation 1**.

  – Show it to a partner. Notice and discuss how Relationship to something affects the text and your experience of it.

- **Relationship**: Create a **Text Relationship Variation 2** by adding a connection to a partner. Try the following: Taking turns both speak your individual lines to, around, behind, past, under, above, each other. Speak your individual lines to each other at the same time, overlapping the text. Save what you like. Name it **Text Relationship Variation 2**.

  – Show these in small groups. Notice and discuss how Relationship to a partner affects these seemingly unrelated texts. Do they now relate? If so, how?

Exploration 22: Keeping track

Take note and review what you have. These are the building blocks for
your piece. Keep the list active adding new discoveries and material as
they develop.

What you now have:

Movement:
Action Phrase
Space Phrase
Effort Phrase
Trial Run
Movement Motif
Movement Motif Developments
(composed of Size, Speed, Strength, Lightness, Body
Developments)
Theme and Variations
(Space, Effort, Action, Body, Relationship with a thing,
Relationship with another)

Text:
Initial Idea
Writing
Title Play
Favorites
Text Motif
Text Motif Developments
(composed of Effort, Relationship, Space Developments)
Theme and Variations
(Space, Effort, Action, Body, Relationship with a thing,
Relationship with another)

PART 4: THINK AND PLAY

Think
Think some more
Think some more again

Figure 5.4 Expanding

Exploration 23: Thinking

You have now created both movement and text, played with and performed that material. Now what? Take some time to deepen your responses by spending time writing and thinking. Is something new emerging? What parts intrigue you? Continue to define and describe your subject. Dig in and spend time researching and studying your subject. View documentaries about it. Read books about it. Read poems about it. Interview people about it. Come to know and love your subject. Put your ideas down, on paper, on a document. Perhaps you can now narrow your focus, refining your Initial Idea. Also, explore the key words you are working with. What does each mean? What are its synonyms, its antonyms? Look up each key word in a thesaurus as well as in a large etymology dictionary.

Exploration 24: General to specific

What happens when you make something general into something specific?

- Look through your writings and pull out a word that is general and make it specific. See where this takes you. Below are examples, which in turn can be made even more specific.

  - **Love** (a general word). More specific: Caress. Idolize. Embrace. Aloha. Cupid. On fire. Beloved. Kiss. Amore. French kiss. Helping George cross the street. Offering Lily a BLT. Listening to your grandmother's story about her uncle George.

  - **Politics** (a general word). More specific: Vote. Voting rights. Ballot box. Lining pockets. Boss. Congress. School Board. Tory. Whig. Labor. State. Fight.

  - **Relationship** (a general word). More specific: Kin. Aunt. Affair. Symmetry. Blood. Gang. George and Alice on Friday. One-upmanship. Poker game. Argument.

- Look through your writings and pull out a short paragraph. Change all the general terms to more specific language. Read both to a partner. Notice its effect. Save what interests you. And see where this leads you.

PART 5: PUTTING IT TOGETHER

There is no correct way to put movement and text together. Jump in, experiment, and play.

Figure 5.5 Organizing

Exploration 25: Putting movement and text together

When you are putting movement and text together you basically have four choices: You can speak without moving. You can move without speaking. You can be still, neither moving nor speaking. And you can speak and move at the same time.

When speaking and moving at the same time, try these possibilities:

- **Choose** a part of your text and some of your movement to be performed together.

- **Overlap** your text and movement: Begin speaking your lines, add the movement, stop speaking, continue moving.

- **Reverse the overlap** of your text and movement. Begin moving, start speaking, stop moving, continue speaking.

- **Emphasize** text and minimize movement. Make the movement very small, as an undercurrent, while amplifying the text.

- **Reverse the emphasis** by softening or eliminating some of the text, amplifying the movement.

- **Practice** what interests you and perform this for the group. As observers, respond to what is intriguing and what keeps your interest. Address why it is intriguing and why it keeps your interest.

Exploration 26: Structuring movement

There are several common structures that are fun to play with. Try the following and then apply these structures to the movement material you have. Save what you like.

- The **ABA** structure begins and ends with the same material with something different in the middle. For example, the movement sequence *Jump, Fall, Jump.* An everyday example might be *Check phone, Do computer work, Check phone.* Try ABA with some of your text. And try it with some of your movement.

- The **Rondo** is a series of movements with a Motif appearing on a regular basis. For example, with Run as a Motif: *Run*, *Fall*, *Run*, *Jump up*, *Run*, *Spiral around*, *Run*. An everyday example might be *Check phone*, *Do computer work*, *Check phone*, *Take a singing lesson*, *Check phone*, *Jog around the block*, *Check phone*. Try the Rondo with some of your text. And try the Rondo with some of your movement.

- **Accumulation** keeps adding one new movement, returning each time to the beginning. For example, try the following. Then make one up yourself with your own text and movement.

  – *Jump*

  – *Jump, Fall*

  – *Jump, Fall, Run*

  – *Jump, Fall, Run, Flail about*

  – *Jump, Fall, Run, Flail about, Stop*

- **De-accumulation** is the opposite of **Accumulation**. For example, try the following, eliminating the last movement.

  – *Jump, Fall, Run, Flail about, Stop*

  – *Jump, Fall, Run, Flail about*

  – *Jump, Fall, Run*

  – *Jump, Fall*

  – *Jump*

- Or a **De-accumulation** eliminating the first movement.

  – *Jump, Fall, Run, Flail about, Stop*

  – *Fall, Run, Flail about, Stop*

  – *Run, Flail about, Stop*

  – *Flail about, Stop*

  – *Stop*

- Then make one up yourself using your own text or movement.

- **Chance** structures are just that—chance organization. The chance can be from a dice roll, from the names of your movement on a piece of paper pulled out of a hat for their order, or from choosing willy-nilly. Create a chance structure and try it with your own text and movement.

Exploration 27: Structuring language

In addition to the **Narrative Structure**, that of storytelling, with a beginning, middle, and end, it is productive to experiment with the **Movement Structures** from above. Try applying the following Movement Structures to language.

- **ABA**: For example, the text sequence
  - *I must go to work*
  - *Maybe have dinner*
  - *I must go to work*
- The **Rondo**: For example, the text sequence
  - *I must*
  - *I won't*
  - *I must*
  - *I will never*
  - *I must*
  - *Don't even think about it*
  - *I must*
- **Accumulation** adds on a new word and then returns to the beginning. For example
  - *Never*
  - *Never on*
  - *Never on Sunday*
  - *Never on Sunday or Monday*
  - *Never on Sunday or Monday or Tuesday!*
- **De-accumulation** subtracts a word.
  - *Never on Sunday or Monday or Tuesday*

- *Never on Sunday or Monday*
- *Never on Sunday*
- *Never on*
- *Never!*

• Now try one or more of these structures with your text. Save what you like.

Exploration 28: Structuring language from the structure of your subject

Does your topic suggest a structure? If you are working with games, consider the structure of a tennis game with a back and forth volley of language. If you are working with *Descent into Deep Sea*, consider the structure of the increasing weight of water. If you are working with a story, consider the narrative structure of beginning, development, climax, resolution, end. Examine the structures inherent in your subject and see what happens when you apply those structures to your language.

Exploration 29: Examples of structuring language

Use the sentence *George taught me how to engage in sleazy rip-off schemes. We just laughed about it.*

ABA: *George taught me. How to engage in sleazy rip-off schemes. We just laughed about it. George taught me.*

Chance shuffling: *We laughed. Loved those rip-offs, those schemes, those sleazy backroom, back slapping, back handed …*

Repetition (of similar meaning): *We lied, fabricated, distorted, made up stuff, pretended, falsified, hatched, concocted, cooked up … a lot of … you know … stuff.*

General to specific: *George taught me to keep my transactions secret. I even used Sally's emails to extract a half mil. How we laughed. What a gas! While it lasted. … And, sure we lied. All the*

*time. Everybody did. In interviews, to reporters, to George's wife
even, yeah, everybody. Got caught, but ...*

Repetition, Accumulation, ABA: *Laughed. Laughed. Laughed.
Laughed some more. It was a hoax. But we got 'em. Good. Until we
were arrested! Then we cried. Cried! And cried. Sobbed. Blubbered.
Tears, rolling down our ... But laugh!*

Work your text with some of these structures. Save what you like.

Exploration 30: Organize your text and movement into a whole

Now put it all together. Remember there is no correct way to do this.
You generated text and generated movement. You have worked on
limiting your ideas. And you have practiced organizing. Return to
Exploration 25 for ideas for combining language and movement. Now
put something together to show. Play with it. Play with it some more.

Exploration 31: Lots and lots of questions and then more questions

When you are ready to take a break, explore playing with some of these
questions.

- **Questions about your Idea, your Subject**
  - How might you go deeper?
  - What is missing?
  - What is emerging? Is there an underlying meaning, a subtext?
  - What is not needed? What happens when you take this out?
  - How does the idea progress from one idea to the next? Can you draw the progression on paper, mapping it out?
  - Can anything from your discarded material now serve the direction you are taking?

- Are you telling the audience what to think or taking them for a ride of discovery?

- **Questions about Body and Action**

  - How does your posture change during the piece?

  - Are you emphasizing upper body over the lower body?

  - Is your spine adapting to your idea? Condensing, expanding, twisting, not twisting?

  - Are your two legs always doing the same thing, staying symmetric, suggesting stability? Can they be asymmetric, suggesting mobility? What about your arms? Symmetric? Asymmetric?

  - Is your head always in line with your spine? Can your neck twist?

- **Questions about Space**

  - Outline on a piece of paper the performing space you are using. Are you using the whole space? Only the downstage area? What about the space above you? Can you hang from the ceiling or get on top of a desk, a chair? Are you exiting and entering, staying on the space?

  - Look at your facings. Are you only facing Downstage? Can you vary your facings? Face the diagonal? Face Upstage? Lie on the floor and face up?

  - How are you using the space around the body, your kinesphere? Are you using only the near space in front of your torso? What about the space behind you? Under you? To the right? To the left? Circuitously? In far reach space? Can you vary the size?

  - Can you deliver your lines when upside down? With you back to the audience?

- **Questions about Effort**

  - Where are the surprises?

  - What is the overall rhythm? What are the internal rhythms?

  - Can you support your idea by revealing an opposite

contrasting idea? For example, if you are exploring power, would a momentary light hummingbird-like touch, reveal your power more clearly?

– Is the rhythm of your speaking always aligned with the rhythm of your movement? Sometimes more interest will occur with off rhythms. And sometimes you might want movement and text exactly together. Are your rhythms always the same or do they vary?

– Where is the climax, if there is one? Where is the evenness?

– Can you vary the delivery of your text, sometimes loud, soft, whispered or mumbled?

– Can you vary the phrasing of both your language and movement? In language, for example, the emphasis within a phrase is revealed by where there is greater Effort. (And this Effort might be forceful like a prize-fighter or its opposite, very soft like a kitten. Or this Effort might be quick as a bug or its opposite, sustained like a sunset.) Try these with varying kinds of Effort emphases.

  – **Emphatic Phrasing**. The emphasis is at the end, as in *You can't leave* **now***!*

  – **Impulsive Phrasing**. The emphasis is at the beginning, as in **You** *can't leave now.*

  – **Middle Phrasing**. The emphasis is in the middle, as in *You* **can't** *leave now,* or *You can't* **leave** *now.*

  – **Even Phrasing**. The emphasis is equal, as in *You can't leave now,* or **You! Can't! Leave! Now!** where each word has equal emphasis.

  – **Beginning/End Phrasing**. The emphasis is at the beginning and end, as in **You** *can't leave* **now***!*

- **Questions about language**

  Are your sentences: Declarative sentences? Questions? (Interrogatory) What if's? (Subjunctive) Demands? (Imperative)

  – **Example 1**: *This sentence is short.* (Declarative)

- *Is this sentence short?* (Question)
- *Might short sentences be the way to go?* (Question)
- *If only we had short sentences.* (Subjunctive)
- *Lengthen this sentence!* (Imperative)
- **Example 2**: *I love you.* (Declarative)
- *Do I love you?* (Question)
- *What if I loved you?* (Subjunctive)
- *If I loved you, this love might be lovely.* (Subjunctive)
- *Love me or else!* (Imperative)
- **Example 3**: *Politics are a mess.* (Declarative)
- *Are politics a mess?* (Question)
- *What if politics were a mess?* (Subjunctive)
- *If I were political, would politics mess me up?* (Subjunctive and Question)
- *Fix the mess!* (Imperative)

- **More questions about language**

  There is a big difference between listening to language and reading language. Here, we are writing text to perform for an audience. With this in mind, some more questions:

  - Notice what is important during each part of your text and movement. Is the language more important than the movement? Does it need to be amplified, diminishing the movement? Or should the movement be amplified, diminishing the importance of the text? With practice and the performing of your choices, you will find answers to these questions of balancing text and movement.
  - What words and movements do you need to repeat?
  - What whole sections could be repeated?
  - Can you eliminate the words, "the" and "a" and "an" from the text? What happens when you do?
  - What ideas need to settle in, ideas that need time, where do you need to slow down?

- **Questions about incorporating music**

  - In thinking through what you have, would it benefit from music or sound? Live or recorded? Music can provide additional Effort life, reaching your audience directly. Your music choices can support what is happening or counteract what is happening. It can add suspense, danger, humor. It can give your audience a break from dense language or movement. Where might music add a needed change?

  - Where and when to insert music/sound? When a mood is especially important, would a musical choice heighten your intention? Might adding music in place of language amplify the mood, supporting your ideas?

- **Questions about incorporating sets, costumes, props**

  - What sets, costumes and props would support what you are delving into? By adding these, your work will change. Once selected, go back and pick up on an earlier Exploration to adjust to these choices. For example, if you've added a costume with pockets, what can you do with pockets? Turn them inside out? Stuff your hands in them? Think of any addition as something to explore and connect to your idea. Be sure that it is not just layered on top but integral to and supporting the piece.

  - Is exaggeration needed? Where? Can the prop/set/costume offer this?

  - Is subtlety required? Where? Can a costume make something more mysterious?

- **Questions about including others**

  - If you are working in pairs or small groups, review what you have made and return to the earlier exercises to examine Relationship. Are you co-workers? Lovers? Enemies? Family? Friends? Are you together against the world? Are you conniving against a third party? Are you distant, close? Would your movements be similar, contrasting? Might you be doing the same thing at the same time (unison)? Or one following the other (in a canon structure)? Might you be opposite spatially, for example, one always up, the other always down? Or one in front, two behind? One leading, the others following?

Exploration 32: Regroup. Take a breather. Use LMA to recuperate

Moving your attention from one aspect of the Star to another can provide a needed break that can re-energize you. See if it works for you.

- Turn to another activity and use the Star Model to recuperate. For example,

  - **Body**: Change something about your Body: Get a massage, do yoga, eat a snack.

  - **Action**: Change your Action: Take a walk. Go for a swim. Read something unrelated. Wash the dishes.

  - **Space**: Change your Space: Go to a coffee shop, a thrift store, a museum, a grocery store. Look out the window.

  - **Effort**: Change your Effort:

    - Watch a funny movie. (Light)

    - Split logs for the fire. (Strong)

    - See a thriller. (Bound)

    - Get on a roller coaster. (Free)

    - Sew on a button. (Direct)

    - Meander through a public garden. (Indirect)

    - Go for a bike ride through the woods. (Light/Strong, Free/ Bound, Direct/Indirect)

- Change your Relationship: Play with your dog, talk with your car mechanic, visit your family, a friend, your neighbors.

PART 6: TEST/EDIT/RETEST

Perform, reflect, perform.

Figure 5.6 Trying out

Exploration 33: Title it

Now step back and, if you haven't already, create a title that captures its essence. Try it out on people. How does it land?

Exploration 34: Final notes

- To understand what you have, show your work to your friends, colleagues, fellow students. Do this in laboratory situations, classes, workshops, showcases, living rooms. For a new work to grow, it is important to perform it.

- Collect feedback. It is valuable to see how your piece is received. Feedback suggests possibilities. Allow it to inform your choices while staying true to your intention.

- If your audience is not getting what you intended, find out what they *are* getting. Perhaps what they are getting might be more interesting to you than what you originally had in mind. You could embrace that or you might choose to rework what you originally intended to more clearly communicate your idea.

- Do let your material have a life of its own. Follow it. This can free you from having to tell an audience what to think or believe. Let them discover what you've made for them.

- Editing is different from creating. When creating, be open to all possibilities. Refrain from judging. When editing and honing in, be tough and demanding.

- How to grow: Study, see work! Be inspired to think for yourself. Attend performances. Research artists and their work. Put your work out in showcases of all kinds. Immerse yourself! Study! Read everything. It's up to you. There is no prescription for you. Experiment and choose.

Exploration 35: Conclusion

You have now made choices, responded to suggestions, generated movement, generated text, organized and shared it and performed it. And as you perform your work, keep open to possibilities. Consider the feedback but don't be led away by it. And finally, discover your work as you invent it and as you reveal it. Keep me posted. Thank you!

Acknowledgments

Thank you Katya Bloom for inviting me into this project. Thank you co-authors Barbara Adrian, Katya Bloom, Tom Casciero, and Jennifer Mizenko for your thoughtful feedback all along the way. Thank you

Mark Armstrong (markarmstrongillustration.com) for your fun illustrations. Thank you dear colleagues for your generous and specific feedback and for your insightful suggestions. In addition, thank you John Pietrowski (Director of Playwrights Theater of New Jersey) for your readings and workshops. Thank you Tracy Pattison (dancer, choreographer, movement/dance teacher) for our work together at Bearnstow Camp. Thank you Rusty Curcio (CMA, choreographer, movement for acting teacher, Wagner College) for your encouragement. Thank you Cynthia Williams (choreographer, teacher, Hobart and Williams Smith Colleges) for your specific and detailed attention to language. And thank you Mary Ellen Childs (composer) for our wonderful collaborations. Enjoy my YouTube performances including *Fund Raiser, Breaking News, Namely, Muscles, Small Stories*.

Further reading

Ashton, Kevin (2015). *How to Fly a Horse: The Secret History of Creation, Invention, and Discovery.* New York: Anchor Books.

Barron, Frank (ed.) (1997). *Creators on Creating: Awakening and Cultivating the Imaginative Mind.* New York: Penguin Group.

Bogart, Anne and Tina Landau (2004). *The Viewpoints Book: A Practical Guide to Viewpoints and Composition.* New York: Theatre Communications Group, Inc.

Bono, Edward de (1970). *Lateral Thinking, Creativity Step by Step.* New York: Harper & Row.

Brook, Peter (1995). *The Open Door: Thoughts on Acting and Theater.* New York: Theatre Communications Group, Inc.

Chicago, Judy (1975). *Through the Flower: My Struggles as a Woman Artist.* New York: Doubleday & Co.

Ciardi, John (1959). *How Does a Poem Mean.* Boston, MA: Houghton Mifflin Company.

cummings, e.e (1923). *six nonlectures.* Cambridge, MA: Harvard University Press.

Dewey, John (1934). *Art as Experience.* New York: The Berkley Publishing Group.

Edwards, Betty (1979). *Drawing on the Right Side of the Brain.* New York: The Penguin Group.

Ghiselin, Brewster (ed.) (1952). *The Creative Process.* California: University of California Press.

Henri, Robert (1923). *The Art Spirit.* New York: J. B. Lippincott Co.

Mamet, David (1997). *True and False: Heresy and Common Sense for the Actor*. New York: Pantheon Books.

Mamet, David (1986). *Writing in Restaurants*. New York: Viking Penguin Inc.

Petrovich, Dushko and Roger White (eds.) (2012). *Draw It With Your Eyes Closed: The Art of the Art Assignment*. New York: Paper Monument.

Provost, Gary (1985). *100 Ways to Improve Your Writing*. New York: New American Library.

Ristad, Eloise (1982). *A Soprano on Her Head: Right-Side-Up Reflections on Life and Other Performances.* Utah: Real People Press.

Shahn, Ben (1962). *The Shape of Content.* Cambridge, MA: Harvard University Press.

Shekerjian, Denise (1990). *Uncommon Genius: How Great Ideas are Born.* New York: Viking Penguin.

Tharp, Twyla (2003). *The Creative Habit: Learn it and Use it for Life.* New York: Simon & Schuster.

APPENDIX A: GENERAL OVERVIEW OF LABAN MOVEMENT ANALYSIS VOCABULARY

BESS (Body, Effort, Shape, Space)

Body, which includes Bartenieff Fundamentals, increases body awareness and range of movement through addressing breath support, grounding, dynamic alignment, initiation, sequencing, body connectedness and organization, spatial intent, and weight shift.

Effort is the energy and dynamics of one's movement. Effort reveals one's inner attitude and motivations for movement. In LMA, we can see/sense these inner attitudes by observing how the Effort Factors of Weight, Space, Time, and Flow occur in movement. Each Effort Factor is represented by two effort elements, which lie at the extreme ends of each Factor.

- Flow Effort (*bound* ↔ *free)* refers to the fluidity of one's movement.

- Weight Effort (*strong* ↔ *light)* is one's active attitude toward the use one's body weight.

- Time Effort (*quick/sudden* ↔ *sustained)* is one's inner attitude toward the duration of time in an action.

- Space Effort (*direct* ↔ *indirect)* describes the quality and manner of one's attention to the environment.

These qualities of movement may be seen or experienced as follows:

- Single Effort: One element from an Effort Factor such as *strong weight*. (See previous list for all single elements.)

- Effort State: Two elements from two different Effort Factors such as *direct space* and *quick time,* which is one configuration of an Awake State. There are six categories of States: Awake, Dream, Remote, Near/Rhythm, Stable, and Mobile. There are four possible configurations of the elements for each State.

- Effort Drive: Three elements from three different Effort Factors. For example, the three elements *light weight, sustained time,* and *indirect space* describe a Float Action Drive. There are four categories of Effort Drives: Passion, Spell, Vision, and Action Drives. Each Drive has eight possible configurations of the elements. Only the eight Action Drives have been assigned specific names: Float, Punch, Glide, Slash, Dab, Wring, Flick, and Press.

Shape describes the ongoing changes in bodily shaping as we relate to others, to our surroundings, and to ourselves. There are two subheadings for Shape. One is Still Shape Forms specifically described as Pin, Ball, Wall, Screw, and Pyramid. The other is the Modes of Shape Change, which is sometimes described as Moving Shape Forms and are designated as the following:

- Shape Flow is self-to-self communication. It is body and breath centered and has an inner orientation.

- Directional (Spoke-like or Arc-like) is goal-oriented movement. It differentiates the self from others and bridges self to the environment locating a person or object.

- Carving/Shaping is process-oriented movement, which embodies a complex, interactive, and creative relationship with the environment.

Space includes general awareness of and connection to all of the space around us.

- Kinesphere is a voluminous sphere of space around the body. It is sometimes referred to as one's personal space.

- Reach Space occurs within an individual's kinesphere and refers to the distance around the body the limbs can reach. Categories for Reach Space are *near-reach, intermediate-reach,* and *far-reach* distance from the body.

- Dimensions describe one-dimensional space: Vertical, Horizontal, and Sagittal lines.

- Planes describe two-dimensional space: Vertical (Door plane), Horizontal (Table plane), and Sagittal (Wheel plane).

- Volume describes the amount of space occupied in three dimensions: Octahedron (diamond), Cube, Icosahedron (geodesic dome), and other crystalline forms.

- Spatial Orientation refers to the direction the body is facing as well as awareness of what is above, below, behind, and beside the body.

- Spatial Pathways refers to movements that occur within one's personal space: Central Pathways move through the core of one's body; Peripheral Pathways move along the outer reaches of one's kinesphere; and Transverse Pathways move in the Space between Central and Peripheral.

APPENDIX B: BODY, EFFORT, SHAPE, AND SPACE CHARTS

BESS Chart 1 – The relationship of Body, Effort, Shape, Space

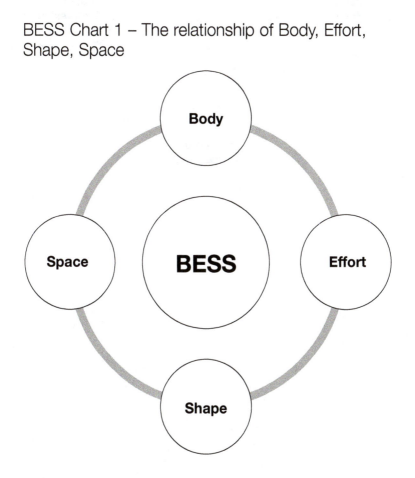

BESS Chart 2 – BESS with Themes

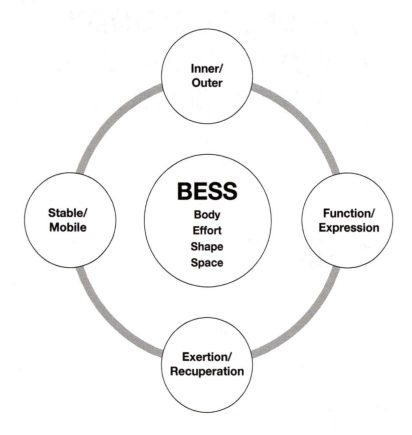

BESS Chart 3 - Effort

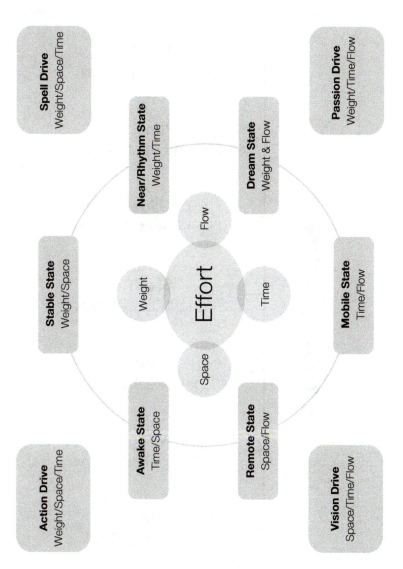

Bess Chart 4 – The eight Effort configurations of Action Drive

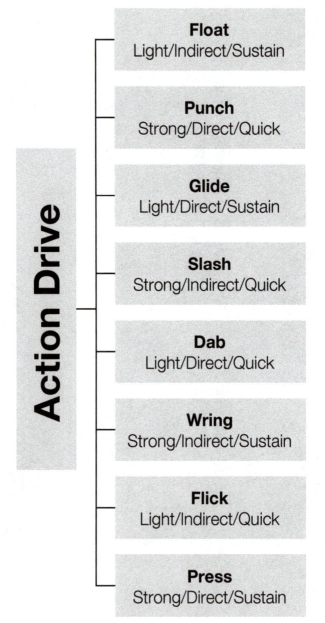

Action Drive

Float
Light/Indirect/Sustain

Punch
Strong/Direct/Quick

Glide
Light/Direct/Sustain

Slash
Strong/Indirect/Quick

Dab
Light/Direct/Quick

Wring
Strong/Indirect/Sustain

Flick
Light/Indirect/Quick

Press
Strong/Direct/Sustain

BESS Chart 5 - Shape

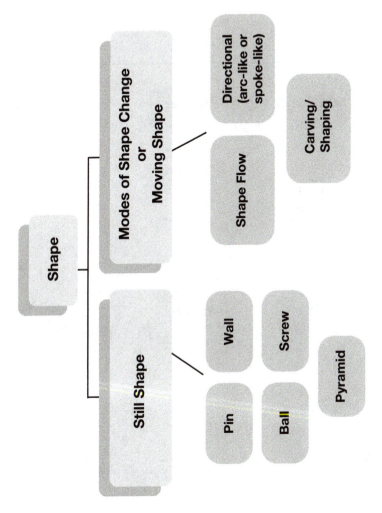

BESS Chart 6 - Space

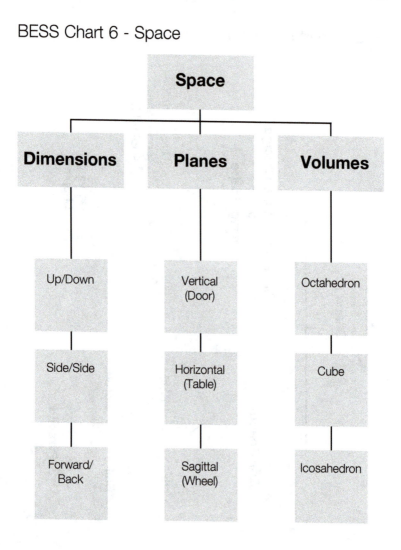

LABAN TRAINING PROGRAMS

1 Laban/Bartenieff Institute of Movement Studies: http://www.limsonline.org/ Belgium, China, Israel, Scotland, U.S.A.

2 Integrated Movement Studies: http://www.imsmovement.com/ U.S.A.

3 Laban-Eurolab: http://www.laban-bartenieff-berlin.de/programs/ Germany

4 Laban Guild: http://www.labanguild.org.uk/ London

5 Giles Foreman Center for Acting—Movement Psychology: Yat Malmgren/Laban Technique: http://www.gilesforeman.com/ character-analysis-movement-psychology/ Europe, U.S.A.

6 Trinity Laban Conservatoire of Music and Dance: https://www. trinitylaban.ac.uk/study/dance/professional-development/ specialist-diploma-choreological-studies U.K.

BIBLIOGRAPHY AND FURTHER READING

Adrian, Barbara (2008). *Actor Training the Laban Way: An Integrated Approach to Voice, Speech, and Movement*. New York: Allworth Press.

Adrian, Barbara (2017). "An Introduction to Laban Movement Analysis for Actors: A Historical, Theoretical, and Practical Perspective," in N. Potter, M. Fleischer, and B. Adrian (eds), *Movement for Actors* (rev. edn). New York: Allworth Press, 92–104.

Bainbridge-Cohen, Bonnie (1993). *Sensing, Feeling and Action*. Northampton, MA: Contact Quarterly.

Bartenieff, Irmgard with D. Lewis (1980). *Body Movement: Coping with the Environment*. London: Routledge.

Bloom, K. and R. Shreeves (1998). *Moves: A Sourcebook of Ideas for Body Awareness and Creative Movement.* London: Routledge.

Bloom, Katya (2003). "Moving Actors: Laban Movement Analysis as the Basis for a Psychophysical Movement Practice." *Contact Quarterly* 28: 11–17.

Bloom, Katya (2006). *The Embodied Self: Movement and Psychoanalysis*. London: Karnac.

Brook, Peter (1987). *The Shifting Point: 1946–1987*. New York: Theatre Communications Group.

Casciero, Thomas (1996). "Laban Movement Studies and Actor Training: An Experiential and Theoretical Course for Training Actors in Physical Awareness and Expressivity." Doctoral Thesis, Union Institute, NY.

Casciero, Thomas (2000). *Laban Movement Studies for Actors*. Course Booklet.

Cerullo, Jessica and F. Sloan (2009). *MICHA Workbook*. Hudson, NY: The Michael Chekhov Association Inc.

Chekhov, Michael and D. H. Du Prey (1985). *Lessons for the Professional Actor*. New York: Performing Arts Journal Publications.

Chekhov, Michael and S. Callow (2002). *To the Actor, On The Technique of Acting*. New York and London: Routledge.

Chekhov, Michael, M. Gordon, and M. Powers (1991). *On the Technique of Acting*. New York: HarperCollins Publishers, Inc.

Esper, William and D. DiMarco (2008). *The Actor's Art and Craft, William Esper Teaches The Meisner Technique*. New York: Anchors Books.

Goldman, Ellen (1994). *As Others See Us: Body Movement and the Art of Successful Communication*. Lausanne, Switzerland: Gordon and Breach.

Hackney, Peggy (2002). *Making Connections, Total Body Integration Through Bartenieff Fundamentals*. London: Routledge.

Hagen, Uta (1973). *Respect for Acting*. New York: Macmillan.

Hodgson, John and V. Preston-Dunlop (1990) *Rudolf Laban: An Introduction to his Work and Influence*. Plymouth: Norcote House Publishers Ltd, 1 England.

Inspirees Institute for Creative Arts Therapy (n.d.). "Introduction to Bartenieff Fundamentals." Available online: www.dancetherapy.cn/content/en-us/p1687.aspx (accessed 10 May 2017).

Jung, C. G. (1971). *Psychological Types, Collected Works of C. G. Jung, Volume 6*. Princeton, NJ: Princeton University Press.

Kawalski, Juan Pablo (2013). "Using Alba Emoting to work with Emotions in Psychotherapy." *Clinical Psychology and Psychotherapy* 20: 180–7.

Laban, Rudolf (1975). *A Life for Dance*, trans. and ed. Lisa Ullmann. New York: Theatre Arts Books.

Laban, Rudolf (1950). *The Mastery of Movement on the Stage*. London: Macdonald and Evans.

Laban, Rudolf von and L. Ullmann (1975). *Mastery of Movement* (rev. 3rd edn). London: Dance Books.

Labanarium (2017). Available online: www.labanarium.com (accessed 28 April 2017). (The focus of the website and network is to explore human movement in all forms, in the tradition of Rudolf Laban.)

Lamb, Warren and E. Watson (1979). *Body Code: The Meaning of Movement*. London: Routledge.

Lessac, Arthur (1978). *Body Wisdom: The Use and Training of the Human Body*. New York: Drama Book Specialists.

Maletic, Vera (1987). *Body, Space, Expression*. Berlin, New York, and Amsterdam: Mouton de Gruyter.

Meisner, Sanford and D. Longwell (1987). *On Acting*. New York: Random House.

Moore, Carol-Lynne and K. Yamamoto (2012). *Beyond Words: Movement Observation and Analysis*. London: Routledge.

Newlove, Jean (1993). *Laban for Actors and Dancers*. Reading: Cox & Wyman Ltd.

Newlove, Jean and J. Dalby (2004). *Laban for All*. New York: Routledge.

Porter, Claire (2008). *Dynamics in a Bag*. Self-published cards.

Preston-Dunlop, Valerie (1980). *Modern Educational Dance*. London: Macdonald & Evans Ltd.

Richards, Thomas (1995). *At Work with Grotowski on Physical Actions*. London and New York: Routledge.

Silverberg, Larry, H. Foote, and S. Stern (1994). *The Sanford Meisner Approach, An Actor's Workbook*. Lyme, NH: Smith & Kraus.

Stanislavski, Konstantin (1989). *The Actor Prepares*. London and New York: Routledge/Theatre Arts Books.

Stanislavski, Konstantin and J. Benedetti (trans.) (2008). *An Actor's Work, A Student's Diary*. London and New York: Routledge.

Studd, Karen and L. Cox (2013). *EveryBody is a Body*. Indianapolis, IN: Dog Ear Publishing.

Tipton, Charles M. (2014). "The History of 'Exercise is Medicine' in Ancient Civilizations." *The American Physiological Society* 38: 109–17.

Toporov, V. S. (1998). *Stanislavski in Rehearsal: The Final Years*. New York and London: Routledge.

Woodruff, Diane (1986). "Somatic Patterns in the Performing Artist." Dialogs, *ALMA NEWS* 2.4 19. Conference.

LINKS TO WORKBOOK VIDEO

To view a particular video, please visit its URL below, or go to https://vimeo.com/channels/thelabanworkbook

Chapter 1: Foundations of Movement, by Tom Casciero

1 Demonstration of the Spiral
https://vimeo.com/channels/thelabanworkbook/199987581

2 Demonstration of the Thigh Lift
https://vimeo.com/channels/thelabanworkbook/199996287

3 Demonstration of the C-curve Squat
https://vimeo.com/channels/thelabanworkbook/199987680

4 Demonstration of the Arm Circle Sit-up
https://vimeo.com/channels/thelabanworkbook/199987606

Chapter 3: Moving Your Voice: Expanding Your Vocal Creative Potential Through LMA, by Barbara Adrian

5 Explorations 2, 3, 4: Shape Flow→Shape Forms→Standing with Unstructured Sound
https://vimeo.com/channels/thelabanworkbook/199996417

6 Exploration 9: Repeating Articulatory Shape=Repeating Sound=Emotional Reveal with Caliban's Text
https://vimeo.com/channels/thelabanworkbook/200001763

7   Explorations 12, 13, 14: Modes of Shape Change and
     Pathways with Unstructured Sound and Words
     https://vimeo.com/channels/thelabanworkbook/199997315

8   Exploration 18: Partner Work: Vocal Gestures with
     Unstructured Sound
     https://vimeo.com/channels/thelabanworkbook/200002743

9   Exploration 20: Unstructured Sound into Caliban's Text with
     Modes of Shape Change and Pathways
     https://vimeo.com/channels/thelabanworkbook/199998212

10 Exploration 22: Effort Elements with Unstructured Sound and
     Body
     https://vimeo.com/channels/thelabanworkbook/199999450

11 Exploration 27: Caliban and Action Drives: Punch, Dab, and
     Wring
     https://vimeo.com/channels/thelabanworkbook/200000784

Chapter 4: Links Between LMA and Key Acting Techniques, by Jennifer Mizenko

12 Inner/Outer Exploration 1
     https://vimeo.com/channels/thelabanworkbook/200008928

13 Inner/Outer Exploration 3
     https://vimeo.com/channels/thelabanworkbook/200009017

14 Inner/Outer Exploration 4
     https://vimeo.com/channels/thelabanworkbook/200009069

15 Inner/Outer Exploration 4: PG into Memorized Text
     https://vimeo.com/channels/thelabanworkbook/200009176

16 Function/Expression Exploration 1
     https://vimeo.com/channels/thelabanworkbook/200009209

17 Exertion/Recuperation Exploration 1
     https://vimeo.com/channels/thelabanworkbook/200009254

18 Exertion/Recuperation Exploration 3
     https://vimeo.com/channels/thelabanworkbook/200009315

19 Stability/Mobility Exploration 1
     https://vimeo.com/channels/thelabanworkbook/200009370

20 Stability/Mobility Exploration 4: Embodying the Imaginary Body
https://vimeo.com/channels/thelabanworkbook/200009480

21 Stability/Mobility Exploration 4: Body Organization—Breath
https://vimeo.com/channels/thelabanworkbook/200009524

22 Stability/Mobility Exploration 4: Body Organization—Core/Distal
https://vimeo.com/channels/thelabanworkbook/200013244

23 Stability/Mobility Exploration 4: Body Organization—Spinal
https://vimeo.com/channels/thelabanworkbook/200009648

24 Stability/Mobility Exploration 4: Body Organization—Upper/
Lower
https://vimeo.com/channels/thelabanworkbook/200012626

25 Stability/Mobility Exploration 4: Body Organization—Body Half
https://vimeo.com/channels/thelabanworkbook/200009574

26 Stability/Mobility Exploration 4: Body Organization—Cross
Lateral
https://vimeo.com/channels/thelabanworkbook/200009699

NOTES ON CONTRIBUTORS

Barbara Adrian, MFA, CMA is a Professor of Theater Arts at Marymount Manhattan College, teaching voice, speech, and movement for the actor. She has taught integrated movement and text workshops in London, Glasgow, and Berlin. She is an Associate Artist with New York Classical Theater (http://www.newyorkclassical. org) and coaches professional actors for television, film, and stage. She has coached productions directed by such notables as Robert Brustein, David Rabe, Elizabeth Swados, Tina Landau, and Stephen Burdman. She is the author of *Actor Training the Laban Way: An Integrated Approach to Voice, Speech, and Movement* (2008) and earned her MFA in Acting from Brooklyn College.

Katya Bloom, PhD, CMA is a movement artist, writer, teacher, and therapist. She taught Laban-based movement in the core actor training at the Royal Academy of Dramatic Art (RADA) in London for twenty years, 1989–2009. Katya is author of *The Embodied Self: Movement and Psychoanalysis* (2006), co-author of *Moves: A Sourcebook of Ideas for Body Awareness and Creative Movement* (1998), and co-editor of *Embodied Lives* (2014). She has also written three plays, with performances in New York and London. Since 2010, Katya lives in Santa Barbara, CA. She offers her work, Depth Movement (www.depthmovement.com), in theater and other settings in the U.S.A. and internationally.

Tom Casciero, PhD, CMA is a Professor of Theater at Towson University. He trains professional and academic actors in Laban Movement, embodied character, and neo-surrealist approaches to devising. He is a Research Associate for the Laban/Bartenieff Institute, author of "Laban Movement Studies and Actor Training" (PhD Thesis), and was an Overseas Fellow and Visiting Scholar at University of Pretoria. Tom has directed movement for over forty university productions and toured his solo performances of comedy and physical theater nationally and internationally. He has taught and presented at universities and conferences in the U.S.A, Brazil, Costa Rica, Slovakia, and South Africa.

Jennifer Mizenko, MA, CMA is a Professor of Dance and Movement for the Actor at the University of Mississippi. Expanded studies include: period dance with Wendy Hilton and Richard Powers, T'ai Chi with Maggie Newman, the work of Jerzy Growtowski with the Teatr Piesn Kozla in Poland, and Michael Chekhov acting technique with MICHA. In addition to Laban Movement Analyst, Jennifer also earned certifications in Alexander Technique and yoga. She has presented internationally at Laban and Alexander conferences and specializes in the teaching of character physicalization, integrating dance, LMA, Chekhov, and Alexander Technique. She earned her a BA in Psychology from Kenyon College, and her MA in dance from the Ohio State University.

Claire Porter, MA, CMA is the creator of Claire Porter/PORTABLES (www.cportables.com). She is a writer, performer, and choreographer whose work has been presented in Europe, Asia and in the U.S.A. at the American Dance Festival, Lucille Ball Comedy Festival, Jacob's Pillow Dance Festival, the Joyce Theater, and the Kennedy Center, among others. Claire is a Guggenheim Fellow, has received Fellowships from the National Endowment for the Arts, New Jersey State Council on the Arts, and Mid-Atlantic Arts Foundation. She has received many university commissions, has an MA in Dance from Ohio State, a BA in Mathematics, and teaches Movement Analysis at New York University.

INDEX

The letter *f* following an entry indicates a page that includes a figure.
The letter *t* following an entry indicates a page that includes a table.